Battersby

Battersby

Extraordinary Food
from an
Ordinary Kitchen

Joseph Ogrodnek *and*
Walker Stern
and Andrew Friedman

Photographs by
Tuukka Koski

GRAND CENTRAL
Life & Style
NEW YORK • BOSTON

Grand Central Life & Style
Hachette Book Group
1290 Avenue of the Americas
New York, NY 10104
GrandCentralLifeandStyle.com

Printed in the United States of America

Q-MA

First Edition: October 2015
10 9 8 7 6 5 4 3 2 1

Grand Central Life & Style is an imprint
of Grand Central Publishing.
The Grand Central Life & Style name and logo
are trademarks of Hachette Book Group, Inc.

The Hachette Speakers Bureau provides a wide range
of authors for speaking events. To find out more, go to
www.HachetteSpeakersBureau.com or call (866) 376-6591.

The publisher is not responsible for websites (or their content)
that are not owned by the publisher.

Library of Congress Cataloging-in-Publication Data
has been applied for.

ISBN: 978-1-4555-5332-7

Contents

Battersby

From Our Kitchen to Yours

Every night, at our restaurant Battersby, in Brooklyn, New York, three cooks toiling in a tight open foxhole of a kitchen turn out more than seventy meals in a matter of hours. It's a feat that demands careful choreography and more than a little improvisation. Sharing a single oven, a six-burner stove, a slim prep counter, and about the same square footage as a studio apartment's kitchenette, we work next to and around each other, playing a game of culinary Twister from the time the doors open until we serve our last dinner sometime after midnight.

Against all odds, the formula works: At five o'clock, people begin lining up for one of our twenty-three seats (thirty-eight in the spring and summer, when our backyard garden is open) before the wait creeps into the one- to two-hour zone. Of course, most guests flock to Battersby because they enjoy and appreciate the food. But part of the appeal is also how we cook: That kitchen, situated at the back of the dining room for all to see, has become a source of fascination, offering our own version of dinner and a show. People are puzzled and pleased by the fact that we can generate such solid food out of such a minuscule galley.

We didn't choose Battersby's space so the kitchen could double as a conversation piece; we ended up there for strictly practical reasons, to open the place on a modest budget. But it's turned out to be our defining feature, and has also provided the inspiration for this book, which builds on the natural connection between our kitchen and yours: In order to function in our cramped quarters, we've devised a repertoire of space-and-equipment-efficient dishes that can be largely prepared in advance and finished quickly when it's time to serve them, which translates beautifully to the needs of home cooks, whether you want to get a head start on a one-course, weeknight family dinner or have a multicourse dinner party ready to go, allowing you to actually spend time at the table with your guests while still serving a sophisticated, memorable meal.

In fact, because of its small size, Battersby often feels like a home, and our staff feels like a family getting ready to host a dinner party. We don't serve lunch, so our days are spent right in the dining room, prepping food. One cook might be at the stove, searing or braising fish and meats, while another sets up camp at the bar, turning artichokes right from the box they were shipped in or peeling potatoes into a bowl. The third team member might be making sauces or parcooking vegetables so they can be quickly reheated and finished with a little olive oil or butter when they are ordered by our guests. Late in the afternoon, our service team pulls in and pretties the place up: folding napkins, setting tables, placing votive candles along the bar and in the recesses in the wall.

Add it all up, and it's not that different from what it's like when you cook for your family or get ready to host guests in your home; we prep right where we serve, and our success depends on how well we plan.

Our Food

The two of us were classmates at the Culinary Institute of America, then trained at such restaurants as Gramercy Tavern, Blue Hill, and Alain Ducasse at the Essex House, which was where we reconnected after cooking school. Over those years and during our time running pre-Battersby kitchens for various employers, we developed a complementary repertoire of dishes, and that repertoire has expanded exponentially since we opened Battersby, and its sister restaurant, Dover, which has a more generously apportioned kitchen and from which we've borrowed a few recipes for this book.

We're young, barely in our thirties, but by today's culinary standards, we're old souls. We believe steadfastly in the merits of traditional cooking: the beauty of fresh ingredients, simply presented; the searing of meat in a pan or the char imparted by a grill; the surprising alchemy created by the right amount of lemon juice and olive oil and judicious seasoning. There's not a dish on our menus that requires modernist additives or equipment, and we don't see that changing any time soon, if ever.

Our dishes draw mainly on French tradition, with Mediterranean and Asian influences. Our time working for Alain Ducasse was especially formative: We loved and absorbed his notion of taking a simple idea and executing it to perfection, or as close to perfection as possible. (Those who know his body of work might recognize a few homages in these pages, such as our chicken Albufera, duck with radishes, and stuffed rabbit.) A few breakout dishes have already emerged, like the little rosemary breads we serve as a welcome, warm from the oven, with a sidecar of whipped ricotta for spreading or dipping, which has become something that regulars look forward to. Our Crispy Kale Salad with Brussels Sprouts and Kohlrabi (page 49) was named the Dish of the Year by *Bon Appétit* and the Best Salad in town by *New York* magazine. There are always a few pastas on our menu and they are popular, even such simple ones as Farfalle with Gorgonzola and Pistachios. As for main courses, they change all the time, but a few mainstays included in this book are Grilled Mackerel with Summer Vegetable Salsa (page 187) and Short Rib Pastrami with Braised Cabbage and Red Bliss Potatoes (page 246). We've also honed a roster of make-ahead desserts such as Fennel Seed Panna Cotta with Lemon Confit (page 295).

How It Works

This book is organized more or less the way most cookbooks are, with one notable exception: The recipes are divided into two parts—To Prep and To Serve—to help you organize your cooking the same way we do. A few recipes are so simple that there's no prep section; they can and should be prepared entirely à la minute. Other dishes, although divided into two parts, are essentially wholly prepared ahead of time, with just a quick reheat, assembly, and/or garnishing required when it's time to serve them. Those dishes include the aforementioned rosemary bread; an amuse-bouche of Greek Yogurt with Root Vegetable Muesli (page 24) and Tomato and Strawberry Soup with Basil and Balsamic Vinegar (page 21).

Similarly, some of our dishes are prepared ahead of time and served cold or at room temperature, with a hot element or garnish added at the last second. There's no better example of this than the kale salad (page 49),

the breakout signature dish of our first season. Inspired by a crispy watercress salad at a Thai restaurant in Queens, it features kale, Brussels sprouts, kohlrabi, and aromatic herbs tossed with a sweet dressing of lime juice and fish sauce. All of those elements are prepared ahead of time and simply tossed together to order. The two finishing touches that imprint the dish with a just-made vibe are crispy, freshly fried kale and Brussels sprout leaves and a scattering of crushed peanuts. The dish exemplifies how we work and what we offer home cooks: It's no exaggeration to say that it can be prepared just as successfully at home as it can at our restaurant, both in terms of efficiency and flavor.

The majority of our repertoire are hot dishes for which we do the heavy lifting ahead of time, then finish and freshen at the last second. For example, a dish of grilled tuna with piperade (a Basque pepper stew; page 194) enlivened with Spanish ham and paprika asks you to do little more than reheat the stew and quickly grill the tuna when it's time to serve the dish. Similarly, the only cooking that needs to happen to serve the Chicken with Crispy Potatoes, Feta, and

Arugula (page 215) is cooking the chicken and frying the parcooked potatoes.

If it seems hard to believe that this much work can be done in advance and still produce great food, we promise you that it's done in restaurants you like and frequent all the time. In our case, the advance work is also balanced by finishing techniques that add freshness and vibrancy, no matter how far ahead they were prepared, such as finishing them with minced shallot and fresh herbs, often followed by a shake of sherry vinegar or a squeeze of lemon juice, or drizzling everything from salads to pastas to main courses (especially fish) with a buttery, slightly floral extra-virgin olive oil. We also frequently incorporate ingredients in both raw and cooked form, another tendency inspired by Ducasse. For example, Striped Bass with Braised Fennel and Tomato Confit (page 197) is finished with a scattering of raw fennel on top; one of our most popular duck dishes is a duck breast with a variety of caramelized and braised radishes, topped with shaved raw radish (page 228); and pasta served over dandelion pesto is topped with fresh dandelion leaves (page 156).

Our Philosophy

We believe that most great cooking results from making a lot of little decisions correctly. For example, the difference between a good pasta and a great one can be the choice of pasta itself (we use readily available De Cecco), the oil used as a cooking medium (extra-virgin, in our case), a last-second addition of fresh garlic (we often toss a smashed clove into the pot for the final minute of cooking, then take it out), and other decisions that are unique to individual dishes.

Throughout this book, in headnotes and elsewhere, we share our tips and advice for making those decisions, from which tools and implements to use for different tasks to the best way to hold prepared foods until you're ready to serve them. Some of it may seem a little "cheffy" or fussy, but trust us, the proof is in the final result, and these little directions add up to better cooking.

Cooking From This Book

Ingredients

We have tried to use commonly found ingredients as much as possible throughout this book, although just what constitutes "commonly found" is changing before our eyes. Certain spices, seasonings, herbs, and cheeses that were once elusive are now encountered in more and more gourmet shops or even well-stocked supermarkets. If they are not there, they are easily ordered over the internet.

If you haven't already used them, we think you'll fall in love with some of our favorite ingredients the way we have. For example, we use Korean chili powder and Calabrian chilies in a few of our dishes because they impart a distinct heat perfectly suited to those recipes. You can probably find these ingredients somewhere in your community, whether you live in a major metropolis or a small town. If not, you can have them shipped to your door in a day or two via the internet, and we think you'll find all kinds of ways to use them in your cooking.

Those items that may require a trip to the web are listed in the back of the book in the Sources section (page 321), along with a recommended purveyor. Where we don't think it will diminish the dish, we offer substitutions for those items, although in some cases they really are worth a little extra planning.

→ **EXTRA-VIRGIN OLIVE OIL**

Most cookbooks use olive oil for cooking and extra-virgin olive oil as a finishing element, but we use extra-virgin olive oil for both cooking *and* finishing. We do this for the simple reason that it tastes better, and while extra-virgin olive oil may be slightly more expensive than regular olive oil, it's usually used in very small amounts in cooking, so the cost is negligible. Extra-virgin olive oils come in a range of flavor profiles, from smooth and fruity to almost astringent, and also span a wide price range, from inexpensive to extravagant. We suggest having a mild, slightly floral extra-virgin olive oil on hand at all times. Generally speaking, a Greek, French, or northern Italian olive oil will fit this profile, while a Spanish or southern Italian oil might be too pronounced. If you want to keep another, more special olive oil on hand for finishing dishes, or even a few olive oils for different finishing effects, that's well worth doing, although we don't insist on it in our recipes.

Recipes

We have organized this book according to the courses of a meal, starting with snacks and breads and ending with dessert. In between are salads and starters, soups, pasta and risotto, and main courses divided up into fish and shellfish and poultry, meats, and game. There's also a chapter of versatile side dishes you can serve with our food or with whatever cooking you do.

To help you get the most out of our approach, most recipes in the book are divided into "To Prep" and "To Serve" steps. The prep step features the portion of the recipe that can be prepared ahead of time and held, sometimes for up to several days or longer, until you are ready to finish and serve the dish. In cases where several components of a dish can be prepared in advance, we have separated them, with the one that can be made the furthest ahead of time coming first.

A few notes on our approach:

- In most cases, you can proceed directly from the prep steps to the serving steps, so if you want to prepare an entire dish from start to finish in one fell swoop, that's fine. The exceptions are when the advance work requires something to cure, marinate, or firm up over a period of time.

- For the most part, we don't include subrecipes in the prep section because if the serve section requires, say, a stock, you might have some on hand, or choose to use a store-bought product, rather than make the one in the back of this book. So you should read the entire recipe from start to finish to see if there are any subrecipes you might want to make ahead of time; these would include any that are followed by page references, either to another recipe, or to the Basic Techniques and Recipes section at the back of the book (page 313). (The one exception to this are the pasta recipes that offer the option of fresh pasta, which we call out in the "To Prep" sections of those dishes.)

- The ingredients lists for many dishes are, ultimately, shorter than they might seem because certain ingredients, especially basics like olive oil, butter, salt, and pepper, often appear in more than one subrecipe, or in both the prep and serve sections of the dish. Read all subrecipes to be sure you know the total amount of each ingredient required to make the dish.

- Also note that some recipes are looser than others: In cases where a specific amount of, say, lemon juice, olive oil, and/or grated cheese is indicated, that's the amount you should measure and use. In other cases, the amounts are more subject to personal taste, so the ingredient list simply calls for a lemon that will be grated and/or squeezed, cheese that will be grated, olive oil that will be drizzled, and so on. In these cases, your own palate and judgment should be your guide as you add those ingredients.

- Another good reason to read all recipes from start to finish is that some prep sections feature steps that require a component to simmer for several hours or rest overnight in the refrigerator. Be sure you have the time available to wait for these steps to reach completion.

- At the back of the book, you will find a short collection of basic techniques such as how to blanch and shock green vegetables or toast nuts and spices, and recipes for some simple items called for throughout the book such as croutons, toasted bread crumbs, and stocks.

Common Sense Cooking

Generally speaking, the recipes in this book offer quantities and cooking times that will produce the desired result. But it's also important to recognize that your own instincts, common sense, and personal taste are essential factors in any cooking. If, for example, your Dutch oven is larger than ours, then you may need more stock than we did to cover the solids in your braises, and it might take a little longer than the indicated cooking time to reduce the braising liquid at the end of the recipe. Power varies from stove to stove, so if a meat isn't searing in the pan as described by a given recipe, then you probably need to turn the heat up higher than the indicated level. If a dressing doesn't taste acidic enough to your palate, go ahead and add more lemon juice or vinegar until you are happy with it. In many cases we incorporate these real-time decisions by suggesting that ingredients be added to taste, or giving a time range rather than a specific number of minutes for particular steps, but the truth is that you need to be attuned to what's going on at *every* stage of the process, and use your judgment as you cook your way through these, or any, recipes.

This is especially true of the finishing stage of our recipes, where some combination of acid (lemon juice and/or vinegar), shallots, and herbs is often added just before serving to really bring a dish alive with fresh, vibrant flavors. Add these ingredients and taste judiciously as you execute this step until the individual characteristics of the dish really pop, and don't be afraid to vary the quantities slightly until your own palate is satisfied.

Tools and Equipment

In addition to the usual battery of equipment required for cooking out of any book (knives, spoons, pots and pans, colanders and strainers, and so on), some tools and equipment called for in this book deserve special mention. A few, such as a juicer or food mill, only occur once or twice, but the following are used repeatedly throughout the book.

CHINOIS   Thought of by most as a professional kitchen tool, a chinois, or conical strainer, has a place in the home kitchen as well. You can get a similar result with a fine-mesh strainer, but a conical strainer is much easier to work with, especially when handling large quantities of food, because the pointed end neatly guides liquids into the pots or pans into which you are straining them. We don't insist you use a chinois for any recipe, but highly recommend you get your hands on this invaluable kitchen tool.

DUTCH OVEN   The gold-standard cooking vessel for braising and stewing is a ceramic, enameled, or cast-iron Dutch oven. The surface produces the dark, crisp sears often required by these recipes, and the thick walls and tight-fitting lid conduct and contain the heat during long, slow turns in the oven. The ideal size will vary from recipe to recipe; generally speaking, you want a Dutch oven that will hold the solids comfortably, but with minimal extra space because close quarters intensify flavors. So, it's desirable to have small (3.5-quart), medium (5-quart), and large (8-quart) Dutch ovens on hand.

MANDOLINE For thinly slicing fruits and vegetables, there's no substitute for this tool, which produces flawlessly even cuts. For our money (literally), Japanese mandolines are the best option. They cost only about $20, their plastic casings are lightweight and compact, and their blade is set at an angle, making it easier to produce a smooth, consistent cut without a lot of force. They last for several years, after which you can simply discard them and purchase a new one.

MICROPLANE The Microplane grater originated as a woodworking tool and has morphed into a standard-issue piece of kitchen equipment. It's not as uncommon as it once was, but we call your attention to it because we use it more than most cooks, whether grating lemon zest over a dish as a finishing touch or grating garlic to help it integrate into a dish.

HAND-CRANK PASTA ROLLER We provide homemade options for many of the pastas in this book, and a hand-crank roller is really the only way to get the dough as thin as it should be before cutting or shaping it for specific uses. These rollers are not very expensive, and you may find other uses for them as well, such as for making the crackers on page 16.

→ **CAKE TESTER**

One of our favorite tools doesn't show up in many cookbooks. It's inexpensive, retailing anywhere from $1 to $10, but is priceless in our professional kitchens. It's a cake tester, a small, thin, steel rod originally used to tell if a cake was done baking by plunging it in, then withdrawing it; if it comes out clean, the cake is done, while batter clinging to the tester indicates more baking is needed. Cake testers can also be used to determine the doneness of other foods, especially fish and meats. Because steel conducts heat, you can get a good sense of how warm those foods are at the center by inserting a cake tester into their thickest part, holding it there for 30 seconds, then removing it and touching it to your wrist or just under your lower lip, which are relatively sensitive areas. If the tester feels cold, the center of the cooked item has a ways to go. Because body temperature is 98.6°F, a warm tester indicates you've passed 100°F, with increasing degrees of heat indicating more well-done. (An additional consideration when cooking fish is that if you slide the tester in at an angle and it encounters resistance, the fish isn't done.)

It takes some practice to develop finesse with a cake tester, in part because ideal doneness is often a matter of personal taste: Different people prefer different fish and meats at different temperatures and/or degrees of doneness. After using a cake tester a few times, you will develop a feeling for when things are cooked to your liking. To help guide you, we have indicated a heat level that will indicate doneness where cake testers are used throughout the book.

Additionally, a cake tester is less intrusive than a thermometer, so thin that it doesn't cause juices or fats to leach out, and can be repeatedly inserted without marring the food. Although we provide other options, we use it as an indicator of doneness in this book, and can't recommend it highly enough.

Breads and Snacks

Rosemary Flatbread with Whipped Ricotta

Makes 8 loaves

These little loaves of crusty bread, exquisitely soft on the inside, and topped with rosemary and fleur de sel, epitomize the connection between our kitchen and yours. We devised them as a welcome for guests at Battersby; it was important to us to have a freshly baked bread to set a tone of hospitality, but with just three cooks in the kitchen, we needed something turnkey. We came up with this recipe: The bread can be baked ahead of time and simply reheated when ready to serve.

You don't need to be an accomplished baker to make these. The dough is very forgiving, and the cool, creamy, whipped ricotta cheese with which they are served is a breeze to prepare. The technique of whipping ricotta in a food processor makes the cheese smoother and more spreadable than it is naturally. When whipped, it can be used to add richness to a dish like the carrot dish on page 277, substituting whipped ricotta for the yogurt.

If serving less bread, you can divide the recipe, or keep the unused loaves frozen for another time. Like many baking recipes, this one is a little safer when ingredients are weighed rather than measured by volume, so if you have a scale, go by the metric amounts. (See photo on page 7.)

To Prep

Rosemary Flatbread

3¼ cups (400 grams) all-purpose flour, plus more for dusting

1¼ teaspoons (4 grams) active dry yeast

1¼ teaspoons (8 grams) kosher salt

2 teaspoons (8 grams) sugar

1 tablespoon extra-virgin olive oil, plus more for greasing

Leaves from 2 fresh rosemary branches, chopped

Fleur de sel

Put the flour, yeast, salt, sugar, and 1½ cups (350 grams) water in a large bowl and mix by hand just until a dough comes together (it will be very loose and wet). Cover the bowl with plastic wrap and let rest at 70 to 80°F for 4 hours or up to 6 hours; during this time, the dough will double in size.

When ready to proceed, line a large baking sheet with parchment paper, and lightly grease it with olive oil. Lightly flour a work surface and turn the dough out onto the surface. Divide the dough into 8 equal pieces, and fold each one over once, tucking the edges under, but do not knead or work them, and set them on the parchment-lined sheet. (Dust them with flour as necessary to keep the dough from sticking to your hands.) Rub the tops with a total of 1 tablespoon of olive oil and top with another, inverted rimmed baking sheet to keep them from drying out. Let rest in a warm space, ideally 80 to 90°F for about 1 hour. (Near the oven while it is preheating is often perfect for this.)

Position a rack in the center of the oven and preheat the oven to its highest setting, preferably at least 500°F. Press into the dough with three fingers on each hand and pull gently from the center outward to stretch it out, making small dimples; repeat two more times to make a total of 18 dimples. Top with the rosemary and season with fleur de sel. Bake until the crust is a dark golden brown, 10 to 14 minutes, rotating the sheet 180 degrees after 7 minutes. Remove the baking sheet from the oven, transfer the loaves to a rack, and let cool. The loaves may be held at room temperature for up to 1 day, or frozen in plastic bags for up to 1 month.

(continued)

→   **FLEUR DE SEL**

A good, finely ground sea salt makes a fine finishing touch in many dishes, but for a more pure salt flavor and more subtle crunch, there's nothing like fleur de sel ("flower of salt"), the exquisitely light, almost fluffy, salt that's hand-harvested from the surface of marshes. The labor-intensive means of collecting fleur de sel results in a relatively high price, but it's worth having some on hand to sprinkle over certain savory baked preparations, sliced grilled or roasted meats, and other dishes.

Whipped Ricotta Cheese
1 cup ricotta cheese
1 tablespoon extra-virgin olive oil
Kosher salt

Put the ricotta cheese in the bowl of a food processor fitted with the steel blade. Add the olive oil and pulse a few times to whip the cheese and incorporate the oil. Season with salt, pulse again, and transfer to a ramekin or other small vessel suitable for serving, or into four to eight smaller vessels for serving individually. Use right away or cover with plastic wrap and refrigerate for up to 24 hours.

To Serve

Position a rack in the center of the oven and preheat the oven to 350°F.

Remove the whipped ricotta cheese from the refrigerator and let it come to room temperature.

For frozen bread, wrap the loaves individually in aluminum foil. Bake until warmed through, about 8 minutes. For fresh bread, bake for 2 minutes with no foil.

Serve the bread on small plates, with the whipped ricotta alongside for spreading or dipping.

Gougères with Sauce Mornay

Makes about 50 gougères

We serve these little cheese puffs to welcome guests at our second restaurant, Dover, and they are a valuable, all-purpose hors d'oeuvre to have in your repertoire as well. Topped with fleur de sel and Parmigiano-Reggiano, they are a natural pairing with many cocktails, and sublime with a glass of champagne. You can make them without the Sauce Mornay, but we think it adds an invaluable, decadent creaminess.

¼ cup milk

4 tablespoons (½ stick) unsalted butter, cut into pieces

½ teaspoon kosher salt

½ cup all-purpose flour

2 large eggs

Fleur de sel

About ¼ cup finely grated Parmigiano-Reggiano or Grana Padano cheese

¾ cup Sauce Mornay (recipe follows)

Preheat the oven to 400°F.

Put the milk, butter, salt, and ¼ cup water in a pan and bring to a boil over high heat, whisking to incorporate the ingredients, about 1 minute. Remove the pan from the heat and whisk in the flour, whisking just enough to eliminate any lumps and make a smooth paste, about 10 seconds. Reduce the heat to low and use a rubber spatula to further smooth the batter for 10 seconds.

Transfer the batter to the bowl of a stand mixer fitted with the paddle attachment. Beat on medium speed to release any steam and cool the mixture, 1 to 2 minutes. With the motor running, add the eggs one at a time, beating until each is fully incorporated before adding the next one, about 1 minute per egg. (If you were to add both of the eggs at once, the mixture would break; you will see that as each egg is added, the batter becomes wet, but a single egg is quickly reabsorbed into the batter.)

Transfer the mixture to a pastry bag fitted with a wide, plain tip. (Alternatively, the batter can be used for many other dishes; see page 14.)

Line a baking sheet with parchment paper (see Note, page 14). With a swirling motion, pipe the batter onto the lined baking sheet into blobs about ½ inch in diameter and ½ inch tall. (You can freeze the gougères on the baking sheet until hard, transfer them to a resealable plastic bag, and freeze; when ready to bake, thaw and proceed with the directions.)

Top the gougères with a sprinkling of fleur de sel and cheese.

Bake the gougères until firm and very lightly browned, about 20 minutes, rotating the pan 180 degrees after 10 minutes.

To serve, pour the Sauce Mornay into a squeeze bottle or into a piping bag fitted with the smallest plain attachment you have, no wider than $\frac{1}{16}$ of an inch. Poke a hole in the bottom of each gougère with a paring knife and pipe in some room-temperature sauce. The gougères are best when freshly baked, filled, and served, but may be made and held at room temperature for up to 1 hour before serving.

Note: *When baking on parchment paper, a cool trick is to use a few dabs of your batter—one in each corner of the pan under the paper—to "glue" the parchment paper in place.*

→   PÂTE À CHOUX

This batter, called pâte à choux, has many applications. One use is to make gnocchi Parisienne: Put the pâte à choux in a piping bag fitted with a wide, plain tip and pipe it directly into simmering, salted water, cutting the batter into 1-inch lengths with a pair of kitchen shears as you pipe. Simmer until the gnocchi float to the surface, then drain, shock in ice water, and dry them. (See the spaetzle recipe on page 288 for guidance in these steps.) Pâte à choux can also be used to make pommes dauphine: Put some of the batter in a bowl, stir together with leftover potato puree, and deep-fry in small spoonfuls.

Sauce Mornay

Makes about 1½ cups

Sauce Mornay is a béchamel made with both Parmigiano-Reggiano and an Alpine cheese. Classically you might see it over vegetables; we prefer it in small doses, as in the gougères. You can also use it to make a quick macaroni and cheese by tossing it with freshly cooked, drained elbow macaroni, transferring to a baking dish, topping with grated Comté cheese, and baking until browned on top.

1 tablespoon unsalted butter

1 tablespoon all-purpose flour

1 cup heavy cream

Kosher salt and freshly ground black pepper

¼ cup finely grated Comté or other Alpine cheese, such as Emmenthal or Gruyère

1 tablespoon finely grated Parmigiano-Reggiano or Grana Padano cheese

Melt the butter in a small heavy pot over medium heat. Sprinkle the flour over the butter and cook, whisking, until they come together to form a roux—do not allow to brown. Whisk in the cream and let the roux come to a boil, whisking all the while, until the roux is amalgamated and thick, about 2 minutes. Season with salt and pepper, then remove the pot from the heat and whisk in the cheeses until the mixture is thick.

For making gougères, use the sauce while still warm, no more than 1 hour after preparing it; leftover sauce can be refrigerated in an airtight container for up to 2 days, then reheated before using.

Fennel Crackers with White Bean Puree and Tapenade

Serves 4 to 6, with leftover crackers

The simplicity of the presentation here allows the big Provençal flavors to sneak up on you—the salty, fennel-dusted cracker, the herb-infused beans, and the briny, bracing tapenade. If you don't want to make your own cracker, you can purchase crisps or flatbreads, just be sure that they are crunchy and salted. Because there are so many high-quality tapenades available for purchase, we encourage you to use your favorite brand here. The recipe calls for a pasta machine to roll out the crackers; if you don't have one, you can cut the crackers and roll them out individually as thin as possible with a rolling pin before baking.

To Prep

White Bean Puree

1 cup dry white beans
3 garlic cloves, smashed with the
    side of a knife and peeled
¼ Spanish onion
½ small carrot, halved
½ celery stalk, halved
1 bay leaf, preferably fresh
1 small fresh rosemary sprig
2 fresh thyme sprigs
¼ cup plus 3 tablespoons extra-virgin olive oil
Kosher salt
3 tablespoons sherry vinegar
Freshly ground black pepper

Put the beans in a medium pot, cover with cold water, and soak overnight. Drain.

Return the beans to the pot and cover with cold water by 1 inch. Bring to a gentle simmer over medium heat. Add the garlic, onion, carrot, celery, bay leaf, rosemary, thyme, and 3 tablespoons of the olive oil. Simmer until the beans are very soft, about 1 hour, seasoning with salt after 30 minutes. If the water level reduces enough that the beans are exposed, add just enough water to cover them. (When finished, you want the water to be just level with the top of the beans.)

Use tongs or a slotted spoon to pick out and discard the vegetables, garlic, and herbs. Drain the beans in a colander set over a bowl; reserve the cooking liquid. Transfer the beans to a blender while still hot. Add just enough of the reserved cooking liquid to cover them, and puree. If the mixture isn't creamy, slowly add a little more of the liquid and blend, then slowly add the remaining ¼ cup of the olive oil and blend to produce an emulsified puree,

about 1 minute. Season with the vinegar, salt, and pepper and pulse to incorporate. Transfer the beans to a bowl or airtight storage container and let cool in the refrigerator. Once cool, the beans may be used right away or covered and refrigerated for up to 2 days.

Note: *This makes about 3 cups, a bit more than you need, but it's difficult to produce a smaller batch because you must make enough to engage the blade of the food processor. Save the extra for up to 2 days and spread it on crostini (see pages 34–39), serve it as a side for braised lamb, or make it the base of a vegetarian sandwich, adding cucumbers and other vegetables.*

Fennel Crackers

1½ cups all-purpose flour, plus
    more for dusting

6 cloves garlic confit (see page 315)

Finely grated zest of 2 lemons

1½ tablespoons extra-virgin olive oil

½ teaspoon sugar

1 teaspoon kosher salt

3 tablespoons fennel seed, toasted
    (see page 314) and coarsely cracked

Fleur de sel

Put the flour, garlic, lemon zest, olive oil, sugar, and salt in the bowl of a food processor fitted with the steel blade. Pulse until the garlic is minced. With the motor running, slowly add about ¼ cup cold water until the dough comes together in a ball. Generously flour your work surface and transfer the dough to it; it should pour out of the bowl, but hold its shape if pushed together. Generously flour your hands to keep the dough from sticking to them and knead until the dough comes together in a ball, 1 to 2 minutes. Wrap the dough in plastic wrap and refrigerate until cold, about 20 minutes, or for up to 24 hours.

Preheat the oven to 450°F.

Roll out the chilled dough, ideally with a pasta machine, repeatedly rolling it and lowering the setting on the machine until you reach the second-thinnest setting. If the dough sticks, lightly dust it with some flour (this might not be necessary).

Use a bench cutter or large chef's knife to cut the dough into triangles or rectangles, pressing down on the dough rather than pulling or dragging the blade through it. Alternatively, bake the sheets whole and break them into shards after baking.

Set the dough on a large baking sheet (do not oil the sheet). Put water in a spray bottle and mist water over the dough, or lightly apply the water with a pastry brush. Scatter fennel seeds and fleur de sel over the dough. Spray with a little more water, then bake until crispy and lightly browned, 3 to 4 minutes. Remove from the oven and let the crackers cool to room temperature.

The crackers can be held in an airtight container at room temperature for up to 24 hours but are best served as soon as possible.

To Serve

½ cup store-bought tapenade

Serve the white bean puree and the tapenade in separate serving vessels, or side by side in the same vessel, with the crackers alongside. The presentation is highly adaptable and you should customize it to your available serving vessels and personal style.

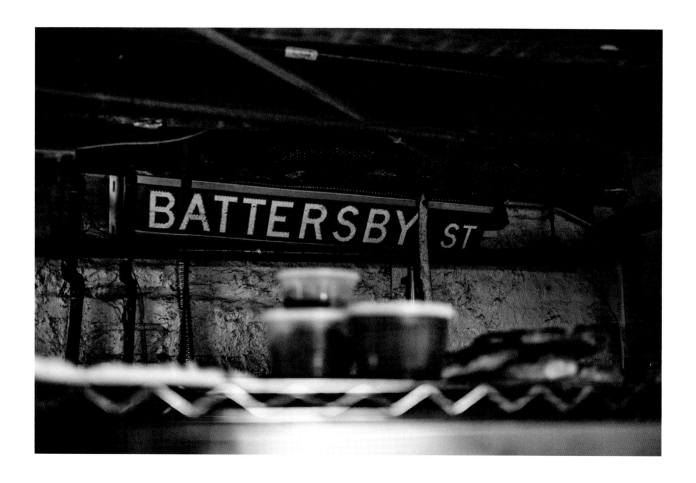

Tomato and Strawberry Soup with Basil and Balsamic Vinegar

Makes 2 cups; serves 8 as an amuse-bouche

This soup, intended to be an amuse-bouche, should be served only in early summer, when strawberry and tomato growing seasons intersect. Because the flavor of individual fruits vary so dramatically, use your personal taste to balance the sweetness and acidity by adjusting the amount of strawberry or tomato after blending the soup. For the drizzle of balsamic vinegar to have the desired impact, it's important to use an authentic variety from Modena or Reggio Emilia; they are expensive but a valuable high-impact condiment to have on hand.

To Prep

1½ cups strawberries (about 8 ounces), stemmed

1 large beefsteak tomato (about 12 ounces), peeled (see page 313) and coarsely chopped

Pinch of sugar

Pinch of kosher salt

Freshly ground black pepper

2 tablespoons extra-virgin olive oil

1 teaspoon sherry vinegar

Put the strawberries, tomato, sugar, salt, pepper (to taste), oil, and vinegar in a blender, and blend to a soup. Taste and add a little more strawberry (if not sweet enough) and/or tomato (if not acidic enough), then blend again. Transfer the soup to a large bowl, cover with plastic wrap, and chill in the refrigerator for as long as possible, but serve the same day.

To Serve

Extra-virgin olive oil

Authentic balsamic vinegar from Modena or Reggio Emilia

Freshly ground black pepper

8 small fresh basil leaves, or torn larger leaves

Pour the soup into eight small, preferably chilled, glasses. Drizzle with oil and vinegar and dust with a pinch of pepper. Garnish each glass with a basil leaf and serve.

Crudités with Aioli

Serves 4

This is a straight-up version of crudités, or raw vegetables served with a dip, in this case an aioli (garlic mayonnaise). You can use other vegetables if you like, or just one type. You can also serve the raw vegetables with Caesar Dressing (page 89), White Bean Puree (page 16), or tapenade.

To Prep

½ cup snow peas

4 large asparagus stalks, halved crosswise

2 celery stalks, peeled and cut into batons

4 small radishes, peeled and halved

8 romaine lettuce leaves

2 Belgian endives, leaves separated

6 baby carrots

½ fennel bulb, thinly shaved, preferably on a mandoline

2 golden beets, thinly shaved on a mandoline

4 baby turnips, halved

1 zucchini, halved crosswise and cut into spears

Fill a large bowl halfway with ice and water. Submerge the vegetables in the ice water for at least 10 minutes to crisp them. The vegetables can be refrigerated in the bowl of ice water for up to 2 hours.

To Serve

Aioli (page 193)

Drain the vegetables and pat them dry with paper towels. Decoratively arrange them on four individual plates, or on a platter to serve them family-style. Serve the aioli in a cup in the center of the table, or in smaller ramekins placed on or alongside the individual plates.

Greek Yogurt with Root Vegetable Muesli

Serves 4

This is our savory take on a breakfast favorite, with root vegetables instead of grains used to make a crunchy condiment that we use in an amuse, contrasting it with the cool, creamy yogurt. You can also scatter the muesli over salads and vegetable dishes to add flavor and texture, or change up the vegetables according to what you have on hand or to suit your personal taste.

To Prep

Note: *Ideally, slice each vegetable with a mandoline.*

1 cup thinly sliced carrots
1 cup thinly sliced sunchokes
1 cup thinly sliced red beets
1 cup thinly sliced celery root
1 cup thinly sliced parsnips
1 cup peeled, thinly sliced sweet potato
1 cup peeled, thinly sliced yam
About 1 quart canola oil or other
    neutral oil such as grapeseed
Kosher salt
3 tablespoons Crispy Fried Quinoa
    (recipe follows; optional)

Put the vegetables in separate bowls, cover each with ice water, and refrigerate overnight to crisp them and draw out some of their starch.

When ready to proceed, pour the oil into a heavy deep pot to a depth of 3 inches and heat the oil over medium-high heat to 300°F.

While the oil is heating, drain the vegetables individually and spin them dry in a salad spinner. When the oil is hot, fry the vegetables individually by type until lightly golden and crispy, adjusting the heat level as necessary to maintain the temperature; each vegetable will take between 2 and 3 minutes, depending on the thickness of the cut and the vegetable's moisture content.

Use a slotted spoon to transfer the vegetables to paper towels to drain, and immediately season each batch with salt.

Once all the vegetables have been fried, drained, and seasoned, put them all in the bowl of a food processor fitted with a steel blade and pulse until finely ground, but not to a powder. Use right away, adding the quinoa, if desired, or store in an airtight container at room temperature for up to 2 days.

To Serve

¾ cup Greek yogurt
1 to 2 teaspoons fresh lemon juice
About 1 tablespoon extra-virgin olive oil
Kosher salt and freshly ground black pepper

Put the yogurt in a bowl and whisk in 1 teaspoon of the lemon juice and the olive oil. Taste and add more lemon juice, if desired, according to your taste. Season with salt and pepper and whisk briefly to incorporate.

Spread about 3 tablespoons of the yogurt over the center of each of four small plates. Sprinkle the vegetable muesli over the yogurt and serve.

Crispy Fried Quinoa

Makes about ½ cup

These crispy grains stay crunchy for a long time and make a wonderful topping for salads and roasted meats. If you make your own granola, add a few tablespoons of this to it.

3 tablespoons quinoa

Kosher salt

Canola oil or other neutral oil, such as grapeseed, for frying

Put the quinoa in a pot. Add just enough cold water to cover and a pinch of salt. Bring to a simmer over medium heat, but do not let the quinoa pop open, about 8 minutes. Drain and rinse under cold running water to stop the cooking, then drain on a paper towel; set aside.

Line a plate with paper towels. Pour canola oil into a heavy deep pot to a depth of 1 inch and heat the oil over medium heat to 350°F. Add the quinoa, stir, and fry, adjusting the heat level as necessary to maintain the temperature, until golden brown and crispy, about 4 minutes.

Strain the quinoa in a fine-mesh strainer set over a heatproof bowl, being careful to not let the hot oil splash. Transfer the quinoa to the paper towel–lined plate and season immediately with salt. Use right away or store in an airtight container at room temperature for up to 3 days.

Hamachi Rillettes Niçoise

Serves 4

Our take on a Niçoise salad came about from the desire not to waste a single scrap of usable food in our kitchen. When butchering a fish, you are always left with unattractive cuts such as the belly, tail, collar, and bits that cling to the bone. We preserve those pieces and make them the focus of a salad. If you butcher your own fish, you can do the same, or simply buy a piece of fish and preserve it; you can also skip the preserving step here and purchase high-quality tuna packed in olive oil. Though not sold as "preserved tuna," seek out brands from Italy or Spain with the tuna in fillets, often in glass jars.

If you are not familiar with them, this recipe also offers a nice introduction to piquillo peppers, delicate, fire-roasted peppers that are super convenient because they are sold ready to use in cans and jars. They traditionally come from Spain, but less expensive South American varieties are available and are perfectly fine; in fact, we use them ourselves.

To Prep

6 ounces hamachi or other fatty fish, such as tuna, mackerel, or salmon

Kosher salt

2 cups extra-virgin olive oil for preserving the fish

1 tablespoon whole-grain mustard

1 teaspoon finely chopped fresh rosemary

½ tablespoon minced drained brine-packed capers

Put the fish in a small bowl, season with salt, and let rest for 10 minutes.

Meanwhile, pour the oil into a small pot, just large enough to comfortably hold the fish with about 1 inch of space all around it, and heat over medium heat to 120 to 130°F.

Carefully lower the fish into the oil and slowly poach, adjusting the heat as necessary to keep the temperature between 120 and 130°F. Cook until the fish is opaque, 10 to 15 minutes; if it begins to leach white albumin, it is overcooking and should be removed

(continued)

½ tablespoon minced shallot

Freshly ground black pepper

About 2 teaspoons sherry vinegar

from the oil. To further test for doneness, remove a piece of fish from the oil with a slotted spoon and transfer it to a clean, dry work surface; if it flakes apart easily, it's done. Remove the pot from the heat and let the fish cool in the oil. Remove the fish from the oil, remove and discard any bones, and flake the fish. You should have about 2 cups flaked fish. If not using immediately, refrigerate the fish in the oil in an airtight container for up to 3 days, then remove it from the oil and flake it. Strain the poaching oil, pour into a small vessel and set aside. (If using store-bought preserved tuna, simply drain off the oil.)

Fill a large stainless-steel bowl halfway with ice and water. Put the flaked fish in a medium bowl and set it over the ice water. Add the mustard, rosemary, capers, and shallots. Mash the fish with a fork while slowly drizzling in 3 tablespoons of the reserved poaching oil. Continue to mash until the fish and other ingredients have come together into a paste and all the oil has been incorporated. Season with salt, pepper, and sherry vinegar. The rillettes can be served right away or refrigerated in an airtight container for up to 2 days.

To Serve

1 large Kirby cucumber, peeled
   and cut into ½-inch discs

4 piquillo peppers (see Sources, page
   321), or 1 roasted bell pepper

4 tablespoons extra-virgin olive oil

2 tablespoons sherry vinegar

Kosher salt and freshly ground black pepper

4 crispy lettuce leaves, ideally
   hearts of romaine

4 hard-boiled quail eggs, peeled and
   halved, or 2 hard-boiled chicken eggs,
   peeled and quartered (see below)

16 black olives, such as Taggiasca olives

4 oil-packed anchovy fillets

8 slices grilled or toasted rustic bread

Put the cucumber slices in a small bowl and the peppers in another bowl. Dress each with 2 tablespoons of the oil and 1 tablespoon of the vinegar and season with salt and pepper. Toss and let marinate for 5 minutes.

You can freely adapt the presentation to suit your own sensibility. To plate this family-style, arrange a bed of lettuce on a platter. Arrange the rillettes, eggs, olives, and anchovies on top. Or divide it among individual plates, arranging the ingredients atop a single piece of lettuce. Serve the bread alongside.

→   HARD-BOILING EGGS

Rather than boiling eggs for an extended period of time, try our method for hard-boiling: Put the eggs in a pot with a tight-fitting lid, cover with cold water by a few inches, and bring to a boil over medium heat. As soon as the water boils, turn off the heat, cover the pot with the lid, remove from the heat, and set aside for 15 minutes, or 5 minutes for quail eggs. Remove the lid, set the pot in the sink, and refresh with cold gently running water until the shells are cool to the touch. This keeps the egg from cooking too quickly and prevents the unsightly green ring that sometimes forms between yolk and white.

Caviar Pie

Serves 4

A dressed-up adaptation of the 1960s cocktail party classic, this starter sets a layer of caviar atop a base of hard-boiled eggs mixed with mayonnaise and a layer of sour cream and cream cheese. It's a decadent, kitschy way to begin a special occasion, and perfect with champagne or vodka martinis.

You can use any black caviar to make this. We use paddlefish roe; you can also use trout roe and, of course, Caspian varieties such as osetra.

To Prep

"The Pie"

3 large eggs, hard-boiled (see page 28)

2 tablespoons mayonnaise

Kosher salt and freshly ground black pepper

1 teaspoon finely chopped fresh dill

1 teaspoon minced scallion whites

2 heaping tablespoons sour cream, at room temperature

2 tablespoons Philadelphia cream cheese

Finely grated zest of 1 lemon

1 teaspoon fresh lemon juice

Peel the eggs and separate the whites from the yolks. Crumble the yolks or pass them through a tamis into a medium bowl. Finely chop the whites and add them to the bowl.

Add the mayonnaise, season with salt and pepper, and stir to combine. Stir in the dill and scallion. Use right away or cover with plastic wrap and refrigerate for up to 24 hours.

Put the sour cream, cream cheese, lemon zest, and lemon juice in a medium bowl, season with salt and pepper, and stir to incorporate.

Transfer the egg mixture to a 1-cup ramekin, filling it three-quarters up the sides and tightly packing it with a rubber spatula. Top with the cream cheese mixture. Cover loosely with plastic wrap and refrigerate for at least 30 minutes or up to 24 hours to firm it up.

(continued)

Buckwheat Blini

⅓ cup milk

½ cup all-purpose flour

½ cup buckwheat flour

1 large egg, separated

½ teaspoon active dry yeast

½ teaspoon kosher salt

2 tablespoons unsalted butter

Warm the milk in a small saucepan over medium heat, until nearly simmering. Meanwhile, in a small bowl, whisk together the all-purpose and buckwheat flours, then whisk in the egg yolk.

When the milk is almost simmering, remove the pan from the heat and whisk in the yeast and salt, then whisk the milk mixture into the flour-yolk mixture, a little at first, to avoid cooking the egg. Cover with plastic wrap and let rise at room temperature until doubled in volume, about 1 hour.

After an hour, whip the egg white until soft peaks form, then fold the whites into the mixture. The batter can be refrigerated in an airtight container for up to 24 hours.

To cook the blini, melt the butter over medium heat in a large pan. Use a tablespoon to spoon out the batter, pushing it off the spoon onto the pan with another spoon. (You can also put the batter in a squeeze bottle and pipe it onto the pan in 2-inch circles.) Cook until the surface of each blini is bubbling, 1 to 2 minutes, then carefully turn them over with a spatula and cook on the other side until the bottom is golden brown, 1 to 2 minutes. Transfer the cooked blini to a plate and repeat until all the batter has been used. The blini can be served right away or loosely covered with plastic wrap and held at room temperature for up to 4 hours.

To Serve

4 thin slices brioche, rye bread, or pumpernickel

2 ounces black caviar (see headnote)

4 lemon wedges

If the blini were made ahead and held, reheat them in a single layer on a baking sheet in a preheated 300°F oven.

Toast the bread, then cut off the crusts and cut the slices in half diagonally to make toast points.

Meanwhile, gently spread the caviar over the pie using a spoon or offset spatula.

Serve the caviar pie in the center of the table, passing the toast points and blini alongside on their own plates or in folded linen napkins. Pass the lemon wedges alongside on a separate small plate.

Cóctel de Mariscos

Serves 4

This festive, refreshing starter (the name translates, simply, to "seafood cocktail") is perfect for summer parties. It's based on the Mexican dish *campechana*, with lightly cooked clams and shrimp, raw oysters, and a ceviche-like flavor thanks to the lime juice, jalapeño, and cilantro. Rather than cook the clams with aromatics, the method here isolates and intensifies their flavor. Feel free to change the seafood, opting for scallops or mussels. For a fun presentation, serve the cocktail in small bowls set in larger bowls filled with crushed ice.

To Prep

8 littleneck clams, scrubbed

¼ cup dry white wine

¼ cup white wine vinegar

1 bay leaf, preferably fresh

½ teaspoon fennel seed

½ teaspoon whole black peppercorns

½ teaspoon coriander seed

Pinch of red pepper flakes

Kosher salt

1 thin round lemon slice, seeds removed

4 jumbo shrimp (about 4 ounces total weight)

Put the clams in a pot just large enough to hold them in a single layer. Add 1 tablespoon cold water. Cover with a lid and set the pot over medium-high heat. Cook, gently shaking once or twice to cause the clams to open, for about 5 minutes. Discard any clams that do not open. Transfer the clams to a plate and let cool. Strain the cooking liquid through a fine-mesh strainer into a small stainless-steel bowl and set over a larger bowl filled halfway with ice to cool.

Make a poaching liquid for the shrimp by putting the wine, vinegar, bay leaf, fennel seed, peppercorns, coriander seed, red pepper flakes, and ½ cup water in a pot. Add 3 tablespoons salt and bring to a simmer over medium-high heat. When the liquid simmers, remove the pot from the heat, add the lemon slice, and set aside to let the flavors infuse for 5 minutes.

Meanwhile, put the shrimp in a stainless-steel bowl. After the poaching liquid has rested for 5 minutes, pour it over the shrimp and poach until firm and pink, about 5 minutes, depending on the size of the shrimp. (If they seem to be overcooking, set the bowl in a larger bowl filled halfway with ice to slow the cooking. Regardless, once fully cooked, set the bowl over ice water to cool the shrimp down and prevent overcooking.) Peel and devein the shrimp and clean them in the poaching liquid (see Note). Cut the shrimp into bite-size pieces.

Refrigerate the shrimp, clams, and clam cooking liquid in separate airtight containers for at least 1 hour or up to 24 hours.

To Serve

4 oysters, preferably smaller West Coast varieties such as Kumamoto or Barron Point, shucked, with their liquor

2 tablespoons thinly sliced red onion

1 teaspoon thinly sliced seeded jalapeño

Juice of 1 lime, plus more as necessary

Kosher salt

½ cup canned tomato juice

1 teaspoon chopped chipotle in adobo

1 teaspoon hot sauce, such as Valentina or Tabasco (see below)

¼ cup diced peeled (see page 313) beefsteak tomato (from about 1 medium tomato), with its juice and seeds

½ avocado, pitted, peeled, and diced

2 tablespoons chopped fresh cilantro

Freshly ground black pepper

Extra-virgin olive oil

Put the reserved shrimp and clams, oysters and their liquor, onion, jalapeño, and lime juice in a stainless-steel bowl. Add a pinch of salt and toss. Set over a larger bowl filled halfway with ice, and allow to marinate for 5 minutes. Add 2 tablespoons of the reserved clam cooking liquid and the tomato juice, chipotle, and hot sauce. Taste and add more lime juice, if necessary. Add the diced tomato, then the avocado and cilantro and toss briefly. Season with black pepper.

Divide among chilled bowls, drizzle each serving with olive oil, and serve.

Note: *Cleaning cooked shrimp in their poaching liquid intensifies flavor rather than diminishing it, as cleaning them under running water does.*

→ HOT SAUCE

Not all hot sauces are created equal. In our kitchens, we use many different brands, each for a different effect or because it gets along with another ingredient particularly well. We like Valentina for this dish because it's mellow, with a classic Mexican flavor profile, and not super spicy. The ridiculously popular dried-chili-and-garlic condiment Sriracha is terrific with lamb—this makes sense, because it has much in common with the Moroccan condiment harissa, which is often paired with lamb as well. *Pique*-style sauce is based on two popular homemade Puerto Rican staples (*pique verde* and *pique criollo*) and is good on meats, especially roasted pork and chicken. Chili oil, popular in Chinese cooking, delivers heat and color that can be used to apply isolated beads or emulsified into a sauce or soup, weaving the heat in and lending an attractive orange tint. Even taken-for-granted Tabasco has its place, offering a way to incorporate the flavor and heat of cayenne into a variety of preparations.

Crostini

Crostini are as valuable at home as they are at a restaurant—a quick and enjoyable way to kick off a meal with an hors d'oeuvre that can be passed or set out, and easily adapted to accommodate a wide range of toppings. Here are four of our favorites, each associated with a particular season.

English Pea Crostini with Mint and Pecorino

Serves 4

This springtime crostini is one of the few recipes in the book that doesn't feature a prep step; it's quick and easy to make à la minute. Use the freshest peas you can find; you do not need to blanch them ahead of time.

4 tablespoons extra-virgin olive oil

1 tablespoon unsalted butter

4 ramps, white bottoms trimmed and thinly sliced, green tops torn by hand into bite-size pieces

1 cup shucked fresh English peas

About 1 cup chicken stock or vegetable stock, preferably homemade (pages 317 and 316), or water

4 thin, angled baguette slices

4 heaping tablespoons ricotta cheese, at room temperature

4 fresh mint leaves, torn by hand

Kosher salt and freshly ground black pepper

1 lemon

Small piece of Pecorino Romano or Manchego cheese, for grating

Heat 1 tablespoon of the olive oil with the butter in a wide medium pot over medium heat. When the butter foams, add the ramp whites and cook, stirring occasionally, until softened but not browned, about 2 minutes. Add the peas and cook, stirring occasionally, for 1 minute. Pour in just enough stock to cover the vegetables, bring to a simmer, and cook until the peas are al dente and there's almost no liquid remaining, about 5 minutes.

Meanwhile, brush the bread with 2 tablespoons of the oil and toast or grill until hard, about 4 minutes. Spread each slice with 1 heaping tablespoon of the ricotta. Set aside.

When the peas are done, use a fork to coarsely mash them, leaving a few larger pieces for a rustic effect. Remove the pot from the heat and stir in the mint and ramp greens and the remaining 1 tablespoon oil. Season with salt and pepper

Spoon the peas and ramps over the ricotta on each crostino. Grate a little lemon zest and cheese over the top. Serve.

Burrata Crostini with Peaches

Serves 4

This summer crostini, so easy to prepare that there's no prep step, was engineered to show off great, fresh peaches and creamy burrata, an Italian cheese that encases a luscious combination of mozzarella and cream within a shell of pure mozzarella; try to use only a high-quality imported burrata because American varieties can be watery. The cheese—and this crostini—are a perfect match with the telltale drinks of the season: prosecco or champagne, a Bellini or Negroni, or a glass of rosé.

1 (4- to 5-ounce) ball burrata cheese

3 tablespoons extra-virgin olive oil, plus more for drizzling

Kosher salt and freshly ground black pepper

4 thin, angled baguette slices

1 small peach, halved, pitted, and thinly sliced

Pinch of sugar

Lemon wedge

Basil, arugula, or watercress, for garnish (optional)

Put the burrata and 1 tablespoon of the olive oil in a medium bowl, season with salt and pepper, and stir them together.

Brush the bread with the remaining 2 tablespoons oil and toast or grill until hard, about 4 minutes.

Arrange the peach slices on a small plate and season with the sugar, a few drops of lemon juice, and salt and pepper. Top with a drizzle of olive oil.

Spread the burrata on the toast. Top with the peaches, overlapping the slices. Finish with basil, if desired. Serve.

Butternut Squash Crostini with Ricotta, Honey, and Walnuts

Serves 4

A terrific way to use one of our favorite autumn crops, butternut squash, complementing its innate sweetness with honey and rounding out the flavor profile with cool, creamy ricotta cheese and walnuts.

To Prep

1 tablespoon extra-virgin olive oil
1 tablespoon unsalted butter
⅔ cup diced butternut squash
Kosher salt and freshly ground black pepper

Heat the oil and butter in a medium sauté pan over medium heat. When the butter has melted, add the squash, season with salt and pepper, and cook, stirring occasionally, until soft and golden brown all over but still holding its shape, 8 to 10 minutes. Transfer the squash to paper towels to drain and let cool to room temperature. Use right away or refrigerate in an airtight container for up to 8 hours.

To Serve

4 thin, angled baguette slices
4 tablespoons extra-virgin olive oil
1 cup ricotta cheese (5 ounces)
Kosher salt and freshly ground black pepper
¼ cup toasted walnuts (see page 314)
2 tablespoons honey
2 tablespoons coarsely chopped fresh
   flat-leaf parsley (optional)

Preheat the broiler or heat a grill. If the squash has been refrigerated, let it come to room temperature.

Drizzle the baguette slices with 2 tablespoons of the oil and broil until nicely toasted and hardened, 2 to 3 minutes.

Meanwhile, put the ricotta in a bowl. Add the remaining 2 tablespoons oil, season with salt and pepper, and stir to incorporate.

Spread the ricotta on the toasted baguette slices. Top with the squash, then the nuts, and drizzle with the honey. Top with parsley (if using) and finish with a few grinds of black pepper. Serve.

Chicken Liver Crostini with Shaved Mushrooms and Aged Balsamic Vinegar

Serves 4

This is probably the most popular and well-known traditional crostini in its home country of Italy. And it's a perfect winter starter—rich and hearty, and made with ingredients available at any time of the year. We give it a French accent with the addition of cream and sherry vinegar. If you can get them, use organic chicken livers, which have the most robust, fresh look and flavor and creamiest mouthfeel.

To Prep

8 ounces chicken livers

Kosher salt and freshly ground black pepper

Pinch of sugar

Pink curing salt (see page 39; optional)

1 tablespoon extra-virgin olive oil

1 shallot, thinly sliced

2 tablespoons apple brandy or cognac

¼ cup heavy cream

4 tablespoons (½ stick) unsalted butter, cut into cubes, at room temperature

1 teaspoon sherry vinegar

Rinse and clean the chicken livers, and pat them dry with paper towels. Separate the livers and remove any large veins by pulling them out; you do not need to remove smaller veins because the livers will be pureed. Put the livers in a bowl and season them with kosher salt, pepper, the sugar, and a pinch of pink curing salt (if using).

In a sauté pan large enough to hold the livers in an even layer, heat the oil over medium heat. Add the livers and sear them well until lightly caramelized on both sides, about 45 seconds per side. Transfer the livers to a blender. Add the shallots to the pan and cook until very soft but not browned, about 2 minutes. Add the brandy to the pan, bring it to a simmer, and cook until the pan is almost dry, about 2 minutes. Transfer the shallots to the blender with the livers and add the cream. Puree, adding the butter one cube at a time, to form an emulsified mixture. Season with salt, pepper, and the vinegar.

Transfer the mixture to a vessel and top with plastic wrap, pressing the plastic wrap directly against the surface of the puree to prevent oxidation. Refrigerate the puree to cool it; once cooled, it can be served right away or covered and refrigerated for up to 4 days. If the topmost part has oxidized and turned dark, trim it away with a paring knife and discard it.

To Serve

4 angled baguette slices, ½ inch thick

2 tablespoons extra-virgin olive
   oil, plus more for serving

1 large button mushroom, stem trimmed

Balsamic vinegar

Fleur de sel

Freshly ground black pepper

Preheat the broiler or heat a grill.

Drizzle the baguette slices with the oil and broil or grill until nicely toasted and hardened, 2 to 3 minutes.

Meanwhile, cut 4 thin slices of mushroom, ideally with a mandoline. Slice from the center part of the mushrooms so that each slice has a mushroom shape that includes the stem.

Divide the mousse among the toasted baguette slices, spreading it on with a small rubber spatula.

Top each crostini with a mushroom slice. Drizzle with vinegar and oil and finish with a pinch of fleur de sel and a grind of pepper.

→   **PINK CURING SALT**

Pink curing salt, or sodium nitrite, is a very strong preservative used in curing that also prevents meats—even chicken livers—from browning. It's optional in terrine making, but essential for making ham, pastrami, and other meats known for their pink color. To purchase it online, see the list of sources on page 321.

Salads and Starters

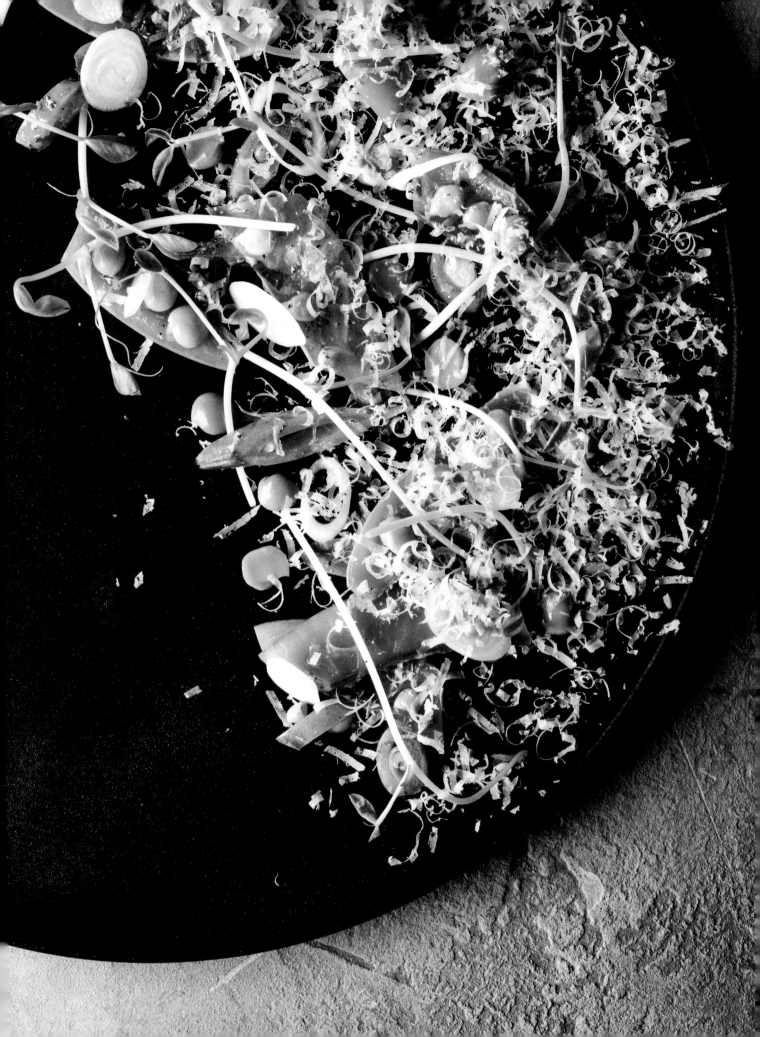

Herbs and Lettuces with Crispy Quinoa and White Mushroom

Serves 4

This salad showcases ingredients that are often taken for granted in salads and other dishes: herbs and lettuces. The more variety you bring to the plate, the better it will be. It offers a perfect place to experiment with the different varieties you might have seen at farmers' markets but not purchased, or to use an abundance of those ingredients if you have extra on hand and want a simple way to prepare them. It also celebrates another underappreciated ingredient, white mushrooms, which are both tossed into and shaved over the salad, an audacious treatment usually reserved for famously expensive white truffles.

To Prep

12 ounces chives, dill, parsley, tarragon, chervil, wood sorrel, wild mustard, dandelion, Lola Rosa, stonecrop, chickweed, upland cress, and/or other herbs and greens (about 16 cups, loosely packed; see headnote)

Note: *Fresh chives, dill, parsley, and tarragon are called for in the fines herbes in the To Serve part of the recipe. If you include them in the mix here reserve enough to make the fines herbes later.*

Wash the greens and spin them dry. Refrigerate in an airtight container with a damp paper towel over them to absorb any lingering moisture until ready to serve, or up to overnight.

To Serve

4 large white button mushrooms,
    stems trimmed and peeled

¼ cup extra-virgin olive oil

2 tablespoons sherry vinegar

2 tablespoons minced shallot

2 tablespoons fines herbes (see below)

¼ cup Crispy Fried Quinoa (page 25)

Kosher salt and freshly cracked black pepper

Thinly slice the mushrooms on a mandoline; slice vertically from the center of the mushrooms so that each slice shows off the shape of the mushroom, including the stem.

Put the greens in a large bowl and dress them with the oil and vinegar. Add the shallot, herbs, quinoa, and about one-quarter of the mushroom slices and season with salt and pepper. Toss well and divide among four small plates. Top each serving with a dome of mushroom slices and serve.

→ **FINES HERBES**

In the Battersby kitchen, we add a blend of equal parts fresh minced chives, dill, flat-leaf parsley leaves, and tarragon to a wide variety of dishes to freshen them at the last second. The mix is essentially the classic combination found in fines herbes, with dill replacing chervil. After the herbs are minced, they may be kept in an airtight container in the refrigerator for up to 24 hours.

Fines herbes are called for throughout this book, although in most cases we offer an alternative, usually thinly sliced fresh flat-leaf parsley leaves.

Spring Peas with Lemon and Manchego

Serves 4

By using a variety of peas of different shapes and levels of sweetness, this starter turns a straightforward idea into something complex, beautiful, and delicious. (See photo on page 41.)

To Prep

Kosher salt

1½ cups sugar snap peas, greens
   reserved for garnish

1½ cups snow peas, greens
   reserved for garnish

1½ cups shucked fresh English peas

Bring a pot of salted water to a boil. Fill a large bowl halfway with ice and water and set aside.

Working with one type of pea at a time, blanch it for 1 minute, then use a slotted spoon to transfer the peas to the ice water to stop the cooking and preserve the color. Once all the peas have been blanched and shocked, drain them. Thinly slice the snap peas and snow peas crosswise.

Refrigerate the peas in an airtight container to chill for at least 2 hours, or up to 24 hours.

To Serve

3 tablespoons extra-virgin olive oil

2 teaspoons minced shallot

2 teaspoons fines herbes (see
   page 44; optional)

Juice and finely grated zest of 1 lemon

Kosher salt and freshly ground black pepper

½ cup pea shoots or pea tendrils

1 small piece aged Manchego,
   Pecorino Toscano, or Pecorino
   Ginepro cheese, for grating

Put the peas in a large bowl. Add the oil, shallot, herbs (if using), and lemon juice. Season with salt and pepper and toss.

Divide the mixture among four salad plates. Scatter the lemon zest and pea shoots over the salads and finish with a grating of cheese.

Watermelon Salad with Shishito Peppers and Feta

Serves 4

This summertime starter marries fresh, juicy watermelon and cucumber with salty feta cheese and the snap and heat of Japanese shishito peppers, which have a complex, bitter flavor that makes an ideal foil for the other elements. Many of the ingredients in this dish can be used in the Watermelon Gazpacho on page 99. Plan your shopping to have this one night for dinner, then have the gazpacho for lunch the next day. The recommended cheese in the ingredient list is a marinated Australian blend that works perfectly in this recipe, as well as on croutons and in other salads; if you cannot find it, use a soft fresh feta.

To Prep

20 ounces seedless watermelon, cubed

¼ small red onion, thinly sliced

2 Kirby cucumbers, peeled and
   cut into small wedges

Refrigerate the watermelon, red onion, and cucumber in separate airtight containers for up to 8 hours, or proceed directly to serving.

To Serve

¼ cup plus 2 tablespoons extra-
　virgin olive oil
4 teaspoons sherry vinegar
Coarse Korean chili powder (see below and
　Sources, page 321) or piment d'Espelette
Kosher salt
Coarsely ground black pepper
20 whole shishito peppers (available
　from specialty and Asian markets,
　or see Sources, page 321)
20 pitted Kalamata olives or
　other black olives
4 ounces soft creamy cheese, either
　Meredith Dairy Sheep & Goat Blend (see
　Sources, page 321) or a soft fresh feta
¼ cup loosely packed fresh soft herb leaves,
　such as cilantro, basil, mint, and/or dill
4 cups loosely packed purslane,
　watercress, or arugula

Put the watermelon, onion, and cucumber on a large plate or platter. Drizzle with ¼ cup of the oil and the vinegar and season with chili powder, salt, and black pepper. Let marinate while you prepare the rest of the dish.

Heat the remaining 2 tablespoons olive oil in a small heavy pan over high heat until smoking. Add the shishito peppers and cook, tossing, until blackened all over, about 2 minutes. Transfer to the plate with the other ingredients, turning the peppers in the marinade to coat them, and season with salt.

Divide the watermelon cubes among four plates, artfully arranging them. Arrange the cucumbers around the watermelon, and set the onions and shishito on top. Top with the remaining marinade from the plate. Add 5 olives to each plate. Scatter the cheese, herbs, and purslane over each plate. Serve.

→　KOREAN CHILI POWDER

Walker first began experimenting with Korean chili powder when he taught himself to make the Korean condiment kimchi, which uses both coarse and fine chili powders, and fell in love with it. The powder has a subtle heat and smokiness (though it's not actually smoked) and is very inexpensive; we use it for crudos, soups, grilled meats, and fish, among other things. It also adds a nice kick to marinades.

Crispy Kale Salad with Brussels Sprouts and Kohlrabi

Serves 4

This dish was inspired by a crispy watercress salad at a Thai restaurant in Queens, and the dressing maintains that influence with the holy trinity of Thai cooking: palm sugar, lime juice, and fish sauce. (Palm sugar may require a special trip or extra effort to obtain; it's available in gourmet markets and Thai groceries, or from the source on page 321, but is worth the trouble for the distinct sweetness it brings to the dressing here.) If you like, you can build this into a main course with the addition of shredded, roasted duck, braised short ribs, or sliced grilled steak.

To Prep

8 ounces Brussels sprouts (large ones, if you can get them)

1 kohlrabi (about 10 ounces)

1 bunch kale, ideally lacinato (about 1 pound), thick stems cut off and discarded

2 scallions, white and light green parts only, thinly sliced on an angle

½ cup fresh cilantro leaves, coarsely chopped

½ cup fresh Thai or regular basil leaves, coarsely chopped

½ cup fresh mint leaves, coarsely chopped

Remove and reserve the outer leaves from the Brussels sprouts, discarding any wilted or blemished ones; you should have about 1 cup loosely packed leaves. Shave the sprouts on a mandoline, holding them by the core to yield as much as possible, or slice them as thinly as possible with a very sharp knife. You should have about 1 generous cup loosely packed shavings. Set the leaves and shavings aside separately.

Peel the kohlrabi, shave it thinly on a mandoline or slice it as thinly as possible with a very sharp knife, then cut the shavings into julienne strips. You should have about 2 cups loosely packed strips.

Set aside 10 kale leaves for frying. Cut the remaining kale into thin strips; you should have about 3 cups loosely packed strips.

Cut the central vein out of each of the reserved kale leaves, then cut each leaf into three equal pieces.

Use the ingredients right away, or put the large pieces of kale and the Brussels sprout leaves in a Ziploc bag or airtight plastic container. Put the sliced kale, kohlrabi, scallions, cilantro, basil, and mint in a separate large Ziploc bag or airtight plastic container and refrigerate for up to 8 hours (put a paper towel in the bag with the greens to absorb any excess moisture).

To Serve

Thai Dressing (recipe follows)

Kosher salt and freshly ground black pepper

3 tablespoons extra-virgin olive oil

Canola oil, for frying

¾ cup chopped or crushed
    roasted salted peanuts

Put the greens in a bowl and dress them with all but ¼ cup of the dressing. Season with salt and pepper and drizzle with the olive oil. Divide among four salad plates.

Line a plate with paper towels. Pour canola oil into a wide heavy pot to a depth of ¼ inch and heat the oil over medium-high heat until it is shimmering. Add the kale and Brussels sprout leaves (careful, they will hiss and spit and may spray a little hot oil) and stir. Cook for about 3 minutes; as the water cooks out of the leaves, they will become crispy and lightly brown. Transfer the leaves to the paper towel–lined plate to drain and season immediately with salt.

Top each salad with some of the hot, crispy kale and Brussels sprouts and spoon the remaining dressing over the salads. Scatter the peanuts over the salads and serve.

Thai Dressing

Makes about 1 cup

We devised this dressing for our signature kale salad, but it can be used on many salads featuring crispy greens and gets along on plates that incorporate braised and grilled meats as well.

3 discs palm sugar (about 2 ounces each)

¼ cup plus 2 tablespoons fresh lime juice

¼ cup fish sauce (see below)

1 garlic clove, grated on a
    Microplane or minced

½ teaspoon thinly sliced seeded Thai chili,
    or 1 teaspoon thinly sliced serrano chili

Put the palm sugar in a small heavy pot and pour in enough cold water just to submerge the sugar. Bring to a simmer over low heat and simmer until the sugar has almost completely dissolved, about 5 minutes. Remove the pot from the heat and let the syrup cool. You should have about ¾ cup syrup. Transfer ⅔ cup of the syrup to a small container (discard the remainder), let cool, and stir in the lime juice, fish sauce, garlic, and chili.

The dressing may be used right away or refrigerated in an airtight container for up to 2 days.

→   **FISH SAUCE**

As with anchovies, fish sauce isn't always meant to add fish flavor to a recipe (although enough of it will), but rather to add an intense, liquid salinity, amping up the other flavors. Like hot sauces, there are many varieties of fish sauce. Different brands produce different effects based on their country of origin; for example, Three Crabs fish sauce imparts a relatively subtle southeast Asian flavor, while Vietnamese Megachef is more potent. Fish sauce acts as a seasoning agent and complements lemon and lime juice especially well. You can also add it to meat ragùs, where it will drive home the flavor of the beef and tomato, although you might opt for a similar Italian product, *colatura*, produced from the juices of pressed anchovies in the coastal town of Cetara. Because of its place of origin, we often use *colatura* in Italian preparations. It's a fine finishing agent for raw and cooked dishes; if anchovies are part of the base of a cooked dish, a finishing drizzle of *colatura* can emphasize the flavor; just be sure to account for the anchovies' salinity and use it sparingly.

Heirloom Tomatoes with Burrata and Sourdough Croutons

Serves 4

Often, cooking means putting your hands on some great ingredients and then getting out of their way. That's certainly the case here, with a salad that involves little more than marinating exceptional tomatoes and bringing them together with burrata cheese for a summery starter that involves no cooking other than making the croutons. Get the tomatoes from a farm stand, garden, or specialty market—the salad lives and dies by how good they are.

To Prep

Sourdough Croutons

1 cup (1-inch) sourdough bread cubes

1 tablespoon extra-virgin olive oil

Kosher salt and freshly ground black pepper

Put the bread in a large bowl. Drizzle with the olive oil and season with salt and pepper. Toss well, then spread out on a rimmed baking sheet and bake until lightly golden, shaking the baking sheet occasionally to ensure even cooking, about 8 minutes.

Let the croutons cool. Use right away or store in an airtight container at room temperature for up to 24 hours.

Marinated Tomatoes

1 pint heirloom cherry tomatoes, ideally different types and colors, halved

Kosher salt and freshly ground black pepper

Sugar

3 teaspoons sherry vinegar

2 teaspoons minced shallot

¼ cup white verjus (see page 54; optional)

4 large heirloom tomatoes, ideally different types and colors, quartered or cut into sixths if especially large

Extra-virgin olive oil

1 tablespoon thinly sliced scallion whites

Put the cherry tomatoes in a large bowl, season with salt, pepper, and a pinch of sugar. Add 2 teaspoons of the vinegar, the shallot, and the verjus (if using). Toss and let marinate at room temperature for at least 20 minutes, or up to 1 hour.

Meanwhile, put the large tomato pieces in a separate large bowl. Season with salt, pepper, and a pinch of sugar. Drizzle with olive oil and the remaining 1 teaspoon vinegar. Add the scallion, toss, and let marinate at room temperature for at least 20 minutes, or up to 1 hour.

To Serve

2 balls burrata cheese (about
   8 ounces each), halved

8 small fresh basil leaves, preferably
   different varieties such as Thai basil,
   bush basil, lemon basil, and purple basil

Divide the large tomatoes and their juice among four plates (the large tomatoes will not give off as much juice as the small ones). Spoon the small tomatoes and their juice over them. Top the tomatoes on each plate with half a ball of burrata. Divide the croutons among the plates, garnish with 2 basil leaves each, and serve.

→   **VERJUS**

Verjus (sometimes called verjuice) is the juice of unripe grapes. It's a softer alternative to vinegar that's especially good with tomatoes, which pick up the floral quality of the verjus. Our favorite verjus is the one made by Wölffer Estate that is more complex than most and gets along well in many preparations. It's also a rare verjus that you can actually drink (we use it in some of our house cocktails), which lives up to our belief, espoused on page 71, that if you wouldn't drink it, you shouldn't cook with it.

Eggplant Caponata with Mozzarella

Serves 4

We appreciate the flavors of caponata, but feel that the essential character of eggplant is often lost in its mushy texture. Our version sautés large batons of eggplant on their own, essentially saucing them with the other caponata ingredients. We also add a small amount of fish sauce to punch up the salinity of the capers, the ingredient from which caponata gets its name.

To Prep

1 eggplant (about 1½ pounds)

Kosher salt

3 tablespoons currants

1 tablespoon plus 1 teaspoon sherry
  vinegar or red wine vinegar

½ cup plus 1 tablespoon extra-virgin olive oil

1 garlic clove, peeled and thinly sliced

5 canned tomatoes, diced (1 cup),
  with just enough juice to cover

Pinch of sugar

½ small red onion, thinly sliced

1 celery stalk, peeled and thinly sliced

1 tablespoon fresh marjoram

1 tablespoon fish sauce

3 tablespoons pine nuts,
  toasted (see page 314)

2 tablespoons brine-packed capers, drained

Freshly cracked black pepper

Peel the eggplant and cut it into 3 x 1 x 1-inch blocks. Arrange the blocks in a single layer on a plate, season all over with salt, and set aside to draw out the moisture (see Note, page 57) while you begin the caponata.

Put the currants in a microwave-safe bowl and add 1 teaspoon of the vinegar and 3 tablespoons cold water. Set a lid loosely over the bowl and microwave on high for 1 minute to plump the currants. Set aside.

Pat the eggplant dry with paper towels.

Heat ½ cup of the olive oil in a sauté pan over medium-high heat until shimmering. Add the eggplant and brown all over, about 10 minutes. Transfer the eggplant to a heatproof bowl. Add the garlic to the pan and lightly brown it, about 20 seconds, then add the tomatoes to stop the cooking. Season with the sugar and cook, stirring, until the tomatoes break down, about 4 minutes. Transfer the tomatoes to the bowl with the eggplant.

Carefully wipe out the pan, add another tablespoon of the olive oil, and heat until shimmering. Add the onion, remaining 1 tablespoon vinegar, and a pinch of salt and cook until the onion is softened but not browned, about 2 minutes. Transfer the onions to the bowl with the other ingredients. Add the celery, marjoram, fish sauce, pine nuts, and capers to the bowl. Drain the currants and add them to the bowl. Season with a few grinds of pepper.

Let cool for 30 minutes, or cover the bowl with plastic wrap and refrigerate for up to 24 hours.

To Serve

1 ball buffalo mozzarella (about 8 ounces)

Extra-virgin olive oil

Freshly ground black pepper

Fleur de sel

Cut the mozzarella into 8 slices.

Spoon one-quarter of the caponata into the center of each of four plates. Top the caponata on each plate with 2 slices of the cheese. (For a more formal presentation, artfully arrange slices of cheese and eggplant alongside each other; see photo.) Finish with a drizzle of oil, a few grinds of pepper, and a scattering of fleur de sel.

Note: *Eggplant is traditionally salted to draw out its bitter juices; we actually don't find it to be unpleasantly bitter, but salt it to dry it slightly and concentrate its flavor.*

Citrus Salad with Castelvetrano Olives and Fennel

Serves 4

This refreshing salad can be made with a wide range of citrus of your choosing. You will want one large citrus fruit such as tangerine, clementine, blood orange, ruby grapefruit, or pomelo, and whatever variety of lemons and limes appeals on the day; Meyer lemons are especially delicious here. You really need to make this with Castelvetrano olives, a sweet, green Sicilian olive that gets on great with both the citrus and fennel. It is easily found in gourmet supermarkets and at olive bars.

To Prep

1 large citrus fruit (see headnote)

4 limes, any variety

4 lemons, any variety

Peel the citrus fruits, removing the bitter white pith. Cut the large fruit into ½-inch circles or separate into sections; cut the lemons and limes into ¼-inch slices. Arrange the pieces on a large plate and use right away, or cover loosely with plastic wrap and refrigerate for up to 12 hours.

To Serve

½ fennel bulb

About 1 tablespoon minced Calabrian chili peppers (see Sources, page 321)

Kosher salt and freshly ground black pepper

Extra-virgin olive oil

Pinch of sugar

8 Castelvetrano olives, halved and pitted

16 fresh mint leaves

16 fresh cilantro leaves

½ lemon

½ cup crushed pistachios

Fill two bowls with ice and water. Cut off the fennel fronds and put them in one of the bowls of ice water. Thinly slice the fennel on a mandoline and set them aside in the other bowl of ice water to crisp them while you prepare the rest of the dish.

Arrange the citrus slices on four plates, first arranging the slices of larger fruit then scattering the lemon and lime slices over them. Use your finger to smear a little minced chili on the larger pieces. Season with salt and black pepper. Drizzle olive oil over each serving, season with the sugar, and top with a scattering of olive halves, mint, and cilantro. Drain the fennel and arrange a few pieces over each serving. Drizzle the fennel with olive oil and a squeeze of lemon juice and season with salt and black pepper. Scatter pistachios and fennel fronds over each portion and serve.

Fall Greens with Apples, Pecans, and Cheddar

Serves 4

This autumn salad is meant to be freely adapted—you can vary the chicories, change up the varieties of cheddar cheese (perhaps even using blue cheese), and select walnuts instead of pecans. The combination of sweet and tart apples balances the flavors and adds a visual flourish.

To Prep

12 ounces assorted chicories such as puntarelle, radicchio, Castelfranco radicchio, Belgian endive, dandelions, watercress, spinach, and/or kale (about 16 cups, loosely packed)

Wash the greens and spin them dry. Refrigerate in an airtight container, with a damp paper towel over them to absorb any lingering moisture, until ready to serve, or up to overnight.

To Serve

1 shallot, minced

1 tablespoon fines herbes (see page 44) or sliced fresh flat-leaf parsley

¼ cup extra-virgin olive oil, plus more for serving

2 tablespoons sherry vinegar, plus more for serving

Kosher salt and freshly ground black pepper

6 ounces aged cheddar, crumbled (about 1 cup crumbled)

¾ cup (about 5 ounces) fried or toasted pecans (see page 314)

1 green apple, cored (see page 61), quartered, and shaved on a mandoline

1 red apple, cored (see page 61), quartered, and shaved on a mandoline

Put the greens in a large bowl and scatter the shallot and herb mix over them. Drizzle the oil and vinegar over the salad and season with salt and pepper. Add the cheddar and pecans and toss.

Divide the salad among four plates and arrange the apples over the salad, covering it. Drizzle a little oil and vinegar over the apples and season with salt and pepper.

→ CORING APPLES AND OTHER FRUIT

Rather than use a coring tool to core apples, quince, pears, and other fruit, try this technique: Quarter the fruit, then cut the core out of each quarter. Then slice the quarters. In addition to saving time, you end up with more usable fruit.

Vanilla-Glazed Beets with Gorgonzola and Walnuts

Serves 4

Beets, Gorgonzola cheese, and walnuts are a classic salad combination that is recast here as the basis of a warm, savory starter. The beets are cut into wedges that are slowly cooked in stock, along with aromatics and vanilla bean, which adds a surprising flavor to the glaze that forms as the stock reduces.

To Prep

3 beets

1 tablespoon extra-virgin olive oil

1 tablespoon unsalted butter

2 garlic cloves, smashed with the side of a chef's knife and peeled

1 fresh thyme sprig

½ vanilla bean

1 teaspoon coriander seed

2 strips orange peel, no pith attached

Kosher salt and freshly ground black pepper

½ teaspoon honey (optional)

About ½ cup chicken stock, preferably homemade (page 317), or water

Cut the greens and stems from each beet; discard the stems and set the greens aside. Peel the beets, cut them into eighths, and set aside.

Heat the olive oil with the butter in a large deep sauté pan over medium-high heat. When the butter foams, add the garlic, thyme, vanilla bean, coriander, and orange peel. Cook, stirring, until the garlic and herbs are aromatic but without allowing the garlic to brown, about 2 minutes.

Add the beets to the pan and season with salt and pepper. If using the honey, drizzle it over the beets. Cook, stirring occasionally, until the beets begin to release their moisture but without allowing them to caramelize, about 4 minutes. Pour in enough stock to come halfway up the sides of the beets. Cover, reduce the heat to low, and gently cook until the beets are tender to a knife tip, about 20 minutes.

Use a spoon or tongs to pick out and discard the garlic, thyme, and orange peel.

Use right away, or let the beets cool and refrigerate them in their glaze in an airtight container for up to 24 hours.

To Serve

1 teaspoon unsalted butter

1 teaspoon extra-virgin olive oil

Kosher salt and freshly ground black pepper

A few drops of red wine vinegar
   and/or raspberry vinegar

4 ounces Gorgonzola cheese,
   cut into small cubes

¼ cup fried or toasted walnuts
   (see page 314)

If necessary, reheat the beets in a sauté pan over medium-high heat, stirring in a tablespoon or two of water to moisten them.

Add the butter and oil to the pan, raise the heat to high, and cook, stirring, to emulsify the fats and create a sauce. Adjust the seasoning with salt and/or pepper if necessary. Add a few drops of vinegar and the reserved beet greens and gently toss.

Divide the beets and greens among individual plates and top with cubes of Gorgonzola. Finish with a scattering of walnuts and serve.

Fluke Crudo with Avocado and Green Apple

Serves 4

Another rare dish in our repertoire that's prepared entirely à la minute, but it only takes about 5 minutes. The flavors and textures of the cold, raw fish; creamy avocado; and tart green apple complement one another and add up to a very fresh, light starter. You can use black bass or kampachi in place of the fluke; be sure to slice the avocado, fish, and apple to the same thickness.

1 sushi-grade fluke fillet (about 8 ounces), thinly sliced on an angle

1 avocado, halved, pitted, peeled, and thinly sliced

1 green apple, cored (see page 61) and thinly sliced

2 tablespoons extra-virgin olive oil

Finely grated zest and juice of 1 lime

Kosher salt and freshly ground black pepper

¼ cup fresh cilantro leaves

Fleur de sel

Lay slices of the fluke, avocado, and apple in a single layer on a large plate. Drizzle with the olive oil and sprinkle the lime zest and juice over the ingredients. Season generously with salt and pepper.

To serve, shingle alternating slices of fluke, avocado, and apple equally on each of four chilled plates. Garnish with the cilantro leaves and finish with a pinch of fleur de sel.

Marinated Scallops with Cherries, Almonds, and Tarragon Tempura

Serves 4

Battersby has a backyard garden with lots of herbs, which gives us a chance to play around with them. We especially love how even the stem of young, tender tarragon is edible, which led us to fry entire branches in tempura batter and incorporate them into dishes. One night we improvised this dish for some regulars pulling various ingredients we had on hand for other dishes, and it immediately became part of our repertoire. The entire thing can be readied and cooked in less than ten minutes. Since the scallops aren't cooked, try to get the freshest you can and ask your fishmonger if they are suitable to be served raw.

2 tablespoons extra-virgin olive oil, plus more for drizzling

10 almonds, peeled and split in half

Kosher salt

About 2 cups canola oil or other neutral oil, for frying

½ cup all-purpose flour

1 cup sparkling water

4 large young tarragon branches

4 large diver scallops

Freshly ground black pepper

1 lemon

10 sweet red cherries, halved and pitted

Heat the olive oil in a medium sauté pan over medium-high heat. When the oil is shimmering, add the almonds, toss gently, and fry for 1 minute. Transfer to paper towels and season immediately with salt. Set aside.

Pour the canola oil into a medium pot to a depth of 1 inch and heat the oil over medium heat to 325°F.

Meanwhile, make a tempura batter by whisking together the flour and sparkling water in a medium bowl, along with a few ice cubes and a pinch of salt. The mixture should be thin, like a crepe batter; whisk to eliminate any lumps.

Dip the tarragon branches in the tempura batter and lift them out, letting any excess batter run back into the bowl. Fry them in the hot oil until light golden brown and crispy, about 90 seconds, adjusting the heat level as necessary to maintain the temperature. Use a slotted spoon to transfer them to paper towels to drain.

(continued)

Season immediately with salt. Set aside in a warm place while you prepare the scallops.

Cut each scallop into 5 round slices and lay them on a plate in a single layer without overlapping. Season the slices with salt and pepper and drizzle a little olive oil over them. Finely grate some lemon zest over the slices, then cut the lemon in half and squeeze a little juice over the slices, catching any seeds in your hand and discarding them.

Divide the scallop slices among four small plates. Scatter the nuts and cherries over the scallop slices and garnish each plate with a tarragon branch. Serve.

Vegetables à la Grecque with Shrimp

Serves 4

The cooking technique à la grecque, or "in the Greek style," refers to preparing vegetables with an acid (wine or lemon juice), olive oil, and coriander seeds; vegetables cooked this way get on very well with shrimp, which are harnessed here in two ways: sautéed as the main protein of the dish, and used to make a sauce flavored with their shells. We use one of our favorite methods here: presenting the vegetables in both raw and cooked form.

To Prep

Shrimp Sauce

20 medium shrimp (about 20 ounces), preferably ruby red

2 tablespoons extra-virgin olive oil

1 large shallot, thinly sliced

1 celery stalk, thinly sliced

1 small carrot, thinly sliced

½ fennel bulb, thinly sliced

4 garlic cloves, smashed with the side of a chef's knife and peeled

½ tablespoon tomato paste

3 tablespoons cognac

¼ cup dry white wine

About 1½ cups chicken stock, preferably homemade (page 317)

1 teaspoon fresh lemon juice

Kosher salt and freshly ground black pepper

Peel the shrimp, saving the shells. Refrigerate the shrimp and shells in separate airtight containers until ready to cook and serve the dish.

Heat 1 tablespoon of the oil in a medium pot over medium-high heat. Add the shrimp shells and cook, stirring occasionally, until bright red, about 2 minutes. Add the shallot, celery, carrot, fennel, and garlic and cook, stirring occasionally, until softened but not browned, about 6 minutes. Add the tomato paste, stirring to coat the vegetables, and cook for 2 minutes. Stir in the cognac, bring to a simmer, and simmer until almost completely evaporated, about 2 minutes. Pour in the wine, bring to a simmer, and simmer until almost completely evaporated, about 4 minutes. Pour in enough stock to cover the solids, bring to a simmer, and simmer until the stock is intensely flavored, 20 to 30 minutes.

Strain the contents of the pot through a fine-mesh strainer set over a bowl, pressing down on the solids with a wooden spoon or the bottom of a ladle to extract as much flavorful liquid as possible. Discard the solids in the strainer.

Carefully wipe out the pot, return the liquid to the pot, bring to a boil over high heat, and cook until it has reduced by half, about 4 minutes.

Fill a large bowl halfway with ice and water and set a medium stainless-steel bowl over it. Transfer the reduced liquid to the empty bowl to chill. Whisk in the lemon juice and remaining 1 tablespoon oil and season with salt and pepper.

Use right away or refrigerate in an airtight container for up to 24 hours.

(continued)

Vegetables à la Grecque

2 tablespoons extra-virgin olive oil

3 garlic cloves, smashed with the side
of a chef's knife and peeled

6 radishes, peeled and halved

2 yellow beets, cut into 6 pieces each

2 carrots, cut into 6 pieces each

Kosher salt

½ teaspoon coriander seed

1 tablespoon white wine vinegar

1 tablespoon dry white wine

12 medium cauliflower florets

Heat the olive oil in a medium pot over medium-high heat. Add the garlic, radishes, beets, and carrots. Season with a pinch of salt and cover with a lid. Cook for 5 minutes without browning the vegetables, then stir in the coriander seed, vinegar, wine, and cauliflower. Cover and cook just until the vegetables are al dente (a paring knife should meet with scant resistance), about 6 minutes. Transfer the vegetables to a heatproof bowl, let cool, cover with plastic wrap, and use right away or refrigerate for up to 24 hours.

Preparing the Plate

12 thin slices red onion

12 thin slices peeled celery

12 thin slices carrot

12 thin slices radish

12 small cauliflower florets

12 thin slices raw yellow beet

Kosher salt and freshly ground black pepper

If desired, this step may be performed up to 30 minutes before serving:

To the bowl with vegetables à la grecque, add the onion, celery, carrot, radish, cauliflower, and beet slices. Season with salt and pepper and toss to coat the vegetables with the marinade.

Artfully arrange the vegetables over four plates and spoon a little marinade over the vegetables on each plate, making sure to include a few coriander seeds on each. The plates can rest at room temperature for up to 30 minutes.

To Serve

Kosher salt and freshly ground black pepper

2 tablespoons extra-virgin olive
oil, plus more for serving

⅓ cup loosely packed watercress

1 teaspoon thinly sliced fresh cilantro leaves

Season the shrimp with salt and pepper.

Heat the olive oil in a pan large enough to hold the shrimp in a single layer. Add the shrimp and cook just until firm and pink, about 20 seconds per side.

Arrange the shrimp over and among the vegetables on each plate and spoon the cold shrimp sauce over the dish. Garnish with a few pieces of watercress and the cilantro. Finish with a drizzle of olive oil and serve.

→ COOKING WINE

We disagree with the conventional wisdom that says any wine will do for cooking. We believe that you shouldn't cook with anything you wouldn't drink on its own. That doesn't mean you have to use an expensive wine for cooking, but don't grab the cheapest bottle from your corner wine store or bodega, either. In general, if a recipe doesn't call for too much wine, you can use the same wine you plan to serve with the meal. Otherwise, we generally like Sauvignon Blanc, Chablis, or a non-oaky Chardonnay for white and a medium-bodied wine such as Pinot Noir for red in our cooking.

Gravlax with Fingerling Potatoes and Watercress

Serves 4

We appreciate gravlax, or cured salmon, for its silken texture and the way it concentrates the flavor of the fish. For home cooks, it's a very achievable way of handcrafting a special dish, something that doesn't require the finesse of, say, charcuterie or cheese making. Here, gravlax is paired with a traditional Swedish accompaniment, potatoes, although we favor American fingerlings for their potent potato flavor. They are incorporated in two ways: sautéed with olive oil and butter and blended into a sauce with heavy cream, thyme, and garlic. Watercress, simply dressed with olive oil and lemon juice, adds crunch and essential acidity.

To Prep

Potato Sauce

1 teaspoon plus 2 tablespoons
  extra-virgin olive oil
1 smoked bacon slice
2 garlic cloves, smashed with the side
  of a chef's knife and peeled
1 fresh thyme branch
1 bay leaf, preferably fresh
1 teaspoon unsalted butter
8 fingerling potatoes, peeled, ends trimmed
  and discarded, held in cold water
Kosher salt
About ½ cup chicken stock,
  preferably homemade
  (page 317)
1 tablespoon heavy cream

Heat a medium heavy pot over medium heat. Add 1 teaspoon of the olive oil and heat it for a few seconds, then add the bacon and cook, stirring with a wooden spoon, until it begins to render its fat but without allowing it to brown, about 1 minute. Add the garlic, thyme, bay leaf, and butter and cook, swirling the pot to help melt the butter. Add the potatoes, season with a generous pinch of salt, and cook, stirring, without allowing the potatoes to brown, for 2 minutes. Pour in the stock, bring it to a simmer, then reduce the heat to low, cover the pot, and simmer until the potatoes are very tender and you can break them apart easily with the wooden spoon, about 25 minutes. Use the spoon to fish out and discard the bay leaf, bacon, and thyme.

Transfer the contents of the pot to a blender (see Note, page 74). Add the cream and 2 tablespoons of the extra-virgin olive oil and blend to the consistency of a thick, pureed soup. (Add a tablespoon or two of stock or warm water, if the sauce seems too thick.) Pass the sauce through a conical strainer or a fine-mesh strainer, pressing down on it with the bottom of a ladle to extract as much flavorful liquid as possible. You should have about ¾ cup sauce. (The sauce may be refrigerated in an airtight container for up to 8 hours.)

(continued)

Potatoes

1 teaspoon extra-virgin olive oil

1 teaspoon unsalted butter

2 garlic cloves, smashed with the side of a chef's knife and peeled

1 fresh thyme branch

12 fingerling potatoes

Kosher salt

About ½ cup chicken stock, preferably homemade (page 317)

1 lemon

Heat the oil with the butter in a medium heavy pan over medium heat. When the butter foams, add the garlic and cook, stirring, until the garlic is softened but not browned, about 2 minutes. Add the thyme and cook, stirring, for 2 minutes. Add the potatoes and a pinch of salt and cook, stirring, for 2 minutes. Add the stock and cover with a tight-fitting lid. Reduce the heat to low and cook until the stock has reduced and emulsified with the fat to coat the potatoes, lifting the lid after 5 minutes to check the amount of liquid and adding another tablespoon of stock or water if the pot seems dry, but only enough to keep things moist. Cook until the potatoes are tender (a paring knife will easily slip in and out of a potato), then stir in a few drops of lemon juice and use a rubber spatula to scoop the glaze over the potatoes.

Use the potatoes right away or refrigerate in an airtight container for up to 4 hours.

To Serve

2 tablespoons extra-virgin olive oil, plus more as needed

3 tablespoons chicken stock, preferably homemade (page 317), or water

1 tablespoon unsalted butter

1 cup loosely packed watercress, well washed and spun dry

1 lemon

Kosher salt and freshly ground black pepper

Gravlax (recipe follows), thinly sliced

If necessary, reheat the potato sauce in a small saucepan. Stir in 1 tablespoon of the olive oil.

Heat a small pan over medium heat and add the potatoes. Reheat them, adding 2 or 3 tablespoons of stock, the butter, and the remaining 1 tablespoon olive oil.

Put the watercress in a bowl. Cut the lemon in half and squeeze a few drops of juice over the watercress, catching the seeds in your hand and discarding them. Drizzle with a few drops of olive oil, season with salt and pepper, and toss.

Spoon some sauce into the center of each of four plates, spreading it around with the bottom of the spoon. Arrange the potatoes around the plate and drape gravlax over the potatoes. Garnish with the watercress, grate some lemon zest over each serving with a Microplane grater (see below), and serve.

Note: *Be careful when blending hot liquids. To prevent them from spraying, do not fill your blender too close to the top; if unsure, do not fill more than halfway and blend in batches, if necessary. To safely allow steam to escape, remove the lid's central piece and cover the hole with a clean, damp kitchen towel while blending.*

→   GRATING

When grating citrus zest, ginger, and other ingredients into recipes with a Microplane grater, it's often most efficient to zest directly into the bowl or pot rather than pregrating: You save yourself from having to clean a vessel and are using the freshest, most vibrantly flavored zest possible.

Gravlax

Makes ¾ pound

This is a useful recipe to have in your repertoire because it's easy and versatile. It's also convenient, made with spices like black pepper, fennel seed, and coriander, that many home cooks already have on hand. In addition to this dish, you can serve gravlax with eggs, drape it on salads made with watercress or frisée, as an amuse or hors d'oeuvre on squares of pumpernickel spread with cream cheese, and, of course, on a bagel. It's also very flexible: To make more, just get a larger piece of salmon and multiply the quantities in the cure accordingly.

We make this with Scottish organic salmon for its superior flavor and texture, but you can also use king, sockeye, coho, and other varieties. You can also use other fresh fish that you'd eat raw such as hamachi, mackerel, or sturgeon.

1 teaspoon coriander seed

1 teaspoon fennel seed

1 teaspoon whole black peppercorns

3 tablespoons sugar

3 tablespoons kosher salt

Finely grated zest of 1 lemon

Finely grated zest of 1 lime

Finely grated zest of 1 orange

2 sprigs fresh dill, coarsely chopped (about 1 tablespoon)

12 ounces skinless salmon fillet, pin bones removed, cold

Heat a wide heavy skillet over medium-high heat. Add the coriander seed, fennel seed, and peppercorns and toast the spices, shaking the pan to keep them from scorching, until they become fragrant, about 3 minutes. Remove from the heat. Let the spices cool in the pan, then coarsely grind them using a mortar and pestle (see below) or in a spice or coffee grinder.

Make the cure: Put the spices in a bowl and add the sugar, salt, lemon zest, lime zest, orange zest, and dill. Toss or mix with clean hands.

Lay out a 12 x 12-inch piece of plastic wrap on your work surface. Scatter half the cure over it in an even layer and set the fish on top. Scatter the remaining cure over the fish and use your hands to pack it in around the fish. Wrap the fish in the plastic wrap, pulling it taut as you seal it to be sure the cure and fish are in contact. Wrap in another piece of plastic wrap to further seal it. Refrigerate the fish for 24 hours to cure it.

Remove the plastic, slice, and serve. Use within 5 days.

→   MORTAR AND PESTLE

Have you ever seen a mortar and pestle in a cooking store or online and wondered why anybody would use them in this day and age? We use a mortar and pestle for grinding because it gives you more control over the size of the grind, allowing you to get it exactly the way you want it for a given recipe.

→   PURCHASING FISH

Freshness matters greatly when buying fish. It's best to get yours from a reputable fish shop. For this recipe, or any recipe that involves curing or smoking, ask the fishmonger to cut the fish from the thicker, head side of the fish, which will make it easier to slice. When you get it home, keep it in the coldest part of your refrigerator and use it as soon as possible.

Braised Octopus with Chorizo and Chickpeas

Serves 8 as an appetizer or 4 as a main course

Caramelized, grilled, or charred octopus is a beautiful thing—smoky on the outside with a meaty texture and slightly sweet, oceanic flavor. It gets along great with starchy components such as potatoes and chickpeas, our choice here. It can also stand up to heat, included here via the sautéed chorizo. We braise octopus before caramelizing it in a pan, a necessary step to soften its toothsome quality. Whether you buy octopus from Greece, New Zealand, Spain, or another country, we recommend that you purchase it frozen, which pretenderizes it by helping to break down its muscle.

To Prep

Octopus
1 octopus (about 3 pounds), preferably pretenderized
Kosher salt
Extra-virgin olive oil

Preheat the oven to 300°F.

Put the octopus in a large ovenproof pot and cover with hot tap water by about 1 inch. Season the water generously with salt; it should taste like seawater. Top the octopus with a heatproof plate to keep it submerged, then cover the pot with a lid and cook in the oven for about 1 hour. During that time, check periodically to be sure the water is not simmering; if it is, reduce the oven temperature slightly just until the water stops simmering. To test for doneness, lift the octopus out of the water with tongs and cut off a portion of one tentacle. When you can bite into it with no resistance, it is done. Remove it from the oven immediately. Uncover and let stand until the water has cooled but is still warm, 30 to 45 minutes.

Use tongs to remove the octopus from the water while it's still warm. Using a fork to hold the octopus in place, cut off the tentacles and discard the head. Put the tentacles in a large heatproof bowl and cover with olive oil. Once cold, the octopus can be refrigerated in the oil in an airtight container for up to 1 week.

(continued)

Chickpeas

1 cup dry chickpeas

1 piece carrot, about 3 inches

1 piece celery, about 3 inches

¼ Spanish onion, cut through the root end

2 garlic cloves, smashed with the side
   of a chef's knife and peeled

1 bay leaf

5 tablespoons extra-virgin olive oil

Kosher salt

Soak the chickpeas overnight in cold water, or use the quick-soak method (see below).

Drain the chickpeas and transfer them to a wide heavy pot. Add enough water to cover the beans by 1 inch. Add the carrot, celery, onion, garlic, bay leaf, and 3 tablespoons of the oil. Simmer over low heat until the chickpeas are al dente, stirring every 10 minutes or so to ensure they cook evenly and skimming any foam that rises to the surface. After about 45 minutes, stir in a generous pinch of salt and simmer for 20 minutes more. Use tongs or a slotted spoon to pick out and discard the vegetables, bay leaf, and garlic. Transfer ¾ cup of the chickpeas to a blender (see Note, page 74), add the remaining 2 tablespoons oil, and puree. Fold the pureed chickpeas into the whole chickpeas.

Use right away or refrigerate in an airtight container for up to 2 days.

To Serve

3 tablespoons extra-virgin olive
   oil, plus more for serving

1 tablespoon unsalted butter

20 thin slices chorizo

1 garlic clove, thinly sliced

4 piquillo peppers (see Sources,
   page 121), halved

Kosher salt and freshly ground black pepper

1 tablespoon minced shallot

1 teaspoon sherry vinegar

2 tablespoons fines herbes (see page 44)
   or thinly sliced fresh flat-leaf parsley

1 tablespoon fresh lemon juice

4 fresh herb sprigs of your
   choosing (optional)

If necessary, let the octopus and beans come to room temperature.

Heat the oil in a sauté pan over medium-high heat. Add the octopus tentacles and cook, turning them until caramelized on both sides, about 3 minutes per side.

Heat a cast-iron pan over medium heat and add the butter. When the butter foams, add the chorizo and garlic and cook, stirring occasionally, until the garlic is softened but not browned, about 2 minutes. Add the chickpeas and cook until the fat in the pan emulsifies and thickens the mixture, about 2 minutes. Fold in the piquillo peppers, just to warm and slightly wilt them. Season with salt and black pepper and fold in the shallot, vinegar, and herbs.

To serve, divide the chickpeas among four plates. Pat the octopus dry and cut the tentacles into ½-inch rounds. Arrange the pieces over the beans on each plate. Finish with a sprinkling of lemon juice, a pinch of salt, and a few grinds of black pepper. Drizzle with olive oil, garnish with an herb sprig, if desired, and serve.

→   QUICK-SOAKING LEGUMES AND BEANS

If you don't have until the next day to wait for legumes and beans to soak, use the following method: Put the beans in a pot, cover with cold water by 3 inches, and bring the water to simmer over medium-high heat. Simmer for 2 minutes, then cover the pot and remove from the heat. Soak for 1 hour, then drain.

Roasted Asparagus with Morels and a Sunny-Side-Up Egg

Serves 4

Asparagus and morels are two of the most anticipated vegetables of spring, and many chefs pair them on their menus at that time of year, like a song that everybody covers in his or her own way. This is our rendition, with a distinctive, almost addictive flavor provided by vin jaune, an oxidized yellow wine from France's Jura mountain region, where chicken and morels cooked with vin jaune are a local classic. If you can't find vin jaune, make this dish with a dry sherry.

To Prep

6 ounces morel mushrooms

3 tablespoons unsalted butter

1 large shallot, minced

1 large garlic clove, smashed with the side of a chef's knife and peeled

1 fresh thyme sprig

Kosher salt and freshly ground black pepper

½ cup vin jaune (see Sources, page 321) or other oxidized yellow wine

About ½ cup chicken stock, preferably homemade (page 317)

Trim the ends off the mushrooms, halve them lengthwise, and rinse them in three changes of cold water, or until the water runs clean. Air-dry them on a kitchen towel or paper towels.

Melt the butter in a medium, heavy pot over medium-high heat. When the butter foams, add the shallot, garlic, and thyme and cook, stirring occasionally, until the shallot is softened but not browned, about 2 minutes. Add the mushrooms and stir to coat them with the butter. Season with salt and pepper. Cook, stirring, until the mushrooms are softened, about 4 minutes.

Stir in the wine, bring to a simmer, and simmer until reduced by two-thirds, about 7 minutes. Pour in the stock, bring it to a simmer, cover, reduce the heat to low, and cook until the mushrooms are tender, about 30 minutes. (Cooking time can vary dramatically; if especially dry, some morels may take as long as 45 minutes. Add more stock if necessary.) Use a spoon or tongs to fish out and discard the garlic and thyme.

Use right away or remove the pot from the heat and set aside to cool. Transfer the mushrooms and their liquid to an airtight container. Cover and refrigerate for up to 3 days.

To Serve

2 tablespoons extra-virgin olive oil

20 pencil asparagus, or 12 jumbo asparagus (if using jumbo, blanch and shock them; see page 313)

Kosher salt and freshly ground black pepper

½ cup chicken stock, preferably homemade (page 317; optional)

Dash of vin jaune (see Sources, page 321) or other oxidized yellow wine

¼ cup lightly whipped cream (from 2 tablespoons heavy cream)

About 2 tablespoons unsalted butter

4 large eggs

Shaved asparagus, watercress, or baby arugula, for garnish (optional)

Preheat the oven to 325°F.

Heat the oil in a wide, deep sauté pan over medium-high heat. Add the asparagus and sauté, turning them as they cook, until lightly browned and tender all over, about 5 minutes. Season with salt and pepper.

Meanwhile, if necessary, reheat the morels in a separate medium pan over medium heat. Add the chicken stock (if using) and a dash of vin jaune, bring to a simmer, and cook until thick and glazed, about 1 minute without chicken stock or 5 minutes with chicken stock. Fold in the whipped cream.

Brush a nonstick ovenproof pan with the butter and heat over medium heat to melt the butter. Crack the eggs into the pan and season with salt and pepper. Transfer to the oven and cook until set. If desired, punch out the egg yolk and some of the white with a 2-inch biscuit cutter.

To serve, arrange 5 pieces of asparagus on each of four plates. Spoon the morels and sauce alongside. Top the morels with an egg, garnish, and serve.

→ WHIPPED CREAM

Whipped cream is a versatile finishing touch for any number of recipes. When you whip cream, you fluff and aerate it so a little goes a long way, allowing it to deliver the body and flavor we all love, but without the heavy, overly rich result. Use whipped cream to finish sauces and stews, or spoon it over soups like the chestnut soup on page 112, allowing diners to stir it in at their own pace.

→ SALAD SPINNERS

We keep extra salad-spinner baskets in the kitchen at Battersby because it's such a versatile piece of equipment. In addition to washing and spinning greens dry, it can be used for cleaning mushrooms, lifting the basket in and out of water while leaving grit behind; for soaking herbs to perk them up; and for blanching cooked vegetables (see page 313). They are also a good medium size that works for many kitchen tasks.

Steak Tartare with Crispy Artichokes and an Herb Salad

Serves 4

Steak tartare is all about the balance between primal, raw, red meat and ingredients that cut and offset its richness—salty cornichons and capers; sharp minced red onion (we substitute shallot); and the kick of Dijon mustard. To those traditional garnishes, we add lemon juice for its brightness and acidity, and our house herb mix for freshness. Everybody has his or her own way of slicing steak for tartare. We like a rustic, varied cut, combining minced and diced meat in every mouthful. The crispy artichokes bring crunch and warmth to the plate, a surprising natural alternative to toast points.

To Prep

10 ounces sirloin or eye round steak, trimmed of fat and silverskin

1½ tablespoons minced shallot

1 tablespoon minced brine-packed capers

1 tablespoon minced cornichons

1 heaping tablespoon fines herbes (see page 44) or thinly sliced fresh flat-leaf parsley leaves

2 tablespoons Dijon mustard

1 tablespoon fresh lemon juice

2 tablespoons extra-virgin olive oil

Kosher salt and freshly ground black pepper

Slice the beef as desired (see headnote) and transfer it to a large bowl. Add the shallot, capers, cornichons, herbs, mustard, lemon juice, and oil. Stir together and season with salt and pepper. Cover with plastic wrap and chill until ready to serve, or for up to 8 hours.

To Serve

2 cups loosely packed fresh herbs of
    your choosing, such as chives, dill,
    tarragon, flat-leaf parsley, and greens
    such as watercress and arugula
Extra-virgin olive oil
Fresh lemon juice
8 curls Pecorino Toscano or
    Parmigiano-Reggiano cheese
Crispy Artichokes (page 124)
8 slices white toast, halved diagonally

Put the herbs and salad greens in a large bowl. Whisk together the olive oil and lemon juice in a small bowl and pour over the salad, tossing to dress it. Add the cheese curls and stir in the artichoke chips.

Remove the beef mixture from the refrigerator and stir to recombine. Divide among four small plates, spooning some salad next to the beef and serve with the toast alongside.

Veal Sweetbreads with Romaine Lettuce and Caesar Dressing

Serves 4

An artfully presented, modified Caesar salad, made with our signature dressing and finished with toasted bread crumbs, proves the perfect backdrop for sweetbreads in this starter, which is rich and satisfying enough to make for a small meal in its own right. If you're unfamiliar with sweetbreads—the glands from the thymus or pancreas of veal, especially young veal or calves, lamb, or, less commonly, beef or pork—they have a relatively mild flavor for offal. Generally speaking, veal sweetbreads have the most appealing flavor and texture. They are popular in French kitchens like the ones we came up in, and are turning up more and more on menus in the United States. We like to poach them, then pan roast them to crisp the outside while leaving the interior soft and luscious. Try to use them soon after purchase because they go bad after a few days. (If you buy your sweetbreads in a supermarket, they may come frozen, which extends their shelf life.)

To Prep

Kosher salt

1 tablespoon white wine vinegar

1 veal sweetbread (about 10 ounces; see Sources, page 321)

Fill a small pot halfway with cold water. Season generously with salt, add the vinegar, and bring to a simmer over high heat. Add the sweetbread and simmer until slightly firm and opaque, about 6 minutes. Remove the sweetbread from the pot with a slotted spoon, transfer to a work surface, and pat dry with paper towels. Use right away or refrigerate on a plate, wrapped with plastic wrap, for up to 24 hours.

To Serve

¾ cup Caesar Dressing (recipe follows)

12 romaine lettuce leaves

2 tablespoons extra-virgin olive oil, plus more for drizzling

½ lemon

3 tablespoons unsalted butter

½ tablespoon brine-packed capers, drained

2 tablespoons chicken stock, preferably homemade (page 317)

2 tablespoons fines herbes (see page 44) or thinly sliced fresh flat-leaf parsley leaves

¾ cup toasted bread crumbs (see page 315)

Small piece of Parmigiano-Reggiano, for grating

Freshly ground black pepper

If necessary, let the sweetbread come to room temperature.

Spread 2 tablespoons of the dressing on each of four plates. Use a spoon to spread a total of ¼ cup dressing on the lettuce leaves and arrange them over the dressing on each plate. Drizzle the leaves sparingly with olive oil and squeeze a few drops of lemon juice on each leaf. Set the prepared plates aside.

Heat the olive oil in a sauté pan, add the sweetbread, and cook, turning with a wooden spoon, until golden brown all over, about 6 minutes. Add the butter and let it melt. Cook, basting the sweetbread with the butter, until firm, about 5 minutes. Carefully drain the butter from the pan and discard it. Squeeze the remaining juice from the lemon half into the pan, catching any seeds in your hand and discarding them. Add the capers, stock, and herbs, bring the liquid to a simmer, and simmer, basting the sweetbread with the pan sauce, until the sauce has reduced to a glaze, about 30 seconds. Test the sweetbread for doneness with a cake tester (see page 4); it should be medium-hot. Transfer the sweetbread to your work surface.

Sprinkle each prepared plate with bread crumbs and finely grate some lemon zest and cheese, and grind some pepper over each plate.

Slice the sweetbread into four pieces and set one piece in the center of each plate. Use a slotted spoon to remove some capers from the pan to each plate. Serve.

Caesar Dressing

Makes ¾ cup

Our take on the classic Caesar dressing begins with a reduction of chicken stock for a complex baseline of flavor and emulsification-aiding gelatin. Rather than fresh garlic, we use garlic confit for a softer, more elegant effect; the confit further helps the mixture emulsify and become creamy. This is a high-utility recipe in our kitchen—we use it for the sweetbread dish on page 85, and as an alternative to aioli to accompany crudité (page 22).

¼ cup chicken stock, preferably homemade (page 317)
7 oil-packed anchovy fillets
5 cloves garlic confit (see page 315)
½ raw garlic clove
1 tablespoon brine-packed capers,
  drained
1 large egg yolk
1 tablespoon sherry vinegar
Freshly ground black pepper
½ cup extra-virgin olive oil

Bring the stock to a simmer in a small pot over medium-high heat and simmer until reduced to a glaze, about 5 minutes. Transfer the reduced stock to a blender (see Note, page 74) and let it cool slightly. Add the anchovies, garlic confit, fresh garlic, capers, egg yolk, sherry vinegar, and a few grinds of pepper. Blend, drizzling in the olive oil a few drops at a time at first, then in a slow, steady stream, until emulsified, about 1 minute.

The dressing may be used right away or refrigerated in an airtight container for up to 2 days.

Beef Salad with Lettuce, Green Papaya, and Peanuts

Serves 4

The trick to the potent marinade here is that by slicing the ingredients as thin as possible, you get a greater extraction of flavor and intensely flavored beef. You can vary the ingredients to emphasize specific elements to suit your taste, and vary the cut of beef, but larger cuts will require longer marinating. For a cool variation, slice the steak as thin as possible, marinate overnight, then let it dry in a low oven for a beef jerky–like result.

To Prep

1 cup soy sauce

¾ cup sugar

1 shallot, thinly sliced

4 garlic cloves, thinly sliced

2 tablespoons minced peeled fresh ginger

2 Thai red chilies, or 1 large red jalapeño, stemmed and coarsely chopped

4 kaffir lime leaves (available in specialty and Asian markets, or see Sources, page 321), preferably fresh

⅓ cup thinly sliced lemongrass (from about ½ stalk)

5 tablespoons fish sauce

12 ounces skirt steak, trimmed (hanger steak or sirloin may be substituted)

Make a marinade by putting the soy sauce, sugar, shallot, garlic, ginger, chilies, lime leaves, and lemongrass in a large, heavy pot and bringing the mixture to simmer over medium heat. Whisk or stir until the sugar has dissolved, 3 to 4 minutes, then remove the pot from the heat and set aside to cool.

Once the marinade is cool, stir in the fish sauce.

Set the meat in a baking vessel just large enough to hold it without crowding, pour the marinade over it, cover with plastic wrap, and refrigerate for 2 to 3 hours, or up to overnight.

To Serve

2 tablespoons canola oil

20 small romaine lettuce leaves
 or halved larger leaves

2 cups julienne strips peeled seeded
 papaya (from about ¼ large papaya)

¼ cup loosely packed coarsely chopped
 fresh mint, Thai basil, or cilantro

¼ cup thinly sliced red onion

⅓ cup thinly sliced peeled Kirby cucumber

6 tablespoons Thai Dressing (page
 51), plus more to finish

Extra-virgin olive oil, for drizzling

Kosher salt and freshly ground black
 pepper

Fried shallots (see page 314)

¼ cup crushed peanuts

Let the meat come to room temperature, then trim the meat so it fits in a cast-iron pan; if it fits in one piece, there is no need to trim it. Lift the beef out of the baking vessel, letting any excess liquid run off, and brush off the marinade solids. Pat dry with paper towels.

Heat the canola oil in the cast-iron pan over high heat. Carefully add the beef to the pan and sear until nicely charred, about 2 minutes, then use tongs to turn the beef over and sear on the other side for 2 minutes more. Transfer the beef to a cutting board and let rest for 3 minutes.

Meanwhile, make the papaya salad: Put the romaine, papaya, mint, onion, and cucumber in a bowl. Drizzle with the dressing, toss, drizzle with olive oil, and season with salt and pepper.

Cut the meat crosswise into ½-inch-thick slices.

Mound some salad on each of four salad plates. Drape the beef slices over the salad and garnish with a scattering of fried shallots and peanuts. Serve.

Foie Gras Confit with Roasted Pear and Brioche

Serves 4

Foie gras is paired here with pear prepared two ways: poached and roasted, and in an aromatic chutney that comes alive with lemon and basil. The pear preparations fulfill the traditional requirement of cutting the foie gras with something sweet and/or acidic, and the textures here are also varied—creamy foie gras confit, al dente poached pear, and meltingly soft chutney—which makes for compelling eating. Because of how it's cooked, less expensive Grade B foie gras works fine in this recipe, and because it cannot be made with less than an entire lobe, you will have some leftover. Eat the remaining foie gras confit on its own, or on toast.

To Prep

Foie Gras Confit
1 foie gras lobe (see Sources, page 321)
Kosher salt and freshly ground black pepper
Pinch of sugar
About 1 quart duck fat (see
   Sources, page 321)

Season the foie gras lobe well with salt and pepper, covering it entirely, then season it with the sugar. Wrap the lobe in parchment paper and refrigerate for at least 12 hours or up to 24 hours to cure it.

After curing the foie gras, remove it from the refrigerator, let come to room temperature for about 1 hour, then remove the parchment paper.

Pour the duck fat into a pot wide enough to comfortably hold the foie gras to a depth of about 6 inches and heat the fat over medium heat to 130°F. Add the foie gras and cook for about 20 minutes on each side, turning it over with tongs or a slotted spoon. To test for doneness, remove the foie gras from the oil and set it on your work surface. If a cake tester inserted into the center is warm to the touch when removed, the foie gras is done. You can also test by pressing your finger into the center to gauge if it is warm.

Set the foie gras on a plate and let cool for 30 to 45 minutes. (If you work with it when it is too hot, it will melt away.)

Once cool to the touch, separate the halves of the lobe. Remove the large veins by hand and use a paring knife to loosen and remove any small veins.

Overlap two pieces of plastic wrap, roughly 14 x 14-inches each, on your work surface. Reassemble the foie gras lobe over the plastic wrap, stacking the halves of the lobes. Wrap the plastic around the foie gras, pulling it taut. Use a paring knife to pop any air pockets in the plastic, then roll the plastic over again to encase it. Turn the ends of the plastic over and over, as if you were wringing out a towel, until the foie gras is shaped into a neat cylinder (this is called a torchon).

Refrigerate the torchon overnight or for up to 3 weeks.

Roasted Pear

2 cups verjus (see Sources, page 321) or dry white wine

3 strips of lemon peel, removed with a vegetable peeler, no pith attached

1 bay leaf, preferably fresh

1 allspice

1 whole clove

4 whole black peppercorns

1 tablespoon sugar

1 pear, preferably Bartlett or Bosc

Put the verjus, lemon peel, bay leaf, allspice, clove, and peppercorns in a pot just large enough to hold the pieces of a quartered pear in a single layer. Add the sugar. Bring the liquid to a gentle simmer over medium heat.

Meanwhile, peel the pear and halve it lengthwise. Use a teaspoon or melon baller to remove the core. Cut each half in half again to form quarters.

Add the pear pieces to the simmering liquid and gently simmer until very tender to a knife tip, about 20 minutes. Let cool in the liquid; use immediately or refrigerate in the liquid in an airtight container for up to 1 week.

Pear Chutney

1 pear, preferably Bartlett or Bosc

2 tablespoons extra-virgin olive oil

2 cipollini onions, peeled and cut into julienne strips

Kosher salt and freshly ground black pepper

Pinch of sugar

1 tablespoon coarsely chopped unsalted pistachio nuts

1 lemon

4 large fresh basil leaves, diced

Peel the pear and halve it lengthwise. Use a teaspoon or melon baller to remove the core. Cut the pear into small cubes.

Heat the olive oil in a sauté pan over medium-high heat until shimmering. Add the onions and sauté, stirring occasionally, until softened but not browned, about 3 minutes. Add the pear, season with salt, pepper, and the sugar and cook, stirring occasionally, until tender and releasing their natural juices but without allowing the pear or onion to caramelize, 6 to 8 minutes. Remove the pan from the heat and fold in the pistachios. Finely grate some lemon zest over the pan, then cut the lemon in half and squeeze some juice into the pan, catching any seeds in your hand and discarding them.

Fold in the basil (if you will be refrigerating the chutney, wait to add the basil until you plan to serve the chutney). The chutney can be cooled and used right away at room temperature or refrigerated in an airtight container for up to 2 days.

To Serve

Extra-virgin olive oil

½ lemon

Fleur de sel

Freshly cracked black pepper

2 tablespoons unsalted butter

1 teaspoon sherry vinegar

4 slices brioche, toasted

If necessary, let the chutney come to room temperature and fold in the reserved basil leaves. Finish the chutney by folding in a drizzle of olive oil and a squeeze of lemon juice.

With the torchon still wrapped in plastic, cut 4 slices, about 2 ounces per slice (the thickness will vary based on the diameter of the torchon), then remove the plastic from each slice. Set 1 slice on each of four plates and season with fleur de sel and some cracked pepper.

Remove the poached pear pieces from their liquid, reserving ¼ cup of the liquid. Pat the pear pieces dry with paper towels. Melt the butter in a sauté pan over medium-high heat. When the butter foams, add the pear pieces to the pan and cook to lightly caramelize on all sides, about 2 minutes per side. Transfer 2 pear pieces to each plate.

Add the reserved poaching liquid to the pan, bring to a simmer, and cook, stirring to loosen any flavorful bits of pear that have cooked onto the pan. Cook to reduce slightly, then stir in the vinegar and dress the pear pieces on each plate with a spoonful or two of the pan sauce.

Spoon some chutney onto each plate and serve, passing the toasted brioche alongside.

Soups

Watermelon Gazpacho

Serves 4

In its native Spain, gazpacho isn't just made with tomatoes, although that's the most popular version and the one that's most well known internationally. Gazpacho can be made with a wide variety of vegetables and fruits; though there's some debate, most agree that the essential ingredients are olive oil, sherry vinegar, and bread, which acts as a thickening agent. This gazpacho focuses on the flavor of watermelon, emphasizing it in a granité and in cubes of watermelon. Tomatoes are incorporated in the gazpacho and also in a garnish of slow-roasted tomato confit.

To Prep

Lime-Watermelon Granité

10 ounces peeled seedless watermelon (weighed after peeling), cut
 into large cubes (about 2 cups)
Finely grated zest and juice of 1 lime
1 tablespoon sugar
Kosher salt

Put the watermelon in a blender and blend until liquefied. Strain through a fine-mesh strainer into a medium bowl. Add the lime zest and juice and sugar and whisk until the sugar has dissolved. Stir in a pinch of salt. Pour into a temperature-proof vessel (see Note) and put in the freezer. Cover loosely with plastic wrap and freeze for at least 4 hours, scraping the ice with a fork every half hour or so to create a snowy granité. The granité may be frozen for up to 2 days.

Note: *Put the vessel in which you will make granité in the freezer ahead of time to speed the chilling and freezing process.*

(continued)

Gazpacho

¾ cup tomato pulp (5 ounces) (save the
    tomatoes from which you squeeze the pulp
    to make the confit called for in To Serve)
½ red bell pepper, stemmed,
    seeded, and thinly sliced
1 heaping tablespoon thinly
    sliced seeded jalapeño
1 Kirby cucumber, peeled and thinly sliced
4 large fresh basil leaves
¼ cup thinly sliced red onion
20 ounces peeled seedless water-
    melon (weighed after peeling), cut
    into large cubes (about 4 cups)
3 thin slices peeled fresh ginger
½ teaspoon kosher salt
1 heaping cup loosely packed torn baguette
3 tablespoons red wine vinegar
3 tablespoons sherry vinegar
¼ cup extra-virgin olive oil

Put the tomato, bell pepper, jalapeño, cucumber, basil, onion, watermelon, ginger, salt, baguette, red wine vinegar, sherry vinegar, and oil in a bowl, stir together, cover, and refrigerate overnight.

The next day, transfer the mixture to a food processor or blender, in batches if necessary, and blend until no solids remain. Refrigerate in an airtight container for up to 24 hours.

To Serve

12 (½-inch) cubes peeled
    seedless watermelon
12 pieces tomato confit (see page 313)
8 large fresh basil leaves

Scrape the granité one last time before serving. Incorporate the granité as you like, either spooning about 3 tablespoons, or as much as you like, into each of the bowls that will hold the gazpacho, or into a small cup alongside. Put 3 watermelon cubes in the bottom of each of four bowls. Lean a piece of tomato confit against each cube. Ladle the gazpacho over the watermelon and tomato. Garnish each bowl with 2 basil leaves and serve.

Melon Soup with Black Pepper and Chorizo

Serves 4

A variation on the Italian theme of melon and prosciutto, with slightly spicy chorizo replacing the cured ham, this soup is one of the simplest recipes in our repertoire and a crowd-pleasing way to start a summer meal. You can play around with the selection of melon, trying different varieties throughout the season. At Battersby, we serve this soup as an amuse, in small cups or glasses with a slice or two of sautéed chorizo speared on a toothpick suspended across the mouth of the vessel; you can do the same, and will get anywhere from 8 to 16 amuse portions from this recipe, depending on the serving size.

To Prep

1 honeydew, sprite or musk melon, or cantaloupe (about 3 pounds), peeled, seeded, and chopped

Put the melon in a blender, in batches if necessary, and blend until liquid. Strain through a fine-mesh strainer into a storage container with a tight-fitting lid. (It will appear frothy, but the froth will dissipate naturally.) Cover and chill the soup until ice cold, at least 1 hour, or for up to 24 hours.

To Serve

16 (¼-inch-thick) chorizo slices
Extra-virgin olive oil
Freshly ground black pepper

Heat a cast-iron or grill pan over high heat until very hot. Add the chorizo in a single layer and quickly char it on both sides, about 30 seconds per side, turning the slices with tongs or a spatula. Transfer to paper towels to drain.

Divide the soup among four bowls. Drizzle a little olive oil and grind some pepper over each serving. Garnish with 4 slices of chorizo per bowl and serve.

Cauliflower Soup with Apple and Curry

Serves 4

With a mild mustard flavor and a texture that lends itself to pureeing, cauliflower makes a versatile soup that can be dressed up with a variety of spices and garnishes; it's often paired with salty capers or sweet currants. Here, a pinch of curry, both sautéed with the garnishing florets and scattered over the finished soup, complements its natural flavor, and tart green apple—also present in two ways, pureed in the soup and diced as a garnish—offers a pleasing contrast.

To Prep

1 head cauliflower (1 pound)

1 Granny Smith apple

2 tablespoons extra-virgin olive oil

3 shallots, thinly sliced

4 garlic cloves, smashed with the side of a chef's knife and peeled

1 fresh thyme sprig

Kosher salt and freshly ground black pepper

4 cups chicken stock, preferably homemade (page 317), or water

¼ cup heavy cream

2 tablespoons browned butter (see page 315)

Cut the stem from the cauliflower and discard it. Separate the cauliflower into florets, cutting especially large ones in half so the pieces will cook at the same rate. Set aside ½ cup of the smallest florets for garnish.

Peel the apple, cut it into quarters, and cut out the core (see page 61). Cut it into small cubes, setting aside 2 tablespoons for garnish. (If making the soup in advance, wrap the 2 tablespoons for the garnish tightly in plastic wrap and refrigerate to keep from oxidizing and turning brown.)

Heat the olive oil in a medium pot over medium heat until shimmering. Add the shallots and garlic and cook, stirring occasionally, until softened but not browned, about 3 minutes. Add the thyme and cauliflower, season with salt and pepper, and cook, stirring occasionally, until the cauliflower is slightly softened but not browned, about 4 minutes. Add the stock and apple, bring the stock to a simmer, then reduce the heat to low and simmer until the cauliflower is tender to a knife tip, about 20 minutes.

Fish out and discard the thyme, transfer the contents of the pot to a blender (see Note, page 74), in batches, if necessary, and puree until smooth. Blend in the cream and butter then taste, adjusting the seasoning and adjusting the consistency with more stock or water, if necessary. For a more refined, luxurious result, pass the soup through a chinois or fine-mesh strainer into a large bowl.

Use right away or let cool, then refrigerate in an airtight container for up to 24 hours.

To Serve

2 tablespoons extra-virgin olive oil

Kosher salt and freshly ground black pepper

1 teaspoon curry powder, plus more for serving

1 tablespoon fresh lemon juice

If necessary, reheat the soup in a medium pot over medium heat, stirring occasionally.

Meanwhile, heat the olive oil in a sauté pan over medium-high heat. Add the reserved small cauliflower florets and season with salt and pepper. Cook, stirring occasionally, until slightly softened but not browned, about 4 minutes. Stir in the curry powder and cook, stirring, just to release its aroma, about 1 minute. Stir in the lemon juice, then gently stir in the reserved 2 tablespoons diced apple.

Divide the cauliflower and apple among four bowls. Dust with a pinch of curry powder and pour the soup over the garnish in each bowl. Serve.

→ **BROWNED BUTTER**

We use browned butter in much of our cooking to add a nutty flavor and aroma. Where unsalted butter actually tones down flavors and enriches texture, browned butter elevates flavor; to us, it's almost a seasoning. You can make browned butter in large quantities and refrigerate it; see page 315 for the method.

White Asparagus Soup with Smoked Trout

Serves 4

White asparagus have a gentle, understated flavor and elegant color that's celebrated here with a complement of smoked trout and a subtle infusion of orange and herbs. As in many of our dishes, a few elements are cooked into the main preparation (the soup) and underscored with a fresh addition at the end via a garnish of asparagus tips and a grating of fresh orange zest. If you like, you can serve this without the smoked trout and it will still be delicious.

To Prep

1 pound white asparagus

4 tablespoons extra-virgin olive oil

1 teaspoon unsalted butter

4 garlic cloves, smashed with the side
   of a chef's knife and peeled

3 shallots, thinly sliced

1 bay leaf, preferably fresh

1 fresh thyme sprig

1 teaspoon coriander seed

3 slices orange peel, removed with a
   vegetable peeler, no pith attached

Kosher salt and freshly ground black pepper

About 4 cups chicken stock, preferably
   homemade (page 317), or water

Cut the tips off the asparagus and trim the woody ends. Coarsely chop the stalks and set them aside. If the tips are firm to the touch, blanch and shock them (see page 313), then quarter them and reserve them for garnish; if the tips are especially fresh and tender, you can skip blanching and simply quarter them.

Heat 2 tablespoons of the oil with the butter in a medium pot. When the butter foams, add the garlic and shallots and cook, stirring occasionally, until softened but not browned, about 3 minutes. Add the bay leaf, thyme, coriander, and orange peel and cook, stirring, until fragrant, about 1 minute. Add the chopped asparagus stalks and season with salt and pepper. Pour in the stock and bring to a simmer. Reduce the heat to low and simmer until the asparagus is very tender, about 20 minutes. Use a slotted spoon to remove the bay leaf, thyme, and orange peel and discard them (see page 105).

Carefully transfer the contents of the pot to a blender (see Note, page 74) and blend until very smooth, working in batches, if necessary, and gradually adding the remaining 2 tablespoons olive oil, emulsifying it. Taste and adjust the seasoning, if necessary, with salt and/or pepper, and adjust the consistency by blending in more stock or water if the soup is too thick.

Use right away or let cool and refrigerate in an airtight container for up to 24 hours.

To Serve

Extra-virgin olive oil

1 orange

Kosher salt and freshly ground black
  pepper

1 piece smoked trout (about 6 ounces)

1 cup loosely packed watercress, tough stems removed

If the soup has been refrigerated and you'd prefer to serve it hot, reheat it in a medium pot over medium heat, stirring occasionally; if serving cold, let it come to room temperature for about 10 minutes.

Meanwhile, put the reserved asparagus tips in a bowl. Drizzle with olive oil and grate some orange zest over the pieces. Season with salt and pepper and toss to coat the asparagus.

Flake the trout into another bowl. Drizzle with olive oil and grate some orange zest over the pieces. Season with salt and pepper and toss to coat the trout.

Arrange some asparagus and trout pieces in the bottom of each of four bowls. Scatter some watercress leaves over them and ladle the soup over the garnish. Serve.

→   **HERB SACHET**

When herbs and other aromatics will be removed from a preparation prior to processing or serving it, you can tie them in a piece of cheesecloth to facilitate removing them and ensure you remove everything you want to.

Corn Soup with Shrimp

Serves 6

It doesn't take much to turn fresh corn into a soup—just a base of garlic and onions and an addition of stock. We finish ours with lightly whipped cream and shrimp that underscore the corn's sweetness. For chowderlike effect, put boiled diced potatoes, lightly sautéed diced Spanish onion, and diced peeled celery in each bowl and ladle the soup over them.

To Prep

2 tablespoons unsalted butter

1 Spanish onion, thinly sliced

3 garlic cloves, peeled and thinly sliced

4 cups corn kernels (from 4 ears of corn)

Kosher salt

Pinch of sugar

4 cups chicken stock or vegetable stock, preferably homemade (pages 317, 316), water, or corn stock (see below)

Melt the butter in a soup pot over medium heat until foaming but not browned. Add the onion and garlic, cover, and cook until softened but not browned, about 7 minutes. Add the corn and season with salt and the sugar. Cover and cook until the corn is softened but not browned, about 10 minutes, lifting the lid to give an occasional stir. Pour in the stock, bring to a boil, then reduce the heat to low and simmer for 45 minutes. Use right away or let cool and refrigerate in an airtight container for up to 2 days.

To Serve

2 tablespoons extra-virgin olive oil

18 large shrimp (about 18 ounces total weight), peeled and deveined

Kosher salt and freshly ground black pepper

¼ cup lightly whipped cream (from 2 tablespoons heavy cream)

If necessary, reheat the soup in a medium pot over medium heat, stirring occasionally.

Meanwhile, heat the olive oil in a pan large enough to hold the shrimp in a single layer. Season the shrimp with salt and pepper and add them to the pan. Cook until just firm and pink, about 20 seconds per side.

Transfer 3 shrimp to the center of each of six wide, shallow bowls. Remove the soup pot from the heat and fold in the whipped cream, then ladle the soup around the shrimp in each bowl. Serve.

→ **CORN STOCK**

For a more intense corn flavor, make this soup with corn stock: Cut the cobs crosswise into thirds, cover with 5 cups cold water, season lightly with salt, and simmer over low heat, covered, until the liquid tastes of corn, about 45 minutes. Strain through a fine-mesh strainer and discard the cobs. You should have about 1 quart stock.

Thai Coconut Broth with Mussels and Bok Choy

Serves 4

Our take on a popular Thai preparation benefits enormously from the incorporation of herbs throughout the cooking process: Notice how the cilantro stems are added up front, and especially the steeping step at the end of the prep section. Keep this in mind in your own cooking: Steeping herbs and citrus (or even toasted, dried spices, chilies, and ginger) into prepared liquids such as broths, sauces, and stocks off the heat imparts a fresher layer of flavor than simmering or boiling them.

To Prep

1 tablespoon extra-virgin olive oil

4 shallots, thinly sliced

6 garlic cloves, smashed with the side of a chef's knife and peeled

Stems from 1 bunch fresh cilantro, coarsely chopped, leaves picked and reserved for serving

2 pounds mussels, preferably Prince Edward Island

½ cup dry white wine

Kosher salt

3 tablespoons unsalted butter

1 celery stalk, thinly sliced

1 fresh Thai red chili, halved

1 (2-inch) piece fresh ginger, peeled and thinly sliced

½ fennel bulb

1 teaspoon small dried shrimp (see Sources, page 321; optional)

3 kaffir lime leaves (available in specialty and Asian markets, or see Sources, page 321), preferably fresh

(continued)

Heat the oil in a heavy pot over medium heat. Add half of the shallots, one-third of the garlic cloves, and the cilantro stems and cook, stirring occasionally, until softened but not browned, about 3 minutes. Add the mussels, then the wine and a pinch of salt. Bring to a simmer, then cover and cook until the mussels open, about 6 minutes. Discard any mussels that do not open. Use a slotted spoon to transfer the mussels to a bowl and cool in the refrigerator. Strain the cooking liquid and reserve it.

Melt the butter in a medium pot over medium heat. Add the celery, remaining shallots and garlic, chili, ginger, fennel, and dried shrimp (if using). Season with a pinch of salt. Cover and cook until the vegetables are softened but not browned, about 4 minutes. Add the reserved mussel cooking liquid and kaffir lime leaves and simmer until reduced by half, to about 1 cup, about 7 minutes.

Stir in the coconut milk and simmer gently for 20 minutes. While the soup is simmering, shell the mussels and discard the shells; set the meat aside in a bowl. Strain the soup through a

1 (19-ounce) can unsweetened coconut
   milk, preferably a good brand with a
   high fat content, such as Mae Ploy
1 smashed lemongrass stalk (see below)
Stems from 1 fresh Thai basil or regular
   basil sprig, coarsely chopped, leaves
   picked and reserved for serving

fine-mesh strainer into a medium bowl. Immediately add the lemongrass and Thai basil stems, cover, and let steep for 10 to 15 minutes, then strain again. Use the soup and mussels right away or refrigerate in separate airtight containers for up to 2 days.

To Serve

1 tablespoon unsalted butter
1 garlic clove, thinly sliced
1 tablespoon minced peeled fresh ginger
4 quarts loosely packed bok choy leaves
½ lime
Fish sauce
¼ cup thinly sliced fresh Thai basil,
   mint, and/or cilantro leaves (preferably equal parts of all three; Thai basil
   and cilantro reserved from To Prep)

If necessary, reheat the soup in a medium pot over medium heat, stirring occasionally.

Melt the butter in a pan and add the garlic and ginger. Cook, stirring, until softened but not browned, about 3 minutes. Add the shelled mussels and cook just to warm them through, about 1 minute. Add the bok choy leaves and ½ cup of the soup and cook just until the bok choy is wilted, about 2 minutes, then divide the bok choy among four bowls.

Season the remaining soup with lime juice and fish sauce and divide it among the bowls, pouring it over the bok choy. Garnish with the herb mixture and serve.

→   LEMONGRASS

To peel lemongrass, slice off and discard the root end and the upper portion. Peel off a layer or two of the woody exterior, either by hand or with a paring knife, then slice the lemongrass or smash it with the side of a chef's knife.

Winter Squash Soup with Crab and Green Apple

Serves 4

Many squash soup recipes either roast the squash or cook it in liquid, both of which cause it to sacrifice some of its flavor. Here, the squash is gently cooked on its own until it breaks down, allowing it to maintain as much flavor as possible, with stock added only for the final part of the cooking process. You can make this with blue crabmeat instead of peekytoe, but it will not have the same sweet flavor or delicate texture. If desired, fold some whipped cream into the soup just before serving, as described on page 113.

To Prep

1 butternut squash (about 2 pounds), peeled, halved, and seeded

1 tablespoon extra-virgin olive oil

4 tablespoons (½ stick) unsalted butter

2 smoked bacon slices, preferably slab bacon, diced

4 garlic cloves, smashed with the side of a chef's knife and peeled

2 fresh thyme sprigs

Kosher salt and freshly ground black pepper

3 tablespoons browned butter (see page 315)

Cut the squash into 1-inch dice.

Heat the oil with the butter in a soup pot over medium-high heat. When the butter foams, add the bacon and cook, stirring occasionally, until browned, about 6 minutes. Add the garlic and thyme and season generously with salt and a few grinds of pepper. Add the squash to the pan, reduce the heat to low and cook, stirring every 3 or 4 minutes, until the squash has softened and broken down into a chunky puree, 10 to 12 minutes.

Add just enough cold water to cover the squash, about 3 cups. Raise the heat to high, bring the liquid to a boil, then reduce the heat to low and simmer until the squash is very tender, 15 to 20 minutes. Transfer the soup to a blender (see Note, page 74), working in batches, if necessary. Puree, adding the browned butter, and a little water, if desired, to thin the soup to your preferred consistency. For a more refined result, pass the soup through a fine-mesh strainer into a bowl, pressing the soup through with a rubber spatula.

The soup can be used right away or refrigerated in an airtight container for up to 2 days.

To Serve

½ cup heavy cream

2 tablespoons unsalted butter

Kosher salt and freshly ground black
  pepper

1 cup peekytoe crabmeat

½ cup finely diced green apple

If necessary, reheat the soup in a medium pot over medium heat, stirring occasionally.

Meanwhile, pour the cream into a medium, heavy pot and bring it to a simmer over medium-high heat. Continue to simmer until reduced to a glaze, about 6 minutes. Off the heat, whisk in the butter until it melts and season with salt and pepper. Fold in the crabmeat and let rest for 1 minute to warm it through.

Divide the crab among four bowls, mounding it in the center, and top with the apple. Ladle the soup around the crab and serve.

Chestnut Velouté with Wild Mushrooms

Serves 4 to 6

Chestnuts and mushrooms have a natural affinity for each other, each with their own nuanced, woodsy flavor, and this soup takes advantage of that. For the most interesting dish, use a mix of at least three types of wild mushrooms. Note that the chestnuts go in before the vegetables in order to roast them and create a *fond* (the bits that get cooked onto the bottom of a pan or pot), adding more flavor to the soup. You can replace the mushrooms with an island of smoked mackerel or trout, or by perching a chicken liver crostini (page 38) on the edge of the bowl.

To Prep

1 pound chestnuts

1 tablespoon extra-virgin olive oil

3 ounces smoked bacon, in thin strips

2 tablespoons unsalted butter

½ shallot, thinly sliced

¼ Spanish onion, thinly sliced

¼ fennel bulb, thinly sliced

4 garlic cloves, smashed with the side of a chef's knife and peeled

Kosher salt

½ teaspoon coarsely ground black pepper

Pinch of sugar

⅓ cup cognac or brandy

5 cups chicken stock, preferably homemade (page 317)

Preheat the oven to 400°F. Cut a shallow "X" on the flat side of each chestnut. Arrange the chestnuts in a single layer on a rimmed baking sheet with the flat sides facing upward and roast until they crack open, about 20 minutes. Let cool, then peel.

Heat a wide, heavy pot over medium-high heat. Add the olive oil and warm it to keep the bacon from sticking, then add the bacon. Cook, stirring, until the bacon turns golden brown and renders enough fat to coat the bottom of the pot, about 6 minutes. Add the butter and let it melt and turn lightly brown. Add the peeled chestnuts and cook, stirring, until golden brown, about 5 minutes. Add the shallot, onion, fennel, and garlic, season with salt, the pepper, and the sugar and cook, stirring, until the vegetables are softened but not browned, about 4 minutes.

Pour in the cognac and cook, stirring to loosen any flavorful bits cooked onto the bottom of the pot. Bring to a simmer and simmer until almost completely reduced, about 3 minutes. Pour in the stock, bring to a simmer, and simmer, uncovered, until the chestnuts start to fall apart, about 20 minutes.

Use tongs or a slotted spoon to fish out and discard the bacon. Transfer the soup to a blender (see Note, page 74), working in batches, if necessary, and blend, then pass it through a conical strainer or fine-mesh strainer, pressing down on the solids with the back of a ladle to extract as much flavorful liquid as possible.

The soup can be used right away or cooled and refrigerated in an airtight container for up to 2 days.

To Serve

2 tablespoons extra-virgin olive oil

8 ounces mushrooms, ideally a mix of 3 varieties such as shiitake, king oyster, cremini, black trumpet, or porcini, cut into 1-inch pieces, smaller ones left whole

Kosher salt

1 tablespoon unsalted butter

Sherry vinegar

1 tablespoon cognac or brandy

1 teaspoon minced shallot

1 teaspoon fines herbes (see page 44) or thinly sliced fresh flat-leaf parsley leaves

⅓ cup lightly whipped cream (from 3 tablespoons heavy cream)

If necessary, reheat the soup in a medium pot over medium heat, stirring occasionally.

Meanwhile, heat a medium sauté pan over medium-high heat. Add the oil and tip and tilt the pan to coat it, heating the oil until it is shimmering and almost smoking. Add the mushrooms, season with a generous pinch of salt, and cook, shaking the pan, to keep them from scorching. When they begin to turn golden brown, about 2 minutes, stir in the butter, then stir in a few drops of sherry vinegar, the cognac, the shallot, and the herbs.

Mound some mushrooms in the center of four to six wide, shallow bowls. Ladle some soup around the mushrooms in each bowl, top with some of the whipped cream, and serve.

French Onion Soup with Oxtail and Comté

Serves 4

Because it's made with veal stock, French onion soup is as beefy as it is oniony. We took that tradition in a logical new direction with this version, braising oxtails in a stew of caramelized onions, then using the strained braising liquid as the soup, flaking the beef into it. In many of our recipes, we don't insist that you use homemade stock, but it's really essential for creating the potent flavor here; because the oxtails are so powerfully beefy, we substitute chicken stock for veal to moderate the intense flavor.

To Prep

2 oxtail pieces, cut 2 inches
   thick by your butcher

Kosher salt

3 tablespoons extra-virgin olive oil

4 Spanish onions, thinly sliced

3 garlic cloves, thinly sliced

1 cup brandy, preferably apple brandy

About 4 cups homemade chicken
   stock (page 317)

3 fresh thyme sprigs

1 bay leaf, preferably fresh

Freshly ground black pepper

Season the oxtails generously with salt.

Heat the oil in a large pot or Dutch oven with a tight-fitting lid over medium-high heat. Add the oxtails and brown them well on all sides, about 8 minutes. Transfer the oxtails to a plate and drain off all but 2 tablespoons of the fat from the pot.

Reduce the heat to medium, add the onions and garlic to the pot, season lightly with salt, and cook, stirring occasionally, until well caramelized, about 40 minutes. If the onions begin to stick or scorch during that time, stir in a little water.

Preheat the oven to 275°F.

Stir in the brandy, loosening any flavorful bits cooked onto the bottom of the pot. Bring to a boil and cook until reduced by half, about 6 minutes. Return the oxtails to the pot, cover with the stock, and add the thyme and bay leaf. Cover the pot and braise in the oven until the meat is very soft, about 3 hours. During this time, periodically check to be sure the liquid is just barely simmering; if it is bubbling aggressively, reduce the oven temperature by 25°F; if not bubbling at all, raise it by 25°F.

(continued)

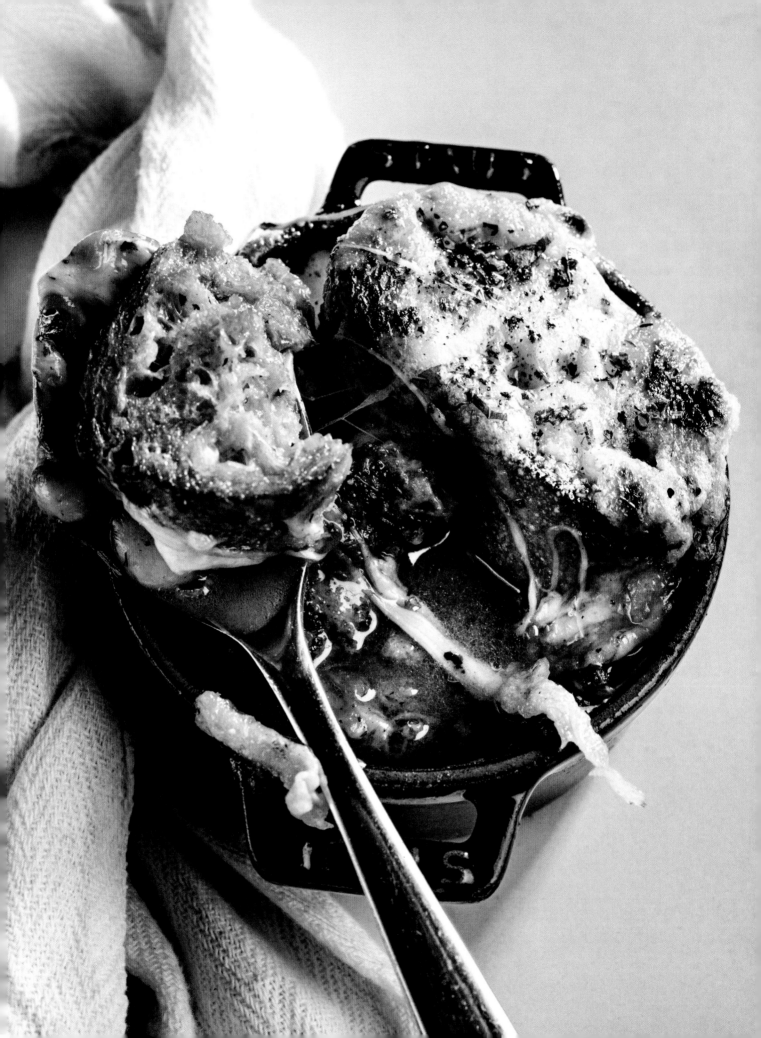

Once the meat is soft, remove the oxtails, and when cool enough to handle, shred the meat, discarding any large pieces of fat. Return the meat to the soup, season with salt and pepper, and use right away, or let cool and refrigerate in an airtight container for up to 2 days.

To Serve

4 (1-inch-thick) baguette slices

8 slices Comté cheese or other Alpine cheese, such as Gruyère or Emmenthal, about 3 inches by 3 inches

If necessary, reheat the soup in a medium pot over medium heat, stirring occasionally.

Meanwhile, toast the baguette slices until hard and crunchy. Preheat the broiler to high.

Ladle the hot soup into ovenproof crocks. Top each crock with a baguette slice and 2 slices of cheese. Broil until the cheese is bubbling and golden. Carefully remove the crocks from the oven, set on heatproof plates, and serve.

Duck Consommé with Foie Gras Won Tons

Serves 4

A French take on a Chinese staple, this is made in the Battersby kitchen with trimmings from duck, such as the neck and wings, that we accumulate over time. We suggest you do the same, saving the trimmings from duck or chicken, or a mix of the two. Simply freeze the pieces as you gather them until you have enough. Alternatively, you can purchase and use a piece of duck or chicken procured expressly to make this soup.

The method for making consommé is unusual: Rather than creating a raft of egg whites to draw out impurities from the stock, it is simply strained repeatedly, once through several layers of cheesecloth. This preserves the flavor of the consommé and results in a greater yield.

To Prep

Consommé

1 small Spanish onion, halved

2 pounds duck or other poultry trimmings (see headnote)

About 6 cups chicken stock, preferably homemade (page 317)

1 (1-inch) piece unpeeled fresh ginger, thinly sliced, plus 4 thin peeled slices

½ celery stalk, thinly sliced

1 carrot, unpeeled, thinly sliced

1 dried shiitake mushroom

1 teaspoon cracked black peppercorns

4 large basil leaves

1 teaspoon soy sauce

1 teaspoon fish sauce (optional)

Heat a medium cast-iron pan over very high heat. Add the onion, cut-side down, and char until nicely blackened, about 5 minutes. Remove from the pan and set aside.

Put the duck trimmings in a medium pot. Add enough stock to cover and bring to a gentle simmer over medium heat. Add the blackened onion, the unpeeled ginger, the celery, carrot, mushroom, and peppercorns. Simmer, adjusting the heat as necessary to prevent boiling, until intensely flavored, 45 minutes to 1 hour, periodically using a spoon to skim off any impurities that rise to the surface.

Strain the broth through a fine-mesh strainer into a heatproof bowl. Line the strainer with three layers of cheesecloth and strain the broth again. While the broth is still hot, add the peeled ginger, basil, soy sauce, and fish sauce (if using). Strain through a fine-mesh strainer into a medium bowl, discarding the solids.

Use right away or refrigerate in an airtight container for up to 2 days.

(continued)

Won Tons

1 large egg

6 ounces store-bought foie gras
    terrine (see Sources, page 321)

12 store-bought won ton skins

Break the egg into a small bowl, add a tablespoon of water, and whisk together to make an egg wash. Set aside.

Cut twelve ½-inch cubes from the terrine.

Working with one won ton wrapper at a time, set a terrine cube in the center of the wrapper, brush the sides lightly with the egg wash, and fold over to form a sealed triangle, pressing down to seal the edges. Bring the ends together in a tortellini-like shape and press them together so they hold, using a little egg wash if they don't hold on their own.

You can use the won tons right away or make them the morning of the day you plan to serve the soup, arrange them in a single layer on a plate, cover loosely with plastic wrap, and refrigerate until ready to use.

To Serve

1¾ ounces enoki mushrooms, root
    system cut off and discarded

1 scallion, white and light green
    parts, thinly sliced on an angle

1 teaspoon finely julienned ginger

4 fresh cilantro sprigs

4 fresh Thai basil or regular basil sprigs

4 fresh dill sprigs

4 fresh chervil sprigs

4 fresh mint sprigs

Freshly ground black pepper

Heat the won tons in gently simmering water over medium-high heat, or steam them in a steamer basket set over simmering water, until the skin is translucent and the foie gras within is soft to the touch (remove a won ton with a slotted spoon and gently press on it to test), about 2 minutes.

Meanwhile, if necessary, reheat the soup in a medium pot over medium heat, stirring occasionally.

Use a slotted spoon to transfer 3 won tons into the center of each of four bowls. Scatter the mushrooms, scallions, ginger, cilantro, basil, dill, chervil, and mint over them, grind some pepper over each bowl, and ladle the soup over the other ingredients. Serve.

Pasta and Risotto

Ricotta Gnudi with Crispy Artichokes, Lemon, and Pecorino

Serves 4

Gnudi means "nude" and these plump little dumplings have been described as everything from ravioli without the pasta to gnocchi without the potato. They are, in fact, a type of gnocchi, since *gnocchi* (probably derived from *nocca*, which means "knuckle") simply refers to any type of dumpling. They are bound together by a combination of creamy ricotta cheese and a modicum of flour. The most well-known version features spinach, but ours focus exclusively on the ricotta (in part because adding spinach can cause gnudi to become too watery and loose) with a boost from Pecorino Romano and an acidic lift from the addition of lemon zest. Crispy fried artichokes and a quick butter-and-lemon sauce are all that's called for to round out the flavors and textures; a little watercress added at the end provides a complementary spinachlike component.

The number of pieces produced by the gnudi recipe will vary depending whether or not you prefer larger or smaller gnudi; we prefer them on the large side which allows them to cook while retaining a creamy center.

To Prep

8 ounces ricotta cheese (about 2½ cups)

2¼ ounces 00 flour (see Sources, page 321) or all-purpose flour (about ½ cup), plus more for dusting

1 large egg yolk

1 tablespoon extra-virgin olive oil

Finely grated zest of 2 lemons

½ cup finely grated Pecorino Romano cheese

Kosher salt and freshly ground black pepper

Put the ricotta, flour, egg yolk, olive oil, lemon zest, and cheese in the bowl of a food processor fitted with the steel blade. Pulse just until the ingredients come together into a slightly sticky batter. Season with salt and pepper and pulse one last time.

Transfer to a disposable pastry bag or a 1-gallon resealable plastic bag. If you have time, refrigerate the batter in the bag for at least 1 hour, or up to 24 hours, to firm it up and help the gnudi hold their shape when cooked.

To Serve

Kosher salt

All-purpose flour, for dusting

¼ cup chicken stock, preferably homemade (page 317)

2 tablespoons unsalted butter

1 tablespoon extra-virgin olive oil

½ lemon

Freshly ground black pepper

1 cup loosely packed watercress or baby arugula

¼ cup finely grated aged pecorino
   cheese, such as Ginepro, Toscano,
   or d'Oro (see Sources, page 321)

Crispy Artichokes (recipe follows)

Bring a large pot of salted water to a boil over high heat.

Meanwhile, dust a large plate with flour. Snip the pastry bag where it's ½ inch wide and pipe the batter onto the plate into uniform dumplings, 1 inch high, using a paring knife to release the batter from the bag. You should have about 20 gnudi. Roll them in the flour and let rest for at least 10 minutes or up to 1 hour to absorb the flour, which will help hold the gnudi together.

Meanwhile, put the chicken stock and the butter in a wide, deep sauté pan over high heat. Cook, swirling, until the butter melts and the stock and butter come together and reduce to a glaze, about 3 minutes. Swirl in the oil and a few drops of lemon juice and season with salt and pepper.

Add the gnudi to the boiling water and cook until they rise to the surface and float, 2 to 3 minutes. Use a slotted spoon to transfer them to the pan with the glaze. Gently toss until the glaze coats the gnudi, about 20 seconds.

Distribute the gnudi among four serving plates and garnish with the watercress and pecorino. Finely grate a little lemon zest over each serving (1 swipe on the grater per plate). Garnish with the artichokes and serve.

Crispy Artichokes

Makes enough to garnish 4 servings

Fried artichokes can add impact to many dishes, lending earthy flavor and crunch. In addition to the gnocchi dish, we serve them with the steak tartare on page 82. They can also be tossed into a salad, and make a nice hors d'oeuvre to share at the table: Double the recipe, spoon some aioli (page 193) onto a plate, and top with the artichoke pieces.

½ lemon
1 large globe artichoke (12 to 16 ounces)
½ cup extra-virgin olive oil
Kosher salt

Fill a medium bowl halfway with cold water and squeeze the lemon into the water.

Turn the artichoke (see below) and very thinly slice it. Hold the pieces in the acidulated water to keep them from browning.

Heat the oil in a wide, deep sauté pan over medium heat to 350°F. (If you do not have a thermometer, you can check the temperature by dipping an artichoke piece into the oil—if it bubbles, you are ready to fry; if the oil begins smoking, it has gotten too hot.)

Working in two batches, remove the artichoke pieces from the water, pat dry with paper towels, and add them to the hot oil, being careful to avoid splashing the oil. Fry, turning the pieces occasionally with a slotted spoon, until golden brown and crispy all over, 6 to 8 minutes, adjusting the heat level as necessary to maintain the temperature. Use the spoon to transfer the finished pieces to a paper towel to drain and season each batch with salt as soon as they hit the paper.

The artichokes can be served immediately or held at room temperature for up to 1 hour.

→ **TURNING ARTICHOKES**

To turn artichokes, first cut off the top inch or so of the artichoke with a chef's knife. Trim the fibrous end of the stem and peel the stem with a vegetable peeler. Snap off the small leaves closest to the stem, then use kitchen shears to snip off the thorny tips of the remaining leaves.

Hold the artichoke in your non-dominant hand and hold a sharp paring knife at a sharp angle against the base of the artichoke. Turn the artichoke, cutting away the leaves until you are left with the heart. Use a tablespoon to scoop out and discard the fibrous portion (choke) inside.

→ **FRYING VEGETABLES**

Frying vegetables is a terrific way to bring texture to many dishes, especially vegetable-based dishes such as salads. We especially like using fried vegetables to build on the flavor of certain fresh vegetables in a dish by presenting them on the same plate in a different way. The technique is also the key to our root vegetable muesli on page 24.

Risotto-Style Strozzapreti with Spring Vegetables and Snail Butter

Serves 6 as a starter or pasta course

The trick to this dish is cooking the pasta the way you'd usually cook risotto, adding stock in small increments and stirring until it has been absorbed. It takes the step of finishing pastas in their sauce to a new level, allowing the pasta to drink up the flavor of the stock and vegetables with which it's cooked. When the cooking is done, the pasta and sauce are seamlessly united. We first learned this method of cooking pasta when we worked at Alain Ducasse's restaurant at the Essex House in New York City.

The size of the pot here is very important because you want the pasta to sit in a single layer so that all the pieces absorb the liquid well and at the same rate. The sauce is made by tossing a compound (flavored) butter and grated cheese with the hot pasta, causing emulsification. Here, snail butter, named for its affinity with escargot, proves the perfect complement to the pasta and vegetables. This dish is somewhat French in character, with the presence of carrots and turnips, two vegetables never seen with pasta in Italian cooking; you can vary the vegetables or simply omit those you do not like or that are not in season.

To Prep

½ pound fava beans in the pod

To Serve

¼ cup extra-virgin olive oil,
   plus more for serving

2 cups dried strozzapreti, penne,
   ziti, or mezze rigatoni

½ cup minced Spanish onion

2 tablespoons unsalted butter

Kosher salt

4 baby carrots, sliced on an angle

3 tablespoons thinly sliced spring garlic

3 cups chicken stock, preferably homemade (page 317)

4 thinly sliced peeled baby turnips

4 scallions, white and light green parts,
   cut on an angle into segments

4 asparagus stalks, woody base trimmed, tip
   quartered, stalk thinly sliced on an angle

¼ cup English peas, blanched and
   shocked (see page 313)

8 ramps, halved (optional)

Small piece of Grana Padano or Parmigiano-
   Reggiano cheese, for grating

½ cup Snail Butter (page 129)

About ¼ cup fresh lemon juice

¼ cup loosely packed thinly sliced
   arugula or watercress

Shell, blanch, shock, and peel the fava beans (see page 313)—this is time consuming, but you can do this up to 24 hours ahead of time.

If you like, prepare the other vegetables in To Serve up to 2 hours ahead of time. You may especially want to blanch and shock the peas; they can be refrigerated in the same container as the fava beans.

Make the Snail Butter (recipe follows) as far in advance as you like. You will need ½ cup for this dish.

Heat the oil in a medium, wide pot over medium-high heat. Add the pasta and cook, stirring, until it's lightly browned, about 1 minute. Add the onion, butter, and a pinch of salt and cook, stirring, until the butter has melted and the onion is softened but not browned, about 2 minutes. Add the carrots and garlic and cook, stirring occasionally, until the garlic is softened but not browned, about 2 minutes

Pour in 1 cup of the stock and cover the pot. When the stock has been absorbed completely, about 5 minutes, add an additional 1 cup of stock and cover. Cook until absorbed, about 5 minutes more, then add the remaining 1 cup stock and the turnips. Cover the pot. When the stock has reduced by about half, about 3 minutes, add the scallions and asparagus and cover the pot. When the stock has been almost totally absorbed, about 2 minutes more, add the peas, peeled favas, and ramps (if using).

Remove the pot from the heat and grate about ¼ cup of the cheese over the pasta and vegetables. Stir in the snail butter until it emulsifies into a sauce. Finish with the lemon juice, adding it in small increments and tasting as you do; you may not use it all.

Toss well, divide the pasta and vegetables among six plates, drizzle each portion with oil, and garnish with the arugula. Serve.

(continued)

We often turn to Grana Padano instead of Parmigiano-Reggiano in our kitchens, not because the former is cheaper (although it is) but because it has a milder flavor than the more internationally famous Parmesan. *Grana* means "grainy," and both Grana Padano and Parmigiano-Reggiano boast an appealing, crystalline texture, but Grana Padano's subtle character recommends it as a default grating cheese, so we save Parmigiano-Reggiano for more robust dishes where the other flavors can stand up to its assertive presence. Both Grana Padano and Parmigiano-Reggiano are nutty and milder than Pecorino Romano, which is sharper, saltier, and more assertive. We often use a mix of the two types for balance.

Snail Butter

Makes about 2 cups

This versatile butter is the foundation of the pasta on page 126 and the lamb dish on page 253. There's no escargot in the butter; rather, this is a wonderful butter for cooking snails, another use you might keep in mind. You can also use it to dress blanched asparagus spears, tossing them with the butter and some lemon juice, or spoon over oysters on the half-shell and broil them.

3 sticks (¾ pound) unsalted butter

Zest and juice of 2 lemons

¼ cup extra-virgin olive oil

Kosher salt and freshly ground black pepper

1 garlic clove

3 cups loosely packed fresh
  flat-leaf parsley leaves

1 cup finely diced prosciutto, preferably di Parma or San Daniele, or
  other cured ham such as pancetta
  (about 7 thick slices; see below)

Put the butter in the bowl of a food processor fitted with the steel blade. Process briefly to soften it. Add the lemon zest and juice and the olive oil. Season with salt and pepper and process briefly to incorporate the ingredients. Grate the garlic right into the processor using a Microplane. Add the parsley and prosciutto and briefly pulse just to incorporate them.

The butter can be used right away, or rolled into a log, wrapped tightly in plastic wrap, and refrigerated for up to 3 days, or frozen for up to 1 month.

→ WORKING WITH PORK PRODUCTS

When dicing or mincing a pork product such as bacon or prosciutto, firm it up briefly in the freezer to make it easier to slice.

Spaghetti alla Chitarra with Sea Urchin and Chili

Serves 6 as a starter or pasta course

No matter where you are when you eat it, or whether you've actually been there, this pasta will remind you of the Italian seaside, with its salty combination of shrimp stock and sea urchin, some of which is melted into the sauce, with an additional piece perched atop each serving. (For an extravagant flourish, add more sea urchin, as in the photo on page 131.) The toasted bread crumbs add essential crunch, and the optional chili flakes, if you include them, provide a counterpoint of heat. *Chitarra*, incidentally, means "guitar" and the name of the pasta itself refers to the instrument usually used to make it, which cuts rather than extrudes the pasta, resulting in a square rather than round shape.

To Prep

If making your own spaghetti (page 166), it can be prepared up to 1 month in advance.

To Serve

Kosher salt

12 pieces sea urchin (see Sources, page 321)

1 pound spaghetti, fresh (page 166) or dried

2 tablespoons extra-virgin olive oil, plus more for serving

2 garlic cloves, thinly sliced

1 Calabrian chili (see Sources, page 321), minced

1½ cups shrimp stock (page 316)

2 tablespoons unsalted butter

Freshly ground black pepper

Juice of ½ lemon

Toasted bread crumbs (see page 315)

Pinch of red chili flakes or piment d'Espelette (optional)

Bring a large pot of salted water to a boil over high heat.

Meanwhile, set aside the 6 nicest pieces of sea urchin for garnish. Put the remaining pieces in a small bowl. Whisk until crushed and liquidy, a few seconds. Set aside.

Add the pasta to the boiling water and cook until al dente, 2 to 3 minutes for fresh, 8 to 9 minutes for dried.

As the pasta cooks, heat the oil in a wide, deep sauté pan over medium-high heat. When the oil is shimmering, add the garlic and chili and cook, stirring occasionally, until the garlic is softened but neither ingredient is browned, about 2 minutes. Pour in the stock, bring it to a simmer, then swirl in the butter until it melts and becomes emulsified, about 1 minute.

Drain the pasta and add it to the pan with the sauce. Toss. It will look very loose but the sea urchin will thicken it when added.

Add the whisked sea urchin to the pan and cook over low heat, tossing, until the sauce emulsifies and thickens slightly, 1 to 2 minutes. Season with salt and pepper. Add the lemon juice and toss to incorporate it.

Divide the pasta and sauce among six plates. Scatter the bread crumbs over the pasta and finish each serving with a piece of sea urchin. Drizzle with olive oil and finish with a pinch of chili flakes, if desired. Serve.

Garganelli with Chicken Sugo and Peppers

Serves 6 as a starter or pasta course

If you break down your own whole chickens, this is a terrific way to use the thighs and/or legs, braising them in a robust, stewlike mix of vegetables, including fennel and bell pepper, then straining and reducing the braising liquid to make a sauce for the chicken and pasta. The sugo can also be made with pork.

To Prep

Garganelli

If making your own garganelli (page 166), it can be prepared up to 1 month in advance.

Chicken Sugo

4 chicken thighs or legs, or a combination

Kosher salt and freshly ground black pepper

¼ cup extra-virgin olive oil

1 small onion, coarsely chopped

½ fennel bulb, coarsely chopped

1 head of garlic, halved

5 thin strips lemon peel, removed with a
  vegetable peeler, no pith attached

1 green bell pepper, seeded
  and coarsely chopped

1 bay leaf, preferably fresh

1 fresh thyme sprig

1 fresh plum tomato, chopped

1 cup dry white wine

4 cups chicken stock, preferably
  homemade (page 317)

Preheat the oven to 325°F.

Season the chicken thighs with salt and black pepper. Heat the olive oil in a Dutch oven or other pot over medium-high heat until shimmering. Add the chicken pieces and brown all over, about 8 minutes. Use tongs or a slotted spoon to transfer the chicken to a large plate and set aside.

Pour off all but 2 tablespoons of the fat from the Dutch oven. Add the onion, fennel, garlic, lemon peel, and bell pepper and cook, stirring occasionally, until softened but not browned, about 4 minutes. Stir in the bay leaf and thyme and cook until fragrant, about 1 minute. Stir in the tomato and cook, stirring occasionally, until the liquid begins to evaporate, about 3 minutes. Pour in the wine, bring to a simmer, and cook until reduced by half, about 6 minutes. Pour in the stock and bring to a simmer.

Return the chicken pieces to the Dutch oven, submerging them. Cover with a lid, transfer to the oven, and braise until the chicken is cooked through and falling off the bone, 90 minutes to 2 hours. During this time, periodically check to be sure the liquid is just barely simmering; if it is bubbling aggressively, reduce the oven temperature by 25°F; if not bubbling at all, raise it by 25°F.

(continued)

When the chicken is cooked, remove the Dutch oven from the oven. Remove the lid and let the chicken cool in the braising liquid for 1 hour. Use tongs or a slotted spoon to remove the chicken from the pot and set aside on a clean, dry surface to cool. Strain the braising liquid through a fine-mesh strainer into a medium pot. Set the pot over high heat, bring to a boil, and cook until reduced to about 2 cups, about 10 minutes.

Meanwhile, when the meat is cool enough to handle, pick it from the bones. Discard the bones. When the sauce has been reduced, put the chicken meat in the sauce. Use right away or refrigerate the meat in the sauce in an airtight container for up to 2 days.

To Serve

Kosher salt

1 pound garganelli, fresh (page 166) or dried (rigatoni or penne may be substituted)

4 tablespoons extra-virgin olive oil

20 shishito peppers (available from specialty and Asian markets, or see Sources, page 321), or padrón peppers, stemmed

Freshly ground black pepper

1 garlic clove, thinly sliced

1 Calabrian chili (see Sources, page 321), minced

2 tablespoons unsalted butter

Small piece of Parmigiano-Reggiano cheese, for grating

½ lemon or a dash of sherry vinegar

If the chicken and sauce have been refrigerated, let them come to room temperature.

Bring a large pot of salted water to a boil over high heat. Cook the garganelli until al dente, about 3 minutes for fresh, 9 to 10 for dried.

Meanwhile, heat 2 tablespoons of the olive oil in a sauté pan over high heat. Add the peppers and cook, tossing, until blistered all over, 2 to 3 minutes. Season with salt and black pepper. Stir in the garlic and chili and cook until softened but not browned, about 2 minutes. Stir in the chicken and sauce and bring to a simmer.

Drain the pasta and add it to the pan. Toss and cook briefly to coat the pasta with the sauce. Add the butter and the remaining 2 tablespoons oil, and grate about 2 tablespoons of the cheese over the pasta. Toss well until the butter has melted.

Divide the pasta among six plates. Finish with a squeeze of lemon juice and serve.

Pappardelle with Duck Ragù, Olives, and Madeira

Serves 6 as a starter or pasta course

Braised duck and pappardelle are one of the quintessential sauce-pasta pairings; the wide, thick noodle proves the perfect foil for the intensely flavored meat and sauce. (Braised rabbit is the other dream matchup for pappardelle.) The olives here provide the kind of relief that sweet components sometimes do, punctuating what threatens to become an overpowering dish with juicy bursts of salinity.

To Prep

Pappardelle

If making your own pappardelle (page 166), it can be prepared up to 1 month in advance.

Duck Ragù

2 duck legs (see Sources,
    page 321), fat intact
Kosher salt
1 teaspoon crushed fennel seed
1 teaspoon crushed black peppercorns
2 teaspoons extra-virgin olive oil
1 teaspoon unsalted butter
1 small celery stalk, cut into large dice
1 small carrot, cut into large dice
1 small onion, cut into large dice
6 garlic cloves, smashed with the side
    of a chef's knife and peeled
2 fresh thyme sprigs
1 bay leaf, preferably fresh
1 heaping tablespoon tomato paste
1 cup Madeira or sherry
2 tablespoons sherry vinegar
About 3 cups chicken stock,
    preferably homemade (page 317)

The night before you make the ragù, season the duck legs all over lightly with salt, and on the flesh side only, with the fennel seed and black pepper. Set in a baking dish, cover lightly with plastic wrap, and let cure in the refrigerator overnight.

The next day, preheat the oven to 325°F.

Heat a teaspoon of the oil in a medium pot over medium-high heat. Add the legs, skin-side down, and cook, turning to brown them all over, about 8 minutes total cooking time. Transfer the legs to a Dutch oven that holds them snugly but comfortably and for which you have a tight-fitting lid. Carefully drain the fat from the pan and discard it.

Heat the remaining 1 teaspoon oil with the butter in the pan in which you browned the duck legs. When the butter foams, add the celery, carrot, and onion and cook, stirring occasionally, until lightly caramelized, 10 to 12 minutes. Add the garlic, thyme, and bay leaf and cook, stirring, until fragrant but not browned, about 1 minute. Stir in the tomato paste and cook, stirring, to coat the other ingredients, 2 minutes. Pour in the Madeira, bring to a simmer, and cook until thick and syrupy, about 6 minutes. Stir in the vinegar and stock and bring to a simmer.

Pour the liquid over the legs in the Dutch oven, cover, and

transfer to the oven. Braise until the meat is very tender, 2 hours to 2 hours 30 minutes. During this time, periodically check to be sure the liquid is just barely simmering; if it is bubbling aggressively, reduce the oven temperature by 25°F; if not bubbling at all, raise it by 25°F.

When the duck is done, remove the pot from the oven and let the legs cool in the liquid for 1 hour. Use tongs to transfer them to a clean, dry surface and, when cool enough to handle, pick the meat from the bones and discard the skin and bones. Strain the liquid into a small pot, set over high heat, bring to a boil, and cook until reduced slightly, to a sauce consistency, about 6 minutes. Skim any fat that rises to the surface.

Use right away or refrigerate the duck in the sauce in an airtight container for up to 2 days.

To Serve

Kosher salt

1 pound fresh pappardelle, homemade (page 166) or store-bought

2 tablespoons unsalted butter

25 pitted Taggiasca olives or other black olives, such as Gaeta

½ cup finely grated Grana Padano or Parmigiano-Reggiano cheese, plus more for serving

2 tablespoons extra-virgin olive oil

Dash of sherry vinegar

¼ cup fines herbes (see page 44) or thinly sliced fresh flat-leaf parsley

Bring a large pot of salted water to a boil over high heat. Add the pappardelle and cook until al dente, 3 to 4 minutes.

Meanwhile, reheat the duck and sauce together in a large, deep sauté pan over medium heat. Swirl in 1 tablespoon of the butter, melting it. Add the olives.

Drain the pasta in a colander and add it to the pan. Toss well. Add the cheese, olive oil, vinegar, and herbs and toss. Finish by swirling in the remaining 1 tablespoon butter, melting it, and grating some more cheese over the pasta.

Divide the pasta among six plates and serve.

→   BRAISING

Successful braising depends on attention to a few crucial details at each step in the process. First, select a cooking vessel that will hold the meats and vegetables comfortably but with very little excess space around them; more space requires more cooking liquid, and the more liquid, the more diluted the flavors become. When searing meats, it's important to not create a dark, hard crust; instead, stop when the meat attains a medium golden brown; otherwise any bits exposed to the hot air will become excessively dry in the oven.

When braising, be sure to check for the desired, gentle simmer described in each recipe, which will help ensure a tender result. We don't insist on it in our recipes, but the ideal way to braise is to cover the meat and liquid with both a cartouche and a lid for a very slow reduction. Finally, when the braising is done, let the meats rest in the braising liquid to reabsorb some of the liquid as they cool; another benefit is that the gelatins in the braising liquid will break down during the resting time and subtly coat the meats.

Potato Gnocchi with English Peas, Ramps, and Chanterelles

Serves 6 as a starter or pasta course

Our method of making gnocchi differs from many: We let the potato cool after ricing it, which keeps the gluten from over-developing and turning the little dumplings gummy. Gnocchi are versatile: You can serve them with spring vegetables as they are served here, or toss them with a quick tomato sauce in the summer or with browned butter and sliced fresh sage in the fall or winter. You can also adapt this recipe to other seasons, replacing the spring garlic with regular garlic or scallion whites.

To Prep

Kosher salt

1 Idaho potato (about 9 ounces), unpeeled

Freshly ground black pepper

¼ cup finely grated Grana Padano or Parmigiano-Reggiano cheese

¼ cup finely grated Pecorino Romano or additional Grana Padano cheese

½ teaspoon finely grated lemon zest

About ⅓ cup all-purpose or 00 flour (see Sources, page 321), plus more for dusting

1 large egg yolk

1 tablespoon heavy cream

Bring a medium pot of generously salted water to a boil over high heat. Add the whole, unpeeled potato and cook at a gentle simmer until it is very tender to a knife tip, about 1 hour.

Drain the potato and set it aside until it is cool enough to handle, then peel it.

While still warm, pass the potato through a food mill or ricer into a medium bowl, or press it through a strainer. Let cool to room temperature. Season lightly with salt and pepper.

Spread the potato out on your work surface and scatter the cheese(s) and lemon zest over it and sprinkle with the flour.

Mound the mixture and make a well in the center. Put the egg yolk and cream in the well.

Briefly knead the dough together, not overworking it. Separate it into two equal pieces. Working with one piece at a time, dust it with flour and roll it out to a 1-inch roll, squeezing it gently to compress it and eliminate any air pockets. Dust it again and cut it at 1-inch intervals, rolling the pieces in flour to keep them from sticking. After rolling and cutting all the dough, you should have about 32 pieces.

(continued)

The gnocchi can be refrigerated on a flour-dusted baking sheet in the refrigerator if you plan to use them the same day; otherwise, set the baking sheet in the freezer to firm up the gnocchi for about an hour, then transfer them to a freezer bag and freeze for up to 1 month.

To Serve

Kosher salt

3 tablespoons unsalted butter

1 cup chanterelles or other wild
    mushrooms, cut into bite-size pieces

5 ramps, white bottoms thinly sliced,
    green tops torn into bite-size pieces

1 cup English peas, blanched and
    shocked (see page 313)

Freshly ground black pepper

½ cup chicken stock or vegetable stock,
    preferably homemade (pages 317 and 316)

Extra-virgin olive oil

⅔ cup finely grated Grana Padano cheese

⅓ cup finely grated Pecorino Romano cheese

¼ cup fines herbes (see page 44) or
    thinly sliced fresh flat-leaf parsley

If the gnocchi have been frozen, defrost them in the refrigerator a few hours before you plan to cook them. (Unlike most pasta, they are too delicate to be cooked directly from a frozen state.)

Bring a large pot of salted water to a boil over high heat.

Meanwhile, melt 2 tablespoons of the butter in a wide, deep sauté pan over medium heat. When the butter foams, add the mushrooms and cook, stirring occasionally, until they begin to give off their liquid, about 3 minutes. Stir in the ramps and peas, season with salt and pepper, and cook, stirring, until slightly softened but not browned, about 3 minutes. Pour in the stock, bring to a gentle simmer, then swirl in the remaining 1 tablespoon butter, melting it to make a glaze, about 1 minute.

Add the gnocchi to the salted water and cook just until they float to the top, 1 to 2 minutes. Use a slotted spoon to transfer them to the pan with the vegetables. Season with salt and pepper, drizzle some olive oil over the pasta, then add the cheeses and herbs. Toss well.

Divide the gnocchi and vegetables among six plates and serve.

Farfalle with Gorgonzola and Pistachios

Serves 6 as a starter or pasta course

This dish finds bow-tie pasta tossed with a rich, creamy sauce dominated by the pungent flavor of Gorgonzola cheese. That richness is cut by the crunch of pistachios, a fresh grating of orange zest, and a scattering of fragrant basil over each serving.

To Prep

Farfalle

If making your own farfalle (page 166), it can be prepared up to 1 month in advance.

Gorgonzola Sauce

2 teaspoons extra-virgin olive oil

1 teaspoon minced garlic

½ teaspoon chopped Calabrian chili (see Sources, page 321)

1 cup heavy cream

Kosher salt and freshly ground black pepper

1 ounce Gorgonzola cheese

1½ tablespoons finely grated Grana Padano or Parmigiano-Reggiano cheese

1½ tablespoons finely grated Pecorino Romano cheese

To make the sauce, heat the oil in a medium pot over medium-high heat. Add the garlic and chili and cook, stirring occasionally, until softened but not browned, about 2 minutes. Add the cream and slowly bring it to a boil. As soon as it boils, remove the pot from the heat, season with salt and pepper, and pour the mixture into a blender (see Note, page 74). Add the Gorgonzola, Grana Padano, and pecorino and blend to emulsify, about 20 seconds.

The sauce may be used right away, or let cool and refrigerate in an airtight container for up to 24 hours.

To Serve

Kosher salt

1 pound fresh farfalle, homemade (page 166) or store-bought

1 tablespoon unsalted butter

½ cup finely grated Grana Padano

¾ cup pistachio nuts, toasted (see page 314) and crushed

1 orange

8 to 12 small fresh basil leaves

Bring a large pot of salted water to a boil over high heat. Add the pasta and cook until al dente, about 2 minutes.

Meanwhile, bring the reserved sauce to a boil in a wide, deep sauté pan over medium-high heat. Swirl in the butter, melting it.

When the pasta is done, drain it in a colander and transfer it to the pan with the sauce. Toss well to coat the pasta. Add the cheese and pistachios and toss well.

Divide the pasta among six plates. Finely grate some orange zest over each serving and garnish with the basil leaves. Serve.

Fresh Squid Ink Tagliatelle with Mussels, Calamari, and Chorizo

Serves 6 as a starter or pasta course

The visual contrast between dark squid ink pasta, freshly cooked squid (calamari), and green parsley here is naturally elegant, and the flavors come together effortlessly. You can purchase the tagliatelle, but you might be surprised how easy it is to make your own by simply adding a small quantity of squid ink to a basic pasta recipe. If you have lobster claw meat or knuckles saved from other cooking, you can replace the mussels with lobster for a more luxurious dish.

To Prep

Squid Ink Tagliatelle
20 mussels

If making your own, the squid ink tagliatelle (page 166) can be prepared up to 1 month in advance.

Pour water into a medium pot to a depth of ½ inch. Add the mussels, bring to a simmer, cover, and continue to simmer until the mussels open, about 5 minutes. Discard any mussels that do not open. Set the pot aside, uncovered, to let the mussels cool slightly, then remove from the shells. Line a fine-mesh strainer with cheesecloth and strain the mussels' cooking liquid through the cheesecloth into a measuring cup. Reserve ¾ cup of the liquid and discard the rest.

The mussels and liquid can be used right away or refrigerated in the same airtight container for up to 24 hours.

To Serve

Kosher salt

20 thin slices chorizo

1 garlic clove, thinly sliced

1 teaspoon minced Calabrian chili
   (see Sources, page 321)

¾ cup shrimp stock (page 316)

1 tablespoon unsalted butter

1 tablespoon extra-virgin olive
   oil, plus more for serving

1 pound fresh squid ink tagliatelle,
   homemade (page 166) or store-bought

2 calamari (about 4 ounces each),
   tubes and tentacles separated

½ lemon

1 cup loosely packed fresh
   flat-leaf parsley leaves

Toasted bread crumbs (page 315)

Bring a large pot of salted water to a boil over high heat. If the mussels and reserved liquid have been refrigerated, remove the mussels from the liquid with a teaspoon and set them aside in a small bowl. Set the liquid aside separately.

Meanwhile, heat a wide, deep sauté pan over medium heat. Add the chorizo and cook, stirring occasionally, to brown the slices all over and render enough fat to coat the bottom of the pan, about 6 minutes. Add the garlic and chili and cook, stirring occasionally, until the garlic is softened but not browned, about 2 minutes.

Add the stock, reserved mussel cooking liquid, butter, and olive oil to the pan, bring to a simmer, and cook until reduced almost to a glaze, about 5 minutes.

Meanwhile, add the pasta to the boiling water and cook until al dente, about 3 minutes. Drain the pasta and add it to the pan with the other ingredients, then immediately add the mussels and calamari. Toss just to coat the pasta and cook the calamari and reheat the mussels, about 30 seconds. Squeeze the juice from the lemon half over the pan, catching the seeds in your hand and discarding them (save the juiced lemon half for grating), add a drizzle of olive oil and sprinkle of parsley, and give a good toss.

Divide the pasta among six plates and finish with a scattering of bread crumbs and grate some lemon zest over each serving.

Bucatini with Fennel Sausage Ragù

Serves 6 as a starter or pasta course

Choose your sausage well for this recipe, because the ragù is made with little more than sausage, wine, and cream, with fresh garlic and fennel seed underscoring certain flavors. The cinnamon might seem an unusual touch but is actually rather common in many Italian meat ragùs and filled pastas.

To Prep

½ pound sweet fennel sausage, casings removed

2 garlic cloves, minced

1 tablespoon ground cinnamon

1 teaspoon crushed fennel seed

1 cup dry white wine

1 cup heavy cream

Pinch of kosher salt

Cook the sausage in a heavy pan over low-medium heat, breaking it up with a fork, until crumbled, loose, and lightly browned all over, about 8 minutes. Remove the pan from the heat and stir in the garlic, cinnamon, and fennel seed to coat the sausage. Return the pan to medium-high heat, add the wine, bring to a boil, and cook until the pan is almost dry, about 8 minutes. Stir in the cream, bring to a simmer, and cook until reduced to a sauce consistency, about 6 minutes. Taste the sauce and, if necessary, season with the salt.

Use right away or refrigerate in an airtight container for up to 24 hours.

To Serve

Kosher salt

1 pound dried bucatini

Freshly ground black pepper

Small piece of Parmigiano-Reggiano or Grana Padano cheese, for grating

Small piece of Pecorino Romano cheese, for grating

Bring a large pot of salted water to a boil over high heat. Add the pasta and cook until al dente, about 11 minutes.

Meanwhile, if necessary, reheat the sauce in a medium pot over medium heat, stirring occasionally.

When the pasta is done, drain it in a colander and toss it with the sauce. Season generously with pepper, generously grate some Parmigiano-Reggiano and pecorino over the pasta, and toss well until the pasta is coated and the sauce is emulsified.

Divide the pasta among six plates and serve.

Pizzoccheri

Serves 6 as a starter or pasta course

This hearty dish, distinguished by the combination of pasta and potato, is based on a classic from the mountains of northern Italy in Valle d'Aosta and was likely influenced by the fact that the region shares a border with Switzerland, where the trio of potatoes, pasta, and cheese is actually rather common. It's hearty enough for the coldest day of winter. The best way to cook and serve this is in individual baking dishes, which are easier to layer, bake more quickly, and have less chance of becoming soupy.

The name *pizzoccheri* refers to both the pasta and the dish itself. When making the dough, be wary of adding too much water. It may look like it's not coming together, but the dryness of the dough is one of the distinguishing characteristics of pizzoccheri. Trust that it will hydrate during its resting time and know that this may be better the second time you make it and have begun to develop an instinct for its unique properties.

To Prep

Duck Sausage

Note: *If you don't own a meat grinder, you can purchase duck sausage and remove it from its casing, or have a butcher grind the duck leg meat for you, mince the pork fat and sage leaves, and knead the ingredients together by hand.*

18 ounces boneless skinless duck
    legs, cut into cubes
6 ounces pork fat (fatback), cut into cubes
5 cloves garlic confit (see page 315)
About 1 tablespoon kosher salt
3 tablespoons chopped fresh sage leaves
3 tablespoons dry red wine
About 1 teaspoon sugar
Freshly ground black pepper

Put the duck, pork fat, garlic confit, salt, sage, wine, and sugar in a medium bowl, season with a few grinds of pepper, and stir together. Cover the bowl and refrigerate for at least 4 hours. Pass the meat mixture through a meat grinder with a small or medium die. To check the seasoning, heat a small pan over medium heat and cook a small piece of the sausage until cooked through. Taste and adjust the sugar, salt, and/or pepper in the mixture accordingly. The duck sausage can be used right away or refrigerated in an airtight container for up to 3 days. You will need 6 ounces of the sausage for this dish; save the rest for another use.

Pizzoccheri Dough

1 large egg
1 large egg yolk
¾ cup 00 flour (see Sources,
    page 321) or all-purpose flour
¼ cup buckwheat flour
1 tablespoon extra-virgin olive oil

In the bowl of a stand mixer fitted with the dough hook, combine the egg, egg yolk, 00 flour, buckwheat flour, and olive oil and mix just until it comes together. If it does not come together, add water in small increments, starting with 2 tablespoons, being wary of adding too much (see headnote). When the dough is ready, a finger pressed into the dough should leave an impression then slowly bounce back.

Remove the dough from the mixer, shape it into a ball, wrap in plastic wrap, and let rest for 1 hour at room temperature or overnight in the refrigerator. During this time, the flour will absorb the moisture of the egg, oil, and water.

Use a bench cutter or chef's knife to cut the dough into four equal pieces. Working with one piece at a time, roll the dough out to ¼ inch thick, folding it over on itself and rolling again, until leathery and tacky but not sticky. Each sheet should be roughly 4 x 12 inches. Let the sheets dry for a few minutes, then cut each one into eight 1½-inch strips, for a total of 32 strips. Stack the pasta in small piles on a plate, wrap loosely in plastic wrap, and proceed to cooking the vegetables and assembling the dish.

(continued)

Pasta and Vegetables

8 fingerling potatoes

1 garlic clove, smashed with the side
   of a chef's knife and peeled

1 fresh thyme sprig

1 teaspoon whole black peppercorns

1 bay leaf, preferably fresh

Kosher salt

2 tablespoons extra-virgin olive
   oil, plus more for drizzling

2 tablespoons unsalted butter

8 large Brussels sprouts, trimmed
   and quartered lengthwise

Freshly ground black pepper

Grana Padano or Parmigiano-
   Reggiano cheese, for grating

½ lemon

2 tablespoons fines herbes (see page 44)
   or thinly sliced fresh flat-leaf
   parsley leaves

8 ounces Fontina cheese, thinly sliced
   or coarsely grated on a box grater

Small piece Parmigiano-Reggiano
   cheese, for grating

To Serve

6 tablespoons toasted bread
   crumbs (see page 315)

2 tablespoons fines herbes (see page 44) or
   thinly sliced fresh flat-leaf parsley leaves

Put the potatoes, garlic, thyme, peppercorns, and bay leaf in a medium pot and add cold water to cover. Bring the water to a simmer over medium-high heat and continue to simmer until the potatoes are tender to a knife tip, 15 to 20 minutes, depending on the size of the potatoes. Drain the potatoes and, when cool enough to handle but still warm, use a paring knife to peel them and slice them into thin rounds. Set aside.

Preheat the oven to 350°F. Bring a large pot of salted water to a boil over high heat.

Meanwhile, heat the olive oil with 1 tablespoon of the butter in a large, deep sauté pan over medium-high heat. When the butter foams, add the Brussels sprouts and cook, tossing occasionally, until lightly browned all over, about 5 minutes. Add the potatoes and sausage and cook, tossing, until both are warmed through, about 3 minutes. Season with salt and pepper and set aside while you cook the pasta.

Add the pasta to the boiling salted water and cook until it floats to the surface, about 2 minutes. Reserve a few tablespoons of pasta cooking liquid in a heatproof vessel, then drain the pasta in a colander and set it aside.

Return the pan with the vegetables to high heat, add a tablespoon or two of the reserved pasta cooking water, along with the remaining 1 tablespoon butter and a drizzle of olive oil, and toss well to emulsify into a sauce. Grate some cheese and squeeze some lemon juice over the pan, catching the seeds in your hand and discarding them, and add the pasta and herbs to the pan. Toss well and set aside.

Spoon the pasta and vegetables into 6 single-serving baking dishes or one large dish, alternating it with layers of Fontina slices. Finely grate about 2 tablespoons of Parmigiano-Reggiano over each serving or about ½ cup over a larger baking dish.

Bake just until the cheese has melted, about 5 minutes, and remove the dish(es) from the oven. Use right away (leave the oven on) or let rest at room temperature, lightly covered with plastic wrap, for up to 4 hours.

If necessary, remove the plastic wrap from the pizzoccheri and return the oven to 350°F. Return the baking dish(es) to the oven and reheat until warmed through, about 8 minutes, checking for doneness by inserting a cake tester or thin paring knife into the center, holding it there for about 30 seconds, and checking to see it is hot when removed (see page 4). Remove the dish(es) from the oven.

Top with the bread crumbs and herbs, and serve.

Rigatoni with Brussels Sprouts, Bacon, and Arugula

Serves 6 as a starter or pasta course

Made via a similar technique as the strozzapreti on page 126, the rigatoni in this dish drinks up the flavor of the Brussels sprouts and bacon with which it cooks. As with that recipe, be sure to cook this one in a vessel that holds the ingredients snugly, but in a single layer.

To Prep

Kosher salt

48 pieces dried rigatoni (about 4 cups), preferably De Cecco

3 tablespoons extra-virgin olive oil

To Serve

2 tablespoons extra-virgin olive oil

4 ounces smoked bacon, cut into ½-inch dice (about ¾ cup)

10 ounces Brussels sprouts (about 12), trimmed and quartered lengthwise

2 tablespoons unsalted butter

Kosher salt and freshly ground black pepper

2 garlic cloves: 1 thinly sliced, 1 smashed with the side of a chef's knife and peeled

About 2 cups chicken stock, preferably homemade (page 317)

2¼ cups grated Parmigiano-Reggiano cheese (about 3½ ounces)

Juice of 1 lemon

¼ cup minced fresh herbs, either a mix of flat-leaf parsley, dill, and tarragon, or just parsley

2 cups loosely packed baby arugula, washed and spun dry

Toasted bread crumbs (see page 315)

Bring a large pot of salted water to a boil over high heat. Add the pasta, give a stir, and cook for 5 minutes. Drain the pasta in a colander, return it to the pot, and toss with the oil. Use right away or spread the pasta out on a rimmed baking sheet to cool, then hold at room temperature for up to 8 hours.

Select a wide, heavy, not-too-deep pot that can hold most of the ingredients in a single layer, or close to it. Heat 1 tablespoon of the olive oil in the pot over medium heat for a few seconds, just to keep the bacon from sticking when added, then add the bacon and cook, stirring occasionally, for 3 minutes. Add the Brussels sprouts and 1 tablespoon of the butter and cook until the bacon is lightly browned, 3 to 4 minutes more. Season generously with salt and a few grinds of pepper. Add the parcooked pasta and remaining 1 tablespoon butter and cook, stirring, until the pasta lightly browns, 1 to 2 minutes. Add the sliced garlic and 1 cup of the stock. Cover and cook until the pasta has absorbed the stock, 3 to 4 minutes. Add another ½ cup stock, cover, and cook until it is reduced and the pasta is cooked through and glazed, stirring in a few more tablespoons of the stock, if necessary, to cause a glaze to form. Stir in the smashed garlic clove, remaining 1 tablespoon oil, 1½ cups of the cheese, the lemon juice, and the herbs. If the pasta seems too dry, stir in a little more stock or water.

(continued)

Remove and discard the smashed garlic clove.

Remove the pot from the heat and stir in the arugula, just wilting it, about 20 seconds.

Divide the rigatoni among six plates or wide shallow bowls. Top with the remaining cheese and bread crumbs, and serve.

→   A FRESH TASTE OF GARLIC

To impart the flavor of fresh, uncooked garlic to sautéed recipes without leaving bits of sliced or minced garlic in the finished dish, add a smashed garlic clove in the last few minutes of cooking, then remove it before serving. For a greater impact, leave it in longer; take it out quickly if just a hint of garlic is what you're after.

Pici with Braised Rabbit, Tomato, and Fennel

Serves 6 as a starter or pasta course

Pici is a spaghetti-like pasta, only fatter and a little looser, so it lands a bit less neatly on the plate, suggesting a rustic effect that gets along well with rabbit ragù. It's especially friendly for home cooks because it doesn't require a pasta roller.

To Prep

Braised Rabbit

2 tablespoons extra-virgin olive oil

4 rabbit shoulders or legs

Kosher salt and freshly ground black pepper

½ cup minced Spanish onion

¾ cup diced fresh fennel

1 garlic clove, thinly sliced

1 teaspoon fennel seed

1 bay leaf, preferably fresh

1 fresh thyme sprig

1 fresh rosemary sprig

½ cup canned diced tomatoes, with their juices

½ cup dry white wine

About 2 cups chicken stock, preferably homemade (page 317)

Preheat the oven to 325°F.

Heat the olive oil in a braising pan just large enough to hold the rabbit shoulders in a single layer without crowding. Season the rabbit shoulders with salt and pepper. When the oil is shimmering, add the rabbit shoulders and brown them lightly all over, about 6 minutes. Use tongs or a slotted spoon to transfer the shoulders to a large plate and set aside.

Add the onion, fresh fennel, garlic, and fennel seed to the pan, reduce the heat to medium, season with salt, and cook, stirring occasionally, until lightly browned, about 10 minutes. Stir in the bay leaf, thyme, and rosemary and cook for 1 minute, then stir in the tomatoes and their juices and cook, stirring occasionally, for 5 minutes. Pour in the wine, bring to a simmer, and cook until reduced by three-quarters, about 3 minutes. Return the rabbit shoulders to the pan. Pour in enough stock to just cover the rabbit shoulders, bring to a simmer, then cover and transfer to the oven. Braise until the rabbit is falling off the bone, about 1 hour 20 minutes. During this time, periodically check to be sure the liquid is just barely simmering; if it is bubbling aggressively, reduce the oven temperature by 25°F; if not bubbling at all, raise it by 25°F.

Remove the pot from the oven and let the rabbit shoulders cool in the braising liquid for 1 hour. Use tongs or a slotted spoon to transfer the rabbit shoulders to a clean, dry surface. Once cool enough to handle, pick the meat from the bones and return it to the liquid with the vegetables. The rabbit and sauce can be used right away or refrigerated in an airtight container for up to 2 days.

Pici

3 cups 00 flour (see Sources, page 321) or
    all-purpose flour, plus more for dusting

2 tablespoons extra-virgin olive oil

In the bowl of a stand mixer fitted with the dough hook, combine the flour and olive oil and mix on low speed, adding 1 cup cold water a few tablespoons at a time, until the mixture comes together in a wet, slack dough, like Play-Doh. (You may not use all the water.)

Wrap the dough in plastic wrap and let rest for 1 hour at room temperature.

To shape the pici, generously dust a work surface and rolling pin with flour. Roll the dough out about ¼ inch thick. Cut the rolled-out dough into ¼-inch-wide strips and roll them out by hand into 12- to 18-inch-long, snakelike strands (we think it looks like goofy spaghetti; the strands do not have to be of a uniform length). Because the dough is so sticky, you might need to redust your surface, rolling pin, and hands frequently.

It's best to cook the pici right away, but you can hold them for an hour or two in a single layer on a well-floured baking sheet in the refrigerator; we do not recommend freezing them.

To Serve

Kosher salt

2 tablespoons unsalted butter

Small piece of Grana Padano
    cheese, for grating

Extra-virgin olive oil

Bring a large pot of salted water to a boil. Add the pasta and cook until al dente, 4 to 6 minutes, depending on thickness.

Meanwhile, reheat the rabbit ragù in a wide, deep sauté pan over medium heat.

When the pasta is done, drain it in a colander and add it to the pan with the ragù. Add the butter and toss well to melt the butter and coat the pasta. Generously grate some cheese over the pasta and drizzle with olive oil. Toss again.

Divide the pasta among six plates and finish with a little more grated cheese. Serve.

Pork Tortellini with Dandelion Pesto and Cherry Tomatoes

Serves 6 as a starter or pasta course

The three components of this pasta deliver layer after layer of flavors that build on each other, upping the ante with each bite. Keep the dandelion pesto in mind for other pasta dishes; even just tossing it with freshly cooked and drained spaghetti and a little of its cooking liquid can produce a quick, delicious sauce.

To Prep

Pork Tortellini

8 ounces ground pork, preferably 80% lean

2 ounces pancetta, finely minced or ground

Kosher salt and freshly ground black pepper

¼ cup dry white wine

2 ounces mortadella, cut into cubes

2 tablespoons unsalted butter,
   at room temperature

1 tablespoon olive oil

Finely grated zest and juice of 1 lemon

½ cup finely grated Parmigiano-
   Reggiano, Grana Padano, or
   Pecorino Romano cheese

2 oil-packed anchovy fillets

1 large egg

All-purpose flour, for dusting

Basic Pasta Dough (page 166)

To make the filling, heat a large sauté pan over high heat and add the pork and pancetta. Season with salt and pepper and cook, stirring frequently, until lightly browned all over, about 4 minutes. Add the wine and stir to loosen any flavorful bits cooked onto the bottom of the pan. Bring to a simmer and cook until the wine has almost completely evaporated, about 2 minutes. Remove the pan from the heat and let cool to room temperature.

Transfer the pork and pancetta mixture to the bowl of a food processor fitted with the steel blade. Add the mortadella and process until semismooth, about 30 seconds. Add the butter, olive oil, lemon zest and juice, cheese, and anchovies and pulse until just incorporated. Taste and adjust the seasoning with salt and/or pepper if necessary. Add the egg and pulse just to incorporate.

Transfer the filling to a medium bowl, cover with plastic wrap, and refrigerate while you prepare the tortellini dough.

Dust a clean, dry work surface with flour and roll out the pasta to a thickness of about 4 millimeters (likely the second-thinnest setting on your pasta machine). Use a 3-inch cutter or glass to punch out rounds, then briefly knead any pasta scraps together, roll it out, and punch out as many additional rounds as you can. You should have about 30 rounds.

To make the tortellini, arrange the rounds on your work surface, dusting it with flour first if necessary. Using a spray bottle, mist a small amount of water over the rounds from a height of

(continued)

about 8 inches. Put a teaspoon of filling in the center of each pasta round. Fold the circle over the filling, sealing the edges by pressing down on them, then wrap the ends around the half-moon to touch each other and pinch them together.

The tortellini can be refrigerated on a flour-dusted baking sheet in the refrigerator if you plan to use them the same day; otherwise, set the sheet in the freezer to firm up the tortellini for about an hour, then transfer them to a freezer bag and freeze for up to 1 month.

Dandelion Pesto

1 small bunch dandelion greens, stems removed and discarded, well washed, and coarsely chopped (about 1½ cups)

1 cup fines herbes (see page **44**) or fresh herbs of your choosing

1 garlic clove, smashed with the side of a chef's knife and peeled

⅓ cup grated Parmigiano-Reggiano, Grana Padano, or Pecorino Romano cheese

¼ cup pine nuts, walnuts, or pistachios, toasted

½ cup extra-virgin olive oil, plus more for topping

Kosher salt and freshly ground black pepper

Put the dandelion greens, herbs, garlic, cheese, and pine nuts in the bowl of a food processor fitted with the steel blade. Process until semismooth; if necessary, stop the machine periodically to scrape down the sides with a rubber spatula. With the motor running, gradually drizzle in the olive oil. Season with salt and pepper.

Use right away, or refrigerate in a jar, topped with a thin layer of olive oil to keep it from oxidizing, for up to 2 days.

To Serve

15 cherry tomatoes, halved

4 large or 2 small dandelion spears

2 tablespoons extra-virgin olive oil

Sherry vinegar

Kosher salt and freshly ground black
    pepper

¾ cup chicken stock, prefera-
    bly homemade (page 317)

2 tablespoons unsalted butter

Small piece of Parmigiano-Reggiano
    cheese, shaved with a vegetable peeler

Put the tomatoes and dandelion spears in 2 separate small bowls. Dress each with 1 tablespoon of the olive oil, a dash of sherry vinegar, and season with salt and pepper. Toss gently and set aside.

Bring a large pot of salted water to a gentle boil. Add the tortellini and cook until they float to the surface, about 2 minutes for fresh, 3 to 4 minutes for frozen.

Drain the tortellini and return them to the pot. Add the chicken stock and butter and cook over medium heat, swirling to emulsify the butter as it melts and glazes the tortellini.

Spread some pesto in the center of each of six plates. Use a slotted spoon to divide the tortellini among the plates. Garnish with the tomatoes, dandelion spears, and shaved cheese. Serve.

Ricotta and Herb Ravioli with Parmesan Broth

Serves 6 as a starter or pasta course

We favor ricotta and herb ravioli to the more classic ricotta and spinach. The herbs have more flavor, and are less likely to make the filling watery. The cheese broth brings all the flavors of the ravioli into high relief.

To Prep

Parmesan Broth

2 cups chicken stock, prefera-
    bly homemade (page 317)
2 tablespoons extra-virgin olive oil
2 tablespoons unsalted butter,
    at room temperature
1 tablespoon browned butter (see page 315)
¼ cup finely grated Grana Padano cheese
¼ cup finely grated Pecorino Romano cheese
Kosher salt and freshly ground black pepper
1 fresh basil sprig
1 thin slice of lemon, seeds removed

Bring the stock to a boil in a medium pot over high heat. Cook until reduced by half, about 6 minutes. Transfer the stock to a blender and, with the motor running, gradually add the following, one at a time, to allow the mixture to emulsify: olive oil, unsalted butter, browned butter, Grana Padano, and Pecorino Romano. Return the mixture to the pot, season with salt and pepper, then add the basil and lemon, cover, and let steep for 10 minutes.

Strain the broth and use right away, or refrigerate in an airtight container for up to 24 hours.

Herb and Ricotta Ravioli

1 cup ricotta cheese

1 tablespoon minced fresh
    flat-leaf parsley leaves

1 tablespoon minced fresh chives

1 tablespoon minced fresh tarragon leaves

½ tablespoon minced fresh marjoram leaves

Finely grated zest of 1 lemon

¼ cup finely grated Grana Padano cheese

¼ cup finely grated Pecorino Romano cheese

¼ garlic clove, minced or grated
    on a Microplane

3 tablespoons extra-virgin olive oil

Kosher salt and freshly ground black pepper

½ recipe Basic Pasta Dough (page 166)

Put the ricotta, parsley, chives, tarragon, marjoram, lemon zest, Grana Padano, Pecorino Romano, garlic, and olive oil in a large bowl. Season with a pinch of salt and a few grinds of pepper. Stir together with a rubber spatula until well incorporated.

Transfer the filling to a medium bowl, cover with plastic wrap, and refrigerate while you prepare the ravioli dough.

Dust a clean, dry work surface with flour and roll out the pasta to a thickness of about ⅛ inch. Use a 3-inch cutter or glass to punch out rounds from the pasta, then briefly knead any pasta scraps together, roll it out, and punch out as many additional circles as you can. (Alternatively, you can make 3-inch squares, cutting them with a straight edge and a knife or pizza cutter.) You should have about 30 circles.

To make the ravioli, arrange the rounds on your work surface, dusting it with flour first if necessary. Working with 1 round at a time, use a spray bottle to mist a small amount of water over the round from a height of about 8 inches. Spoon about ½ tablespoon of the filling in the center of the round. Fold the circle over the filling, sealing the edges by pressing down on them, then use a 2-inch ring cutter to cut the excess dough from the half-circle, setting it over the round edge (avoiding the straight side), and pressing down. Repeat with the remaining rounds and filling.

The ravioli can be used right away, or refrigerated on a flour-dusted baking sheet in the refrigerator if you plan to use them the same day; otherwise, set the sheet in the freezer to firm up the ravioli for about an hour, then transfer them to a freezer bag and freeze for up to 1 month.

To Serve

Kosher salt

Extra-virgin olive oil

Freshly ground black pepper

Reheat the broth in a medium pot over medium heat, stirring occasionally.

Meanwhile, bring a large pot of salted water to a boil over high heat. Add the ravioli and cook until they float to the surface, about 2 minutes for fresh, 3 to 4 minutes for frozen.

When the ravioli are done, use a slotted spoon to transfer them to six bowls. (Do not drain in a colander because they are delicate and may rupture.) Ladle some broth over the ravioli in each bowl. Finish each serving with a drizzle of olive oil and a few grinds of pepper. Serve.

Spring Vegetable Risotto

Serves 6 as a starter or risotto course

This risotto captures springtime both in flavor and visually, with the signature green color of the season captured in the asparagus puree that coats the rice, with asparagus tips and fava beans tossed in for texture. You can add to the vegetables here or replace them with peas, ramps, and other seasonal touchstones.

To Prep

Favas

4 pounds fava beans in the pod

Shell, blanch, shock, and peel the fava beans (see page 313)—this is time consuming, but you can do this up to 24 hours ahead of time.

Asparagus Puree

18 large asparagus stalks

1 tablespoon extra-virgin olive oil

1 tablespoon unsalted butter

½ Spanish onion, minced

1 garlic clove, thinly sliced

1 tablespoon fresh tarragon leaves

1 tablespoon fresh flat-leaf parsley leaves

1 teaspoon coarsely chopped fresh chives

Trim the woody ends off the asparagus. Cut off the tips and set them aside. Slice the stalks crosswise into ⅛-inch pieces. Blanch and shock the tips (see page 313), then drain them and set aside.

Bring 1½ cups of water to a boil in a small pot over high heat.

Heat the olive oil with the butter in a sauté pan over medium heat. When the butter foams, add the onion and garlic and cook, stirring occasionally, until softened but not browned, about 3 minutes. Add the sliced asparagus and the boiling water and cook, stirring occasionally, until the asparagus pieces are very soft, about 4 minutes.

Transfer the asparagus-onion mixture to a blender and add the tarragon, parsley, and chives. Blend until smooth.

Set a stainless-steel bowl over a larger bowl filled halfway with ice and water. Pass the puree through a fine-mesh strainer into the empty bowl, using a spatula to extract as much puree as possible. The puree and asparagus tips can be used right away or refrigerated in separate airtight containers for up to 4 hours.

To Serve

About 2 quarts chicken stock or vegetable stock, preferably homemade (pages 317, 316)

1 tablespoon extra-virgin olive oil

2 tablespoons unsalted butter

½ Spanish onion, minced

1 garlic clove, minced

Kosher salt and freshly ground black pepper

1 pound risotto rice, such as Arborio

½ cup dry white wine

1 cup shelled fava beans (see page 313)

½ cup finely grated Parmigiano-Reggiano cheese

⅓ cup whipped cream (from 3 tablespoons heavy cream)

Bring the stock to a simmer in a medium saucepan over medium-high heat.

Meanwhile, heat the oil with the butter in a medium saucepan over medium heat. When the butter foams, add the onion and garlic, season with salt and pepper, and cook, stirring, until softened but not browned, about 2 minutes. Stir in the rice and cook, coating the rice with the fats, until the rice turns opaque but without allowing it to brown, about 1 minute. Stir in the wine and cook, stirring continuously, until the wine has evaporated or been absorbed by the rice, 3 to 4 minutes. Ladle in 1 cup of the stock and cook, stirring, until the stock has been almost completely absorbed by the rice, about 6 minutes. Add the remaining stock in small, approximately ½-cup increments, stirring continuously until it has been absorbed before adding the next addition. It should take about 10 minutes to incorporate the remaining stock.

Fold in the vegetable puree and favas, the cheese, and the reserved asparagus tips, then fold in the whipped cream.

Divide the risotto among six plates and serve.

Black Truffle Risotto

Serves 6 as a starter or risotto course

Risottos are versatile. The Spring Vegetable Risotto on page 162 turns the rice green, altering its character and flavor. Here, an unadorned risotto serves more as a backdrop against which the unmistakable earthy flavor and aroma of black truffle really pops. The truffle is stirred into the risotto in paste form, then fresh black truffles are shaved over the finished risotto. There's no need to complicate the dish with bells and whistles. If you love the flavor of truffles, serve this dish to begin a special dinner or as a splurge anytime. (Note that you will need a truffle slicer or mandoline for the fresh truffle; there's just no other way to properly slice one.)

About 2 quarts chicken stock or vegetable stock, preferably homemade (pages 317, 316)

2 tablespoons extra-virgin olive oil

4 tablespoons (½ stick) unsalted butter

½ Spanish onion, minced

1 garlic clove, minced

Kosher salt and freshly ground black pepper

1 pound risotto rice, such as Arborio

½ cup dry white wine

1 tablespoon black truffle paste (see Sources, page 321)

½ cup finely grated Parmigiano-Reggiano cheese

½ cup whipped cream (from 3 tablespoons heavy cream)

1 black truffle (about 1 ounce)

Bring the stock to a simmer in a medium saucepan over medium-high heat.

Meanwhile, heat 1 tablespoon of the oil with 2 tablespoons of the butter in a medium saucepan over medium heat. When the butter foams, add the onion and garlic, season with salt and pepper, and cook, stirring, until softened but not browned, about 2 minutes. Stir in the rice and cook, coating the rice with the fat, until the rice turns opaque but without allowing it to brown, about 1 minute. Stir in the wine and cook, continuing to stir, until the wine has evaporated or been absorbed by the rice, 3 to 4 minutes. Ladle in 1 cup of the stock and cook, stirring, until the stock has been almost completely absorbed by the rice, about 6 minutes. Add the remaining stock in small, approximately ½-cup increments, stirring continuously until it has been absorbed before adding the next addition. It should take about 10 minutes to incorporate the remaining stock.

Fold the black truffle paste, cheese, remaining 1 tablespoon olive oil, and remaining 2 tablespoons butter into the risotto, then fold in the whipped cream.

Divide the risotto among six plates, shave black truffle over each serving, and serve.

Basic Pasta Dough

Makes about 1¼ pounds

Our basic pasta dough uses half 00 flour and half semolina for a balanced result: 00 flour is an Italian flour that's unmatched for its ability to create smooth, delicate pasta; semolina, produced by a different milling process, is coarser, resulting in more texture. You can play around with the ratios, perhaps using more semolina for, say, pappardelle, because it's usually paired with heartier sauces made with braised poultry and meats.

2 large eggs

2 large egg yolks

½ cup plus 3 tablespoons semolina flour

½ cup plus 3 tablespoons 00 flour
   (see Sources, page 321)

1 tablespoon extra-virgin olive oil

Note: *To make squid ink pasta, add 1 teaspoon squid ink (see Sources, page 321) with the other ingredients when mixing the dough.*

In the bowl of a stand mixer fitted with the dough hook, combine the eggs, egg yolks, flours, and olive oil and mix until smooth, about 2 minutes; if the dough doesn't come together, you might need to add a little cold water. Continue to mix on low speed for 5 minutes to develop the gluten; the dough will become smooth and slightly paler in color. When done, the dough will bounce back after you press it with your finger.

Remove the dough from the mixer, shape it into a ball, wrap in plastic wrap, and let rest for 1 hour at room temperature or overnight in the refrigerator.

When ready to proceed, cut the dough into two pieces with a chef's knife or bench cutter.

Working with one piece at a time, and covering the other piece loosely with plastic wrap or a clean, dry kitchen towel, roll the dough out with a rolling pin or simply press it down by hand. Run the pasta through a pasta machine repeatedly, narrowing the setting each time, until you have a length of pasta that you can fold. Fold the dough in thirds, like a letter, and roll it again.

Continue to roll the dough, folding in thirds once again, until it is smooth; you may need to repeat the letter-fold a third or fourth time before achieving the desired texture. Continue based

on the desired pasta cuts or shape: For spaghetti alla chitarra and pappardelle, the dough should be about ⅛ inch thick; for fettuccine and tagliatelle, it should be about ¹⁄₁₆ inch thick. Cutting and shaping procedures for individual pastas follow; for filled pastas, see individual recipes.

Cut Pastas

For cut pastas such as spaghetti and pappardelle, you must dry the sheets before you cut them to prevent them from sticking when stacked. Cut the sheets into large rectangles and lay them out in a single layer on parchment paper. Dry for 30 minutes, turning the pasta over after 15 minutes. Once dried, the dough should not be tacky at all but should feel like paper to the touch. The drying will go more quickly in a drafty room or one with an overhead fan. Once dried, trim the imperfect edges and ends to create straight lines.

FETTUCCINE: Stack the pasta rectangles and cut them into ¼-inch-wide strips with a chef's knife.

TAGLIATELLE: Stack the pasta rectangles and cut them into ⅛-inch-wide strips with a chef's knife.

SPAGHETTI: Stack the pasta rectangles and cut them into ¹⁄₁₆-inch-wide strips with a chef's knife.

PAPPARDELLE: Stack the pasta rectangles and cut them into 1 x 5-inch strips with a chef's knife.

Cut pastas can be cooked right away, refrigerated on a flour-dusted baking sheet in the refrigerator for up to 24 hours, or set the sheet in the freezer to firm up the pasta for about an hour, then transfer to a freezer bag and freeze for up to 1 month.

(continued)

Pasta Shapes

For pasta shapes such as garganelli and farfalle, you need to shape the pasta before drying it.

For **garganelli** (see photos on page 168), you will need a garganelli board and a ¼-inch-diameter wooden dowel. Cut the pasta sheets into 1½-inch squares. Working with one square at a time, set it diagonally on the board and roll it up forcefully with the dowel, pressing down at the end to seal it. As they are done, collect the garganelli in a single layer on a parchment paper–lined baking sheet and let dry completely, 30 to 60 minutes at room temperature. The garganelli can be cooked right away or refrigerated on a flour-dusted baking sheet in the refrigerator for up to 24 hours; otherwise, set the sheet in the freezer to firm up the garganelli for about an hour, then transfer them to a freezer bag and freeze for up to 1 month.

For **farfalle** (pictured opposite) cut off the imperfect edges of the pasta sheets to create straight lines. Cut the sheets into 2½ x 2-inch rectangles using a fluted cutter to create ruffled edges. Brush a little water in the center of each rectangle and pinch at the center to create bow ties. As they are done, collect them in a single layer on a parchment paper–lined baking sheet and let dry completely, 30 to 60 minutes at room temperature. The farfalle can be cooked right away, or refrigerated on a flour-dusted baking sheet for up to 24 hours; otherwise, set the sheet in the freezer to firm up the farfalle for about an hour, then transfer them to a freezer bag and freeze for up to 1 month.

Fish and Shellfish

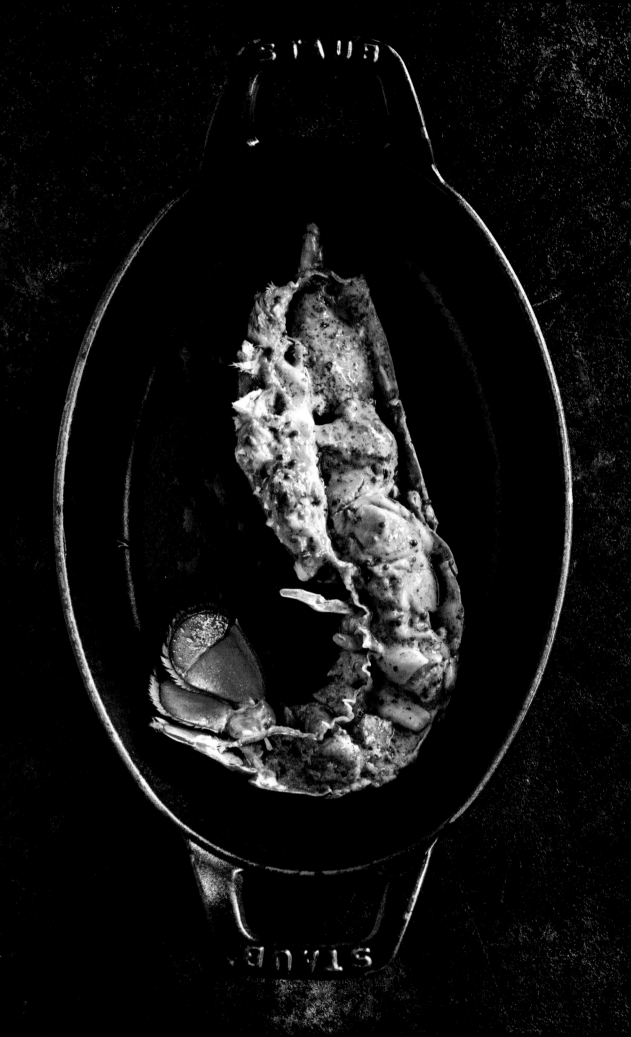

Seared Scallops with Spinach and Aromatic Vegetable Broth

Serves 4

The highlight of this dish is an unusual but easy-to-make broth, based on a dish Juan José Cuevas, one of Walker's mentors, used to make that combines equal amounts of five vegetable juices, punching up their flavors with Melfor (seasoned) vinegar. (Yes, you will need a juicer to make this.) When juicing the vegetables, let the desired yield be your guide, not the approximate quantities of each vegetable in the ingredient list.

To Prep

½ teaspoon coriander seed

½ teaspoon cracked black peppercorns

½ teaspoon fennel seed

1 fresh Thai basil sprig

½ lemongrass stalk, smashed and peeled

1 (1-inch) piece fresh unpeeled
   ginger, thinly sliced

3 thin lemon slices, seeds removed

½ cup red bell pepper juice (from
   about 2 red bell peppers)

½ cup fennel juice (from about 1 fennel bulb)

½ cup carrot juice (from about 1 large carrot)

½ cup green apple juice (from about 1 apple)

½ cup butternut squash juice (from ½ squash)

Kosher salt

2 tablespoons browned butter (see page 315)

2 tablespoons unsalted butter

2 tablespoons extra-virgin olive oil

1 tablespoon Melfor vinegar
   or fresh lemon juice

Toast the coriander seed, fennel seed, and peppercorns (see page 314).

Put the toasted spices, basil, lemongrass, ginger, and lemon slices in a medium, heatproof vessel and set it aside.

Put the pepper juice, fennel juice, carrot juice, apple juice, and squash juice in a pot, season with salt, and bring to a simmer over medium heat. Cook until reduced by about one-third, skimming any foam that rises to the surface, about 6 minutes. Once reduced, stir in the browned butter, unsalted butter, oil, and vinegar.

Pour the broth over the herbs and seeds and let steep for 10 minutes, then strain through a fine-mesh strainer set over a medium bowl, working the mixture with a spoon to extract as much flavorful broth as possible. Use right away or cover the broth and refrigerate for up to 24 hours.

To Serve

About 2 tablespoons unsalted butter

1 teaspoon minced shallot

4 cups loosely packed spinach or
   Swiss chard

½ lemon

3 tablespoons extra-virgin olive oil

12 sea scallops (if very large, only use 8)

2 tablespoons crushed pistachios

Bring the broth to a boil in a medium pot over medium-high heat.

Meanwhile, melt 1 tablespoon of the butter in a sauté pan over medium-high heat. When the butter foams, add the shallot and spinach and cook, stirring, just to wilt the spinach, about 1 minute. Finish with a squeeze of lemon juice and set the pan aside.

Heat another pan over medium-high heat. Add 2 tablespoons of the oil and heat until shimmering. Pat the scallops dry with a paper towel. Add the scallops to the pan and cook, using tongs or a spatula to periodically lift them and set them back down, until they are a nice, even brown (see below). Finish by melting the remaining 1 tablespoon butter in the pan, adding a squeeze of lemon juice, and basting the scallops with the melted butter for 1 minute.

To serve, mound some spinach in the center of each of four wide, shallow bowls. Spoon 3 scallops (or 2, if using larger ones) alongside the spinach in each bowl. Scatter the pistachios over the scallops and spinach. Add the remaining 1 tablespoon oil to the broth and blend the broth directly in the pot with an immersion blender, or transfer to a standing blender and blend. Taste and add a little more butter and/or lemon juice, if necessary. Pour the broth around the scallops in the bowls. (For special occasions, pour the broth over the scallops and spinach at the table.) Serve.

→   COOKING SCALLOPS

Before cooking scallops, pat them dry with paper towels and let them air-dry on a plate in the refrigerator for 10 minutes; eliminating excess moisture will help them sear better. When searing scallops, lifting them as they cook and setting them back down in the hot oil allows the oil to find its way into the scallops' crevices, ensuring an attractive, even sear.

Shrimp with Pimentón Pepper, Potato, and Chorizo

Serves 4

This is a highly efficient and delicious dish in which all parts of the shrimp, potato, and fennel are utilized, in the sauce and on the finished plate, which both pulls all the elements together and really drives home their individual qualities. Be sure that you begin with head-on shrimp, which are intensely flavorful.

To Prep

1 fennel bulb, halved lengthwise

4 Yukon Gold potatoes

24 large shrimp (about 1½ pounds), shells and heads intact

1 tablespoon plus 1 teaspoon extra-virgin olive oil

5 garlic cloves, smashed with the side of a chef's knife, unpeeled

1 large shallot, thinly sliced

1 tablespoon plus 1 teaspoon unsalted butter

Pinch of saffron

½ cup dry white wine

About 2 cups chicken stock, preferably homemade (page 317)

Kosher salt

To make the sauce, remove and reserve the outer layers of the fennel bulb. If not serving the dish right away, wrap the peeled fennel in plastic wrap and refrigerate until ready to proceed; otherwise, simply set it aside while you make the sauce. Chop the outer leaves and trimmings from the fennel and reserve 1 cup of the chopped trimmings, discarding the rest.

Peel the potatoes, cut them into ¼-inch-thick slices, and use a 2-inch cutter to punch circles out of the slices, or cut into similar shapes. Transfer to a medium bowl and cover with cold water; set aside. Reserve the potato trimmings.

Peel and devein the shrimp, reserving the shells. Pull off the heads and set them aside with the shells. Wrap the peeled shrimp in plastic wrap and refrigerate until ready to finish and serve the dish.

Heat 1 tablespoon of the oil in a medium pot over high heat. Add the shrimp shells and heads and cook, stirring, until bright red, about 2 minutes. Add the fennel and potato trimmings, 4 of the garlic cloves, the shallot, 1 tablespoon of the butter, and the saffron. Cover and cook, lifting the lid to stir occasionally, until the vegetables are softened but not browned, 6 to 8 minutes. Stir in the wine, bring to a simmer, and cook until almost dry, about 4 minutes. Add 1 cup of the stock, bring to a simmer, and cook over very low heat until reduced by half, 10 to 12 minutes. Strain the sauce, let cool, and refrigerate in an airtight container for up to 24 hours.

(continued)

To cook the vegetables, heat the remaining 1 teaspoon oil and remaining 1 teaspoon butter in a small pot over medium heat. Add the remaining garlic clove and cook, stirring, until softened but not browned. Drain the potato discs, add them to the pot, and season with salt. Cook over medium-low heat, stirring, just until lightly golden, about 5 minutes. Add the remaining 1 cup stock, or just enough to cover the potatoes. Bring to a gentle simmer, cover, and cook until the liquid has reduced to a glaze, about 12 minutes. Use right away or cool the potatoes on a plate, then refrigerate in an airtight container for up to 24 hours.

If desired, preseason the shrimp, below, during the To Prep stage up to 4 hours before serving.

To Serve

Pimentón de la Vera
    (see Sources, page 321)
2 tablespoons plus 2 teaspoons
    extra-virgin olive oil
Kosher salt
20 thin slices Spanish chorizo
3 teaspoons fresh lemon juice
1 tablespoon unsalted butter
1 garlic clove, smashed with the side
    of a chef's knife and peeled
Freshly ground black pepper

Thinly shave the peeled fennel on a mandoline. Put the slices in a medium bowl and cover with cold water; set aside.

Put the peeled shrimp in a small bowl. Season with pimentón, drizzle with 1 teaspoon of the oil, and season with salt. Toss and set aside.

Heat 1 teaspoon of the oil in a pan over medium heat. Add the chorizo and cook, stirring, until it renders its fat and turns slightly crispy, about 6 minutes. Add the potatoes and cook for 1 minute, then add the strained sauce to the pan and cook until it has reduced enough to coat the back of a wooden spoon, about 2 minutes. Stir in 2 teaspoons of the lemon juice and set aside.

Heat 1 tablespoon of the oil in a pan over medium-high heat. Add the seasoned shrimp and cook until firm, about 30 seconds per side. Add the butter and garlic to the pan and swirl to melt the butter and coat and flavor the shrimp.

Drain the fennel and transfer it to a medium bowl. Dress with the remaining 1 tablespoon oil and remaining 1 teaspoon lemon juice and season with salt and pepper. Toss well.

Evenly divide the shrimp, chorizo, and sauce among four plates. Garnish with the fennel and serve.

Grilled Lobster

Serves 4

The preparation of this dish is a bit involved as the lobsters are parcooked, then the meat is cut into bite-size pieces and "reassembled" in the shell where they are slathered with a butter made with their roe and tomalley. But the advance work pays off, because when the time comes to serve the lobster, you only need to grill them, and doing so in the shell really amps up the lobster flavor. (You can also finish them in a pan or under the broiler, if you prefer.) Serve these with Creamed Corn with Bacon (page 267) or Bomba Rice with Soffrito and Saffron (page 279).

To Prep

Kosher salt

4 Maine lobsters (about 1¼ pounds each)

Note: *Use cold salted water to wash off the gunky white protein from the lobsters after cooking and shocking; rather than diluting their flavor, using salt water maintains it.*

Bring a pot of generously salted water to a boil over high heat. Fill a large bowl halfway with ice and water.

Add the lobsters to the boiling water and cook for 3 minutes. Use tongs to remove the lobsters from the water, twist off their claws, return the claws to the water, and cook for 2 minutes more. Put the lobster bodies in the ice water to cool; when the claws have cooked, transfer them to the ice water as well.

When cool enough to handle, remove the lobster meat from the claws and clean the meat (see Note). Cut the lobster bodies in half lengthwise and remove and discard the vein. Reserve the roe and tomalley for butter (page 182). Note that the lobsters will appear undercooked.

Make the butter (recipe follows).

Remove the tail meat from the lobsters. Cut the bottom off the knuckles and cut them open up the sides; the meat should come out in one piece. Spread some roe butter inside the shells. Cut the tail crosswise into five pieces (to make it easier for the diner to eat it) and reassemble the pieces inside the shell over the butter. Spread

the remaining butter over the top. (If the lobsters are well covered before you use all the butter, save the extra for serving.) Grill right away or refrigerate the prepared lobsters until the butter is hard, then wrap the halves in plastic wrap and refrigerate for up to 24 hours.

To Serve

4 lemon wedges

If refrigerated, let the prepared lobsters come to room temperature, about 15 minutes, before grilling.

Heat a gas grill to high heat or prepare a charcoal grill for grilling, letting the coals burn until covered with white ash.

Cook the lobsters, shell-side down, until the shell starts to char, then move to indirect heat, cover the grill, and cook for about 5 minutes more, until cooked through; test with a cake tester if you are unsure (see page 4); it is done when the tester is medium-hot. Smear any extra butter over the top. Serve with lemon wedges alongside for squeezing over the lobsters.

Roe Butter

Makes about 3 cups butter

Use this butter in any dish featuring lobster or shrimp; it's especially good with pasta and risotto.

4 sticks (1 pound) unsalted butter,
    at room temperature
Roe and tomalley from 4 lobsters
½ cup loosely packed coarsely
    chopped fresh tarragon leaves
¼ cup whole-grain mustard
Zest and juice of 2 lemons
¼ cup extra-virgin olive oil
Kosher salt and freshly ground black pepper

Put the butter, roe, and tomalley in the bowl of a food processor fitted with the steel blade. Pulse just to soften the butter. Add the tarragon, mustard, lemon zest and juice, and olive oil. Season with salt and pepper and process just until creamy.

The butter can be used right away or refrigerated, wrapped in plastic wrap or in an airtight container, for up to 24 hours or frozen for up to 1 week.

Roasted Lobster with Confit Potatoes, Pearl Onions, and Coral Sauce

Serves 4

This luxurious dish uses all parts of the lobster to great effect, especially the knuckles, which are shaped into stunning, shell-on "medallions," and the coral, which brings intense flavor to the sauce. It requires some finesse, but is well worth the effort and appropriate for even the most formal occasions.

To Prep

Kosher salt

4 lobsters (about 1¼ pounds each)

2 tablespoons extra-virgin olive oil

2 tablespoons unsalted butter

1 large shallot, thinly sliced

1 celery stalk, thinly sliced

1 small carrot, thinly sliced

½ fennel bulb, thinly sliced

4 garlic cloves, smashed with the side
    of a chef's knife and peeled

2 tablespoons tomato paste

3 tablespoons cognac

½ cup dry white wine

About 3 cups chicken stock,
    preferably homemade (page 317)

Bring a large pot of salted water to a boil over high heat. Fill a large bowl halfway with ice and water.

Separate the lobster tail and claws from the head, either by simply twisting and breaking them off or by using a knife for the claws. Set the heads aside. Add the tails and claws to the boiling water and cook until bright red, about 2 minutes for the tails, and 5 minutes for the claws. As the parts are done, use tongs or a slotted spoon to transfer them to the ice water to cool.

To make the sauce, coarsely chop 3 of the lobster heads with a cleaver or heavy chef's knife and halve the fourth head. Remove and set aside the tomalley and roe.

Heat the olive oil in a wide, deep sauté pan over medium heat. Add the chopped lobster heads and cook, stirring, until bright red, about 3 minutes. Add the butter. When the butter foams, add the shallot, celery, carrot, fennel, and garlic and cook, stirring occasionally, until softened but not browned, about 4 minutes.

Stir in the tomato paste and cook, stirring to coat the ingredients with the paste, about 2 minutes. Pour in the cognac, bring to a simmer, and cook until it has almost completely evaporated, about 2 minutes. Pour in the wine, bring to a simmer, and cook until it has almost completely reduced, about 6 minutes. Pour in just enough chicken stock to cover the solids. Bring to a simmer and cook until reduced slightly and the flavors have intensified, 20 to 30 minutes.

Strain the contents of the pot through a chinois or fine-mesh strainer into a large, heatproof bowl, pressing down on the solids with a spoon or the bottom of a ladle to extract as much flavorful liquid as possible. Discard the solids. Pour the liquid into a small pot, bring to a boil over high heat, and boil until reduced to about 1½ cups and intensely flavored, about 8 minutes.

Remove the lobster claw meat from the shells. Cut the legs and bottom shell off the tail, leaving the top of the shell intact, and cut between the joints, creating lobster medallions. Clean the meat (see Note, page 179). Use right away or wrap in plastic wrap and refrigerate for up to 6 hours.

To Serve

5 medium Yukon Gold potatoes, quartered

About 3 cups plus 2 tablespoons clarified butter (see page 315)

Kosher salt

2 fresh thyme sprigs

2 garlic cloves, smashed with the side of a chef's knife and peeled

20 pearl onions, trimmed and peeled

2 tablespoons extra-virgin olive oil, plus more for drizzling

Freshly ground black pepper

1 tablespoon unsalted butter

½ lemon

¼ cup lightly whipped cream (from 2 tablespoons heavy cream)

Preheat the oven to 350°F.

Put the potatoes in a pot that can hold them snugly in a single layer. Add 1 tablespoon of the clarified butter, season with salt, add half the reserved lobster head, and cook, stirring occasionally, until glistening but not browned, about 4 minutes. Add 1 thyme sprig and 1 garlic clove and cook over low heat, stirring occasionally, for 2 minutes. When the lobster head turns golden but the vegetables have not yet browned, add just enough clarified butter to cover the potatoes, about 2 cups. Bring the butter to a simmer, then reduce the heat to low and cook slowly until the potatoes are soft to a cake tester or knife tip, 15 to 20 minutes. Remove the pot from the heat and let the potatoes cool slightly in the butter, then remove with a slotted spoon and set aside. (Strain and save any extra butter for making hollandaise sauce or other recipes where the lobster flavor would be welcome. It can be cooled and refrigerated in an airtight container for up to 1 week.)

Meanwhile, put the onions in a separate pot that can hold them snugly in a single layer. Add 1 tablespoon of the clarified butter, season with salt, add the other half of the reserved lobster head, and cook, stirring occasionally, until glistening and lightly browned, about 4 minutes. Add the remaining thyme sprig and garlic clove and cook over low heat, stirring occasionally, for 2 minutes. When the lobster head turns golden but the onions have not yet browned, add just enough clarified butter to cover the onions, about 1 cup. Bring the butter to a simmer, then reduce the heat to low and cook slowly until the onions are soft to a cake tester or knife tip, 10 to 12 minutes. Remove the pot from the heat and let the onions cool slightly in the butter, then remove with a slotted spoon and set aside with the potatoes. (Again, strain and save any extra butter for making hollandaise sauce or other recipes where the lobster flavor would be welcome. It can be cooled and refrigerated in an airtight container for up to 1 week.)

Heat 1 tablespoon of the olive oil in a large sauté pan over medium-high heat. Season the lobster medallions with salt and pepper. When the oil is shimmering, add the medallions, shell-side down, and cook for 1 minute. Add the unsalted butter and let it melt and brown slightly.

Put the claw and knuckle meat on a rimmed baking sheet and season with salt and pepper. Transfer the browned medallions to the sheet, spoon the melted butter from the pan over the claw and knuckle meat and medallions, and season with salt and pepper. You can do this up to 30 minutes before serving and hold the prepared lobster meat at room temperature.

Heat the remaining tablespoon of olive oil in a clean, ovenproof sauté pan over medium-high heat. When the oil is shimmering, add the potatoes and onions and cook, tossing occasionally, until the potatoes are lightly browned all over, about 3 minutes, then transfer the pan to the oven. Put the pan with the lobster pieces in the oven to warm them through.

Meanwhile, heat the sauce in a small pot over medium-high heat. Add the lobster tomalley and roe and blend in the pot with an immersion blender or transfer to a standing blender and blend briefly. Finish with a drizzle of olive oil and a few drops of lemon juice, and season with salt and pepper.

When the potatoes and lobster are warmed through, divide the potatoes and onions among four plates. Divide the lobster pieces among the plates alongside the potatoes.

Pour any accumulated juices from the lobster baking sheet into the sauce and blend briefly to incorporate them, then fold the whipped cream into the sauce. Spoon the sauce over the lobster, potatoes, and onions and serve.

Grilled Mackerel with Summer Vegetable Salsa

Serves 4

To us, this dish epitomizes efficient summer home cooking: a piece of grilled fish finished with a complementary condiment, in this case, a homemade salsa. Rather than pulse the salsa ingredients together in a food processor, we prefer to mince them by hand and toss them together with olive oil just before serving, allowing each one to retain its individual texture and flavor. You can substitute other crunchy summer vegetables for the ones here, or alter the quantities and leave some out.

To Prep

3 tablespoons minced peeled cucumber

2 tablespoons minced peeled radish

2 tablespoons minced peeled zucchini

2 tablespoons finely diced husked tomatillo

2 tablespoons minced tomato

2 tablespoons minced peeled celery

2 tablespoons minced red onion

4 canned anchovy fillets, minced

¼ cup chopped tomato confit (from
    about 4 pieces; see page 313)

1 teaspoon fresh lemon thyme
    or regular thyme leaves

3 tablespoons fresh lemon juice

1 teaspoon minced preserved lemon rind

2 tablespoons minced Taggiasca
    olives or other black olives

1 tablespoon brine-packed capers, drained

Use the prepared salsa ingredients right away or refrigerate in separate containers for up to 2 hours.

(continued)

To Serve

4 skin-on mackerel fillets
    (about 6 ounces each)
Kosher salt
Smoked paprika (see Sources, page 321)
Dried Korean chili powder (see
    Sources, page 321)
¾ cup extra-virgin olive oil
Freshly ground black pepper
½ lemon

Heat a gas grill to high or prepare a charcoal grill for grilling, letting the coals burn until covered with white ash.

Season the mackerel all over with salt, paprika, and chili powder and rub with about ¼ cup of the olive oil. Set in a baking dish and let marinate for 20 minutes at room temperature.

Meanwhile, make the salsa by putting all of the prepped ingredients in a medium bowl. Add the remaining ½ cup olive oil, season with salt and pepper, and stir together gently.

Grill the mackerel, skin-side down, until it begins to turn opaque, 3 to 5 minutes, then turn the fillets and cook on the other side for 1 minute.

Set one fillet in the center of each of four plates. Squeeze some lemon juice over each fillet and spoon some salsa alongside. Serve.

Braised Hake with Tender Vegetables and Aioli

Serves 4

This is our play on bourride, a Provençal fish stew that's usually made with monkfish, and aioli stirred in to thicken and imbue it with garlicky flavor. Our version uses more tender hake, removes the fish and vegetables from the stew, then reduces the liquid into a sauce that's spooned over the fish and vegetables.

To Prep

Fish Stock

3 tablespoons extra-virgin olive oil

1 tablespoon unsalted butter

1 small leek, thinly sliced

1 carrot, thinly sliced

1 small white Spanish onion, thinly sliced

1 head of garlic, halved

1 fresh fennel bulb, thinly sliced

1 Yukon Gold potato, thinly sliced

Scant pinch of saffron threads

1 teaspoon fennel seed

1 teaspoon whole black peppercorns

Kosher salt

1 pound whitefish bones

1 cup dry white wine

2½ cups chicken stock,
   preferably homemade (page 317)

Heat the oil with the butter in a large pot over medium heat. When the butter foams, add the leek, carrot, onion, garlic, fresh fennel, potato, saffron, fennel seeds, and peppercorns, season with salt, and cook, stirring occasionally, until the vegetables are softened but not browned, about 6 minutes.

Stir in the fish bones and cook, stirring occasionally, until the bones give up some of their liquid, about 5 minutes. Pour in the wine, bring to a simmer, and cook until it has reduced by half, about 6 minutes. Pour in the stock, bring to a simmer, and cook for 30 minutes. Use tongs to remove and discard the fish bones, then strain the stock through a fine-mesh strainer set over a bowl. Use the stock right away or refrigerate it in an airtight container for up to 24 hours.

(continued)

Vegetables

4 small fingerling potatoes

Kosher salt

1 garlic clove

1 fresh thyme sprig

1 teaspoon whole black peppercorns

1 bay leaf, preferably fresh

8 sugar snap peas, blanched and
shocked (see page 313)

¼ cup shelled English peas, blanched
and shocked (see page 313)

8 haricots verts, blanched and
shocked (see page 313)

To Serve

1 tablespoon extra-virgin olive oil

4 small turnips, peeled and halved

8 baby carrots

Kosher salt

1 tablespoon unsalted butter

4 skinless hake fillets (about 6 ounces each)

4 small ramps

3 tablespoons Aioli (recipe follows)

½ tablespoon fresh lemon juice

⅓ cup whipped cream (from about
3 tablespoons heavy cream)

Put the potatoes in a large pot, cover by a few inches with cold water, and generously salt the water. Add the garlic, thyme, peppercorns, and bay leaf. Bring to a boil and cook until the potatoes are tender to a cake tester or knife tip, 15 to 20 minutes, depending on the size of the potatoes. Drain in a colander and set aside to cool. (Discard the garlic, thyme, peppercorns, and bay leaf.)

The sugar snap and English peas and haricots verts can be used right away or refrigerated together in an airtight container for up to 24 hours. The potatoes can be used right away or refrigerated for up to 24 hours in their own container.

If necessary, let the sugar snap peas, English peas, haricots verts, and the potatoes come to room temperature.

Choose a small roasting pan or large, deep sauté pan large enough to hold the hake and all the vegetables in a single layer. Heat the oil in the pan over medium-high heat until shimmering. Add the turnips and carrots, season with salt, and cook, stirring occasionally, until softened but not browned, about 4 minutes. Add the butter. When the butter foams, add the potatoes and cook until the vegetables are tender to a cake tester or knife tip but do not allow them to caramelize, about 6 minutes. Pour in 2 cups of the fish stock and bring it to a simmer. Add the hake, cover the pan, and cook over very low heat for 3 minutes. Turn the fillets over and cook for 3 minutes more. (They should be done at this point; test with a cake tester if unsure—see page 4; it should be medium-hot and the fish should offer no resistance.) Add the ramps, sugar snap peas, English peas, and haricots verts and cook for 1 minute to warm them through and wilt the ramps.

Use a slotted spoon to transfer one fillet to the center of each of four plates. Spoon the vegetables around the fish on each plate. Bring the liquid in the pan to a boil over high heat and cook until it has reduced by half, about 1 minute. Remove the pan from the heat and vigorously whisk in the aioli until the sauce is thick and creamy. Whisk in the lemon juice and fold in the whipped cream. Spoon the sauce over the vegetables and fish and serve.

Aioli

This versatile Provençal garlic mayonnaise can be used as a dip, as for the crudité on page 22, spread on toast, or used in sandwiches.

1 large egg yolk
1 tablespoon Dijon mustard
Juice of 1 lemon
1 garlic clove, minced or grated on a
	Microplane
1 cup extra-virgin olive oil
Kosher salt and freshly ground black pepper

Put the egg yolk, mustard, lemon juice, and garlic in a medium bowl. Slowly whisk in the olive oil, a few drops at first, then in a thin stream, whisking continuously to create an emulsified dressing. Season with salt and pepper. The aioli can be refrigerated in an airtight container for up to 3 days.

Grilled Tuna with Piperade and Spanish Ham

Serves 4

The pepper-and-onion stew piperade hails from the Basque region, which bridges France and Spain, and tastes like it. There, each chef takes great pride in his or her distinct piperade; for example, some cook ham into the beginning of the recipe, while others may save it as a garnish. We do both, but the unique touch here is juicing the pepper trimmings and adding them to the stew, intensifying their sweetness.

To Prep

6 red bell peppers

1 medium Spanish onion

2 tablespoons extra-virgin olive oil

1 thin slice Iberico ham or
 prosciutto di Parma

4 garlic cloves, thinly sliced

Kosher salt

1 teaspoon smoked paprika
 (see Sources, page 321)

Trim off the tops and bottoms of the peppers, reserving them. Peel the peppers, cut them in half, and remove and discard the seeds and ribs. Cut the peppers into julienne strips.

Peel the onion and cut it into julienne strips. Set aside.

Juice the tops and bottoms of the peppers. If you do not have a juicer, put them in a blender, blend with just enough water to engage the blender's blade, then strain through a fine-mesh strainer into a small bowl. You should have ½ cup pepper juice.

Heat the oil over medium heat in a pot that will hold all of the ingredients comfortably. When the oil is just shimmering, add the onions and ham and cook, stirring occasionally, until the onions are softened but not browned, about 4 minutes. Add the garlic and cook over very low heat, stirring often, until the garlic and onions are very soft but not browned, about 15 minutes. Add the julienned peppers and season with salt and paprika.

Cover the pot and continue to cook over very low heat. After about 5 minutes, check to see if the onions and peppers have given off a lot of their liquid (if not, continue to cook for a few minutes more), then remove the cover, raise the heat to medium, and bring the juices to a simmer. Cook until the juices have almost completely

evaporated, about 5 minutes. Reduce the heat to low, add the reserved pepper juice, and cook, uncovered, until the peppers are very soft and the mixture is saucy, about 30 minutes.

The piperade can be used right away or refrigerated in an airtight container for up to 2 days.

To Serve

4 (6-ounce) tuna steaks,
    ideally 1½ inches thick

Kosher salt

Korean chili powder (see Sources, page 321)

Sherry vinegar

Extra-virgin olive oil

Freshly ground black pepper

8 thin slices Iberico ham or pro-
    sciutto di Parma

Heat a gas grill to high or prepare a charcoal grill for grilling, letting the coals burn until covered with white ash.

Season the tuna with salt and chili powder. Grill the fillets until the bottoms are lightly charred and the fish is just starting to turn opaque at the bottom, 2 to 3 minutes, or a bit longer for more well-done. (We like the fish rare in this dish.) Turn the fillets over and grill until cooked on the other side, 2 to 3 minutes more.

Meanwhile, gently reheat the piperade. (You can do this in a pot set on the grill.) Freshen it with a drizzle of vinegar and a drizzle of olive oil and season with salt and pepper.

Divide the piperade among four plates or wide, shallow bowls. Top each serving with a tuna fillet and finish by topping each fillet with 2 pieces of ham. Serve.

Striped Bass with Braised Fennel and Tomato Confit

Serves 4

This Riviera-themed combination of fennel, Taggiasca olives, and tomato is as classic as it gets, and striped bass makes a perfect backdrop. It takes a little finesse to glaze the fish; if the reduction breaks, swirl in a little more stock to help it re-emulsify.

To Prep

1 tablespoon extra-virgin olive oil

1 tablespoon unsalted butter

3 garlic cloves, smashed and peeled

2 shallots, thinly sliced

¼ teaspoon coriander seed

¼ teaspoon crushed black peppercorns

¼ teaspoon crushed or coarsely
   ground fennel seed

2 strips orange peel, removed with a peeler
   or paring knife, no pith attached

2 strips lemon peel, removed with a peeler
   or paring knife, no pith attached

1 fresh thyme sprig

1 bay leaf, preferably fresh

½ cup dry white wine

½ cup fresh orange juice (squeeze
   from the orange you peeled;
   you may need 2 oranges)

2 fennel bulbs, outer layer removed,
   halved through the root end

About 1 cup chicken stock, preferably homemade (page 317)

Preheat the oven to 350°F.

Heat the oil with the butter in a pot large enough to hold the fennel in a single layer. When the butter foams, add the garlic and shallots and cook, stirring occasionally, until softened but not browned, about 2 minutes. Add the coriander, pepper, fennel seed, orange peel, lemon peel, thyme, and bay leaf. Cook, stirring occasionally, until the spices are fragrant, 2 to 3 minutes. Add the wine, bring to a simmer, and cook until reduced by half, about 4 minutes.

Add the orange juice, bring to a simmer, then add the fennel bulbs in a single layer and pour over enough stock to just cover them. Bring to a simmer, then cover and transfer to the oven. Braise until the fennel is soft to a knife tip but still holding its shape (like a cooked potato), about 50 minutes. During this time, periodically check to be sure the liquid is just barely simmering; if it is bubbling aggressively, reduce the oven temperature by 25°F; if not bubbling at all, raise it by 25°F. Remove the fennel pieces; strain and discard the other solids, saving the cooking liquid.

Wipe out the pot, return the liquid to the pot, and bring to a boil over high heat. Cook until the liquid has reduced to about 1 cup, about 10 minutes. Trim a little off the back of the fennel pieces so they will rest on their sides when plated. Use right away or refrigerate the fennel and liquid in separate airtight containers for up to 24 hours.

To Serve

1 small fennel bulb

About ½ cup extra-virgin olive
   oil, plus more for serving

Kosher salt and freshly ground black pepper

8 scallions

12 pitted Taggiasca olives or
   other black olives

8 pieces tomato confit (see page 313)

6 tablespoons (¾ stick) unsalted butter

½ lemon

4 skinless striped bass fillets
   (about 6 ounces each)

1 garlic clove, smashed with the side
   of a chef's knife and peeled

1 fresh thyme sprig

¼ cup chicken stock, preferably homemade (page 317)

If necessary, let the braised fennel and its liquid come to room temperature.

About 30 minutes before serving, cut the fronds from the fennel and set aside; shave the fennel thinly on a mandoline. Fill a medium bowl halfway with ice and water and submerge the fennel in the water to crisp it. Select 8 attractive fennel fronds and reserve them for garnish, discarding the rest.

Heat 2 tablespoons of the olive oil in a large sauté pan until just smoking. Add the braised fennel, season with salt and pepper, reduce the heat to low, and cook slowly until the fennel is nicely caramelized, about 5 minutes. Carefully drain the oil from the pan. Add the scallions and olives and cook until the scallions are just slightly wilted, about 2 minutes. Add the tomato confit, the reserved fennel braising liquid, and 2 tablespoons of the butter, raise the heat to high, and cook until the liquid reduces slightly and emulsifies with the butter, about 5 minutes. Add 2 tablespoons of the oil, season with salt and pepper, and finish with a few drops of lemon juice. Remove the pan from the heat and set it aside.

Heat 2 tablespoons of the oil in a large sauté pan over high heat until smoking. Add the striped bass, skinned-side down, reduce the heat to medium, and cook until lightly browned on the skinned side, about 3 minutes, then add the remaining 4 tablespoons butter, the garlic, and the thyme to the pan. Turn the fish over and cook until the garlic and thyme are fragrant, about 1 minute. Pour in the stock, bring to a simmer, and cook until it has reduced to a glaze, about 4 minutes. Finish by drizzling a few teaspoons of olive oil and a squeeze of lemon juice over the fish.

Transfer one fillet to each of four plates, skinned-side down, and spoon the glaze over the top. Arrange the braised fennel alongside the fillet on each plate, caramelized side up. Arrange the tomato and scallions over the fish and fennel. Spoon some sauce over and around the fennel and fish. Drain the raw fennel slices, return them to their bowl, and drizzle the remaining 1 tablespoon olive oil over them. Arrange the fennel slices and fronds over the dish. Drizzle olive oil over and around the fish and vegetables and serve.

Cod Grenobloise

Serves 4

The quintessentially French pan sauce of browned butter, lemon, parsley, and capers has a name: *grenobloise.* It's traditionally served with white fish, especially sole, and fashioned in the pan in which the fish was cooked. We change it up, gently poaching the cod in olive oil for a luxurious texture and making the sauce separately in its own pan.

To Prep

Glazed Cipollini Onions

1 teaspoon extra-virgin olive oil

1 teaspoon unsalted butter

1 garlic clove, smashed with the side
    of a chef's knife and peeled

1 fresh thyme sprig

4 large or 8 small cipollini onions, peeled

Kosher salt and freshly ground black pepper

Heat the oil with the butter in a small pot over medium heat. When the butter foams, add the garlic and thyme and cook, stirring occasionally, until the garlic is softened but not browned, about 2 minutes. Add the onions in a single layer and season with salt and pepper. Pour in ¼ cup cold water, bring to a simmer, cover, and reduce the heat to very low. Braise until the onions are tender to a cake tester or knife tip, about 20 minutes for small, 25 to 30 minutes for large. Drain the onions in a colander and let cool to room temperature. Use right away or refrigerate in an airtight container for up to 24 hours.

Fingerling Potatoes

12 ounces fingerling potatoes,
    ideally 12 small potatoes

Kosher salt

1 garlic clove, smashed with the side
    of a chef's knife and peeled

1 fresh thyme sprig

1 teaspoon whole black peppercorns

1 bay leaf, preferably fresh

Put the potatoes in a large pot, cover by a few inches with cold water, and generously salt the water. Add the garlic, thyme, peppercorns, and bay leaf. Bring to a boil and cook until the potatoes are tender to a cake tester or knife tip, 15 to 20 minutes, depending on size. Drain the potatoes and, when cool enough to handle but still warm, use a paring knife to peel them. (Discard the garlic, thyme, peppercorns, and bay leaf.) Use right away or refrigerate in an airtight container for up to 4 hours.

To Serve

3 tablespoons extra-virgin olive
  oil, plus more for poaching
4 skinless cod fillets (about 6 ounces each)
½ cup coarsely chopped fresh flat-leaf
  parsley leaves, plus ½ cup whole leaves
½ lemon
Kosher salt and freshly ground black pepper
12 Taggiasca olives or other
  black olives, pitted
4 tablespoons (½ stick) unsalted butter
2 tablespoons diced lemon
  supremes (see page 313)
1 tablespoon brine-packed capers, drained
½ cup brioche croutons (see page 314),
  made with butter, garlic, and thyme

Preheat the oven to 350°F.

Pour olive oil into a small pot, just large enough to comfortably hold the cod fillets with about 1 inch of space all around it, to a depth of 6 inches and heat the oil over medium heat to 120 to 130°F.

Carefully lower the fillets into the oil and slowly poach, adjusting the heat as necessary to keep the temperature between 120 and 130°F. Cook until the fish is opaque, 10 to 15 minutes; if it begins to leach white albumin, it is overcooking and should be removed from the oil as soon as possible. To further test for doneness, remove a piece of fish from the oil with a slotted spoon and transfer it to a clean, dry work surface; if it flakes apart easily, it's done. Transfer the fish to a rimmed baking sheet and set aside.

Meanwhile, put the whole parsley leaves in a small bowl. Drizzle with 1 tablespoon of the olive oil, a few drops of lemon juice, and season with salt and pepper. Toss and set aside.

Heat the remaining 2 tablespoons oil in a large sauté pan over medium-high heat. Add the potatoes and cook until lightly golden brown, about 3 minutes. Add the cipollini onions and cook until lightly golden, about 3 minutes. Add the olives, season with salt and pepper, and toss. Finish with a few drops of lemon juice and ¼ cup of the chopped parsley. Spoon the vegetables into wide, shallow bowls or plates and set aside.

To make the sauce, melt the butter in a medium pot over medium heat and let it separate and turn brown, almost black, about 3 minutes. While the butter is hot, add the lemon supremes and capers. Season with salt and pepper and freshen with a few drops of lemon juice. Remove the pot from the heat and toss in the croutons and remaining ¼ cup chopped parsley.

Transfer the baking sheet holding the fish to the oven and bake for 1 minute, just to warm the fish through. Check for doneness with a cake tester (see page 4); it should be medium-hot and the fish should offer no resistance.

Top the potatoes and onions on each plate with a fish fillet. Spoon the sauce over and around the fish. Top each portion with some of the parsley salad and serve.

Halibut with Coco Beans

Serves 4

This light main course pairs flaky halibut with coco beans. Worth special mention is the method used to make the beans: Pureeing a portion and folding them together with whole ones, as you would to thicken an Italian bean soup, creates a creamy effect without the addition of any actual cream. The same technique can be used with just about any white beans, and is also employed with the chickpeas on page 78.

To Prep

1 cup dry coco beans, great northern
   beans, or cannellini beans

1 (3-inch) piece carrot

1 (3-inch) piece celery

¼ Spanish onion, cut through the root end

2 garlic cloves, smashed with the side
   of a chef's knife and peeled

1 bay leaf, preferably fresh

5 tablespoons extra-virgin olive oil

Kosher salt

Soak the beans overnight in cold water, or use the quick-soak method on page 78.

Drain the beans and transfer them to a wide, heavy pot. Pour in enough cold water to cover the beans by 1 inch. Add the carrot, celery, onion, garlic, bay leaf, and 3 tablespoons of the oil. Simmer over low heat until the beans are al dente, stirring every 10 minutes or so to ensure the beans cook evenly and skimming any foam that rises to the surface. After about 45 minutes, stir in a generous pinch of salt and simmer for 20 minutes more. Use tongs or a slotted spoon to pick out and discard the vegetables and garlic. Transfer ¾ cup of the beans to a blender, add the remaining 2 tablespoons oil, and puree. Stir the pureed beans into the whole beans.

Use right away or refrigerate in an airtight container for up to 2 days.

To Serve

¼ cup chicken stock, preferably
 homemade (page 317)

4 (6-ounce) skinless halibut fillets

Kosher salt

4 tablespoons extra-virgin olive oil

2 tablespoons unsalted butter

1 teaspoon fresh lemon juice

1 teaspoon minced shallot

1 teaspoon fines herbes (see page 44) or
 thinly sliced fresh flat-leaf parsley leaves

2 teaspoons sherry vinegar

Reheat the beans in a small, heavy pot over medium heat. Bring the stock to a simmer in a small pot on a back burner.

Season the fish on both sides with salt. Heat a wide, heavy skillet over medium-high heat. Add 2 tablespoons of the oil and 1 tablespoon of the butter to the skillet. When the butter foams, add the fish, skinned-side up, and cook until very lightly golden, about 4 minutes. Turn over and add the stock. Cook on the other side, basting with a tablespoon, until done, about 4 minutes more, adding the lemon juice just before basting for the last time.

Add the remaining 1 tablespoon butter, 2 tablespoons oil, the shallot, herbs, and vinegar to the beans and gently fold them in.

To serve, spoon some beans onto each of four dinner plates and set a fish fillet on top.

Salmon with Artichokes Barigoule

Serves 4

This celebration of artichokes features them braised in a smoky, aromatic riff on the white wine–based Provençal preparation, *barigoule*; blended into a puree and sauce; and in fresh, raw slices scattered over the plate. Artichokes have a distinct flavor that should be carefully matched to others—it's a notorious challenge for sommeliers—and salmon proves the perfect complement to its many forms here.

To Prep

Artichoke Puree

2 tablespoons extra-virgin olive oil

2 tablespoons unsalted butter

1 large shallot, thinly sliced

4 garlic cloves, smashed with the side
  of a chef's knife and peeled

2 artichokes, peeled (see page 124), thinly
  sliced, and held in acidulated water

1 fresh thyme sprig

1 bay leaf, preferably fresh

Pinch of ascorbic acid or vitamin C
  powder (see page 207; optional)

About 1 cup chicken stock, preferably homemade (page 317)

1 tablespoon browned butter (see page 315)

1 teaspoon fresh lemon juice

Heat 1 tablespoon of the oil with 1 tablespoon of the unsalted butter in a medium pot over medium-high heat. When the butter foams, add the shallot and garlic and cook, stirring occasionally, until softened but not browned, about 2 minutes. Stir in the artichokes, thyme, bay leaf, and ascorbic acid (if using). Cook for 4 minutes, stirring occasionally, then add enough stock to just cover the artichokes and simmer until the slices are tender, about 4 minutes.

Use tongs or a slotted spoon to fish out and discard the thyme and bay leaf. Transfer the artichokes and their liquid to a blender. Add the remaining 1 tablespoon unsalted butter, the browned butter, remaining 1 tablespoon olive oil, and the lemon juice and blend to a smooth puree.

Use right away or refrigerate in an airtight container for up to 2 days.

Artichokes Barigoule

2 tablespoons extra-virgin olive oil

1 teaspoon unsalted butter

1 thick slice smoked bacon

1 small carrot, cut into large dice

1 small onion, cut into large dice

1 celery stalk, cut into large dice

1 garlic clove, smashed with the side
    of a chef's knife and peeled

1 fresh thyme sprig

1 bay leaf, preferably fresh

3 artichokes, peeled (see page 124),
    quartered through the stem end,
    and held in acidulated water

Kosher salt and freshly ground black pepper

¼ cup dry white wine

About 1 cup chicken stock, prefer-
    ably homemade (page 317)

Heat the olive oil with the butter in a small pot over medium heat. Add the bacon and cook, stirring occasionally, until it renders much of its fat and turns golden brown, about 6 minutes. Add the carrot, onion, and celery and cook, stirring occasionally, until softened but not browned, about 4 minutes. Add the garlic, thyme, and bay leaf and cook, stirring, until aromatic, about 1 minute. Add the artichokes, season with salt and pepper, and cook, stirring occasionally, until slightly softened, about 2 minutes. Pour in the wine, bring to a simmer, and cook until it has reduced by half, about 2 minutes. Add just enough stock to cover the artichokes, bring to a simmer, and cook until the artichokes are tender to a knife tip, about 30 minutes.

Use right away or let the artichokes cool in their liquid and refrigerate in an airtight container for up to 2 days.

To Serve

1 baby artichoke

1 lemon, halved

2 tablespoons unsalted butter

¼ cup plus 2 tablespoons extra-virgin olive oil

Kosher salt and freshly ground black pepper

4 (4-ounce) skinless salmon fillets

¼ cup lightly whipped cream (from
    2 tablespoons heavy cream)

Trim the baby artichoke (see page 124) and slice it, ideally on a mandoline, gathering the slices in a small bowl. Cover with cold water and squeeze some lemon juice into the water, catching the seeds in your hand and discarding them, to acidulate it and prevent the artichoke from turning brown.

Reheat the artichokes barigoule in about ½ cup of their cooking liquid in a medium pot over medium-high heat. Add the butter and swirl it into the sauce to thicken and enrich it and coat the artichokes, about 2 minutes. Add a squeeze of lemon juice and drizzle with 1 tablespoon of the olive oil. Remove the pot from the heat, cover the pot, and set aside to keep the artichokes warm.

Reheat the artichoke puree in a separate small pot over low heat. If it seems too thick, stir in a little water.

Spoon about ½ cup of the reserved artichoke cooking liquid into a small pot, stir in about ¼ cup of the puree, and bring to a simmer over medium heat. Cook until slightly reduced and thickened, about 4 minutes. (If the mixture seems too thick for a sauce, add a little more water; if it seems too thin, add a little more puree.) Finish by stirring in 2 tablespoons of the olive oil, a squeeze of lemon juice, and a few grinds of black pepper. Set aside, covered to keep the sauce warm.

(continued)

Meanwhile, heat 2 tablespoons of the olive oil in a sauté pan over medium-high heat. Add the salmon fillets to the pan without crowding and cook until opaque on the bottom, 3 to 4 minutes. Turn the fillets over and cook until opaque on the other side, 3 minutes more. If you like, test for doneness with a cake tester (see page 4); it should be warm to the touch for medium-rare, hotter for more well-done.

Spoon some puree onto each of four plates. Set a salmon fillet alongside. Set 2 pieces of artichokes barigoule atop each piece of salmon and 1 piece in the puree. Fold the whipped cream into the sauce and spoon the sauce over the salmon and artichokes.

Drain the shaved artichokes and return them to the bowl. Drizzle with the remaining 1 tablespoon olive oil and a squeeze of lemon juice and season with salt and pepper. Garnish each plate with the raw artichokes and serve.

→   ASCORBIC ACID

Ascorbic acid (vitamin C) doesn't show up in many recipes, but it helps keep the artichokes a beautiful, elegant white color that adds a strong visual component to the plate. You can simply use lemon juice instead but we think it's worth adding this resource to your repertoire; see Sources, page 321.

Sautéed Branzino with Braised Endive

Serves 4

Of all the ways to add impact to a fish dish, the most direct just might be to leave the skin on, for the crispy texture and salty flavor produced when it's seared over high heat. The branzino here is accompanied by endive braised in a trio of citrus juices, adding unexpected tang and providing a convenient pan sauce; a further surprise is the sprinkling of cilantro leaves, another unconventional pairing. Neither component can be prepared in advance, but they cook simultaneously and show how complete a simple, perfect pairing can be.

¼ cup plus 2 tablespoons extra-virgin olive oil, plus more for serving

8 Belgian endives, ends trimmed, halved lengthwise

3 tablespoons unsalted butter

3 tablespoons sugar

1 teaspoon coriander seed, toasted (see page 314) and coarsely cracked

Kosher salt

Juice of 1 grapefruit

Juice of 1 orange

Juice of 1 lemon

4 skin-on pieces branzino (about 6 ounces each—ask your fishmonger to scale them; see page 209)

Freshly cracked and ground black pepper

¼ cup thinly sliced fresh cilantro leaves

Preheat the oven to 325°F.

Heat 2 tablespoons of the olive oil in an ovenproof sauté pan large enough to hold the endive pieces in a single layer. When the oil is shimmering, add the endive, cut-side down, and cook until golden brown, about 4 minutes. Add 2 tablespoons of the butter and the sugar. When the sugar begins to caramelize, 2 to 3 minutes, turn the endive over, scatter the coriander over the pan, and season with salt. Add the grapefruit, orange, and lemon juices. Bring to a simmer and cook until the liquid has reduced by half, about 4 minutes, then transfer the pan to the oven. Cook until the endive are very tender (test with a cake tester or knife tip), about 12 minutes, basting once or twice during that time.

Meanwhile, heat the remaining ¼ cup olive oil over high heat in a sauté pan large enough to hold the fish in a single layer. Season the fish with salt and add it to the pan, skin-side down, pressing down gently to flatten the fish. Cook until the skin starts to turn brown and crispy, 2 to 3 minutes, then turn over, add the remaining 1 tablespoon butter, and cook the fish in the foaming butter for 30 seconds. Season with cracked black pepper, then transfer the fish to paper towels to drain.

Set 1 fillet on each of four plates. Remove the endive from the oven, season with ground black pepper, and scatter the cilantro over it. Arrange 4 pieces of endive alongside the fish on each plate and drizzle the cooking liquid over the plate. Drizzle a little olive oil over the fish and serve.

→ PREPPING SKIN-ON FISH

Before cooking skin-on fish, run the back of a chef's knife along the skin to "squeegee" any excess liquid before cooking. This will help attain a nice, crispy skin in the pan or on the grill.

Poultry, Meats, and Game

Pan-Roasted Chicken with Summer Fruit Panzanella

Serves 4

There's no reason to confine stone fruits, one of the great pleasures of summertime dining, to dessert. Here, cherries and peaches are tossed with croutons, almonds, and blue cheese for a spin on the Italian bread salad panzanella, with lemon juice replacing the traditional red wine vinegar. It's an unexpected foil to the crispy chicken skin and succulent meat, and the interplay between the greens, fruit, and cheese is so satisfying that it could also be a dish or side dish on its own.

¼ cup plus 3 tablespoons extra-virgin olive oil

¼ cup blanched almonds, crushed

Kosher salt

4 boneless, skin-on chicken breasts (about 8 ounces each), preferably organic

Freshly ground black pepper

2 tablespoons unsalted butter

3 fresh thyme sprigs

2 garlic cloves, smashed with the side of a chef's knife and peeled

2 small peaches or 1 large peach, pitted and cut into ½-inch dice

12 sweet red cherries, pitted and halved

1 scallion, white and light green parts, thinly sliced on an angle

Juice of 1 orange

1 tablespoon fresh lemon juice

2 ounces mild blue cheese, preferably Stilton Colston Bassett or Bayley Hazen Blue (see Sources, page 321)

Heat 2 tablespoons of the olive oil in a medium sauté pan over medium-high heat. When the oil is shimmering, add the almonds, toss gently, and fry for 1 minute. Transfer to paper towels and season immediately with salt. Set aside.

Preheat the oven to 350°F.

Season the chicken breasts all over with salt and pepper. Heat a cast-iron pan until very hot and add 2 tablespoons of the olive oil. Add the breasts, skin-side down. When the oil begins to shimmer again, 8 to 10 minutes, add the butter, thyme, and garlic to the pan. Baste the chicken with the melted butter for 2 to 3 minutes. Transfer the pan to the oven and cook until cooked through (check for doneness with a cake tester [see page 4]; it should be medium-hot), 8 to 10 minutes more, although timing may be more or less depending on the thickness of the breasts. Remove the pan from the oven and return to the stovetop over medium-high heat. Turn the breasts over and cook for 1 minute, then transfer the chicken breasts to a cutting board and let rest for 5 minutes.

Meanwhile, make the panzanella by putting the peaches, cherries, scallion, fried almonds, orange juice, lemon juice, remaining 3 tablespoons olive oil, the cheese, and a pinch of

(continued)

Pinch of sugar

1 tablespoon fines herbes (see page 44) or thinly sliced fresh flat-leaf parsley

12 whole leaves greens or chicories such as radicchio, watercress, or arugula (optional)

2 cups brioche croutons (see page 314), made with olive oil

sugar in a large bowl. Season with salt and pepper and toss together. Set aside.

Halve the chicken breasts lengthwise, or leave them whole if you prefer. Set one chicken breast on each of four plates. Add the herbs, greens (if using), and croutons to the bowl with the panzanella and toss well. Spoon the panzanella over and alongside the chicken on each plate. Serve.

Chicken with Crispy Potatoes, Feta, and Arugula

Serves 4

As with the chicken dish on page 213, the accompaniment here is created by tossing together a number of ingredients, including cheese, causing them to meld and create their own sauce. The contrast between the potatoes and feta is especially satisfying, a sophisticated spin on the pairing of sour cream and a baked potato. It's also incredibly simple, one of the few main courses in the book that's essentially prepared entirely à la minute.

20 fingerling potatoes

Kosher salt

2 garlic cloves, smashed with the side of a chef's knife and peeled

2 fresh thyme sprigs

1 teaspoon whole peppercorns

1 bay leaf, preferably fresh

5 tablespoons extra-virgin olive oil

4 boneless, skin-on chicken breasts (about 8 ounces each), preferably organic

Freshly ground black pepper

1 tablespoon unsalted butter

½ cup canola oil or other neutral oil, such as grapeseed

2 ounces feta cheese, preferably Meredith Dairy Sheep & Goat Blend (see Sources, page 321), cut into 4 cubes

2 tablespoons fresh lemon juice

1 tablespoon minced shallot

1 tablespoon fines herbes (see page 44) or thinly sliced fresh flat-leaf parsley leaves

1 cup loosely packed arugula

1 cup loosely packed red watercress or regular watercress

Preheat the oven to 350°F.

Put the potatoes in a large pot, add cold water to cover by a few inches, and generously salt the water. Add 1 garlic clove, 1 thyme sprig, the peppercorns, and the bay leaf. Bring to a boil and cook until the potatoes are tender to a cake tester or knife tip, 15 to 20 minutes, depending on the size of the potatoes. Drain in a colander, transfer to a large plate, crush with the back of a tablespoon, and set aside. (Discard the garlic, thyme, peppercorns, and bay leaf.)

Heat a cast-iron pan until very hot and add 2 tablespoons of the olive oil. Season the chicken breasts with salt and pepper and add them to the pan, skin-side down. When the oil begins to shimmer again, 8 to 10 minutes, add the butter, remaining garlic clove, and remaining thyme sprig. Transfer the pan to the oven and cook, basting occasionally, until cooked through (check for doneness with a cake tester—see page 4; it should be medium-hot), about 5 minutes more, although timing may be more or less depending on the thickness of the breasts. Remove the pan from the oven, return to the stovetop over medium-high heat, and turn the breasts over and cook, basting, for about 3 minutes. Transfer the chicken breasts to a cutting board and set aside.

Working quickly to finish while the chicken is still hot, pour the canola oil into a deep sauté pan and heat the oil over medium heat to 350°F. Add the crushed potatoes to the pan and fry until golden brown and crispy, about 4 minutes, turning once with a slotted spoon and adjusting the heat level as necessary to maintain the temperature. Use a slotted spoon to transfer the potatoes to paper towels, let drain briefly, season with salt, and transfer to a medium heatproof bowl. Add the feta, 2 tablespoons of the olive oil, 1 tablespoon of the lemon juice, the shallot, and the herbs. Season with salt and pepper and toss with a spoon; the feta will break down and become part of the dressing.

Divide the potatoes and cheese among four plates. Put the arugula and watercress in the bowl that held the potatoes. Dress with the remaining 1 tablespoon olive oil and remaining 1 tablespoon lemon juice and toss well to coat with any lingering cheese, shallot, and herbs in the bowl.

Halve each chicken breast lengthwise and arrange the pieces over the potatoes on each plate. Top with the dressed greens and serve.

Whole Roasted Chicken

Serves 2

"Whole Roasted Chicken for Two" is how this dish is called out on our menu at Dover. Like most dishes meant to be shared, it sounds like something a little extra special, and it is: There's the spectacle of the whole bird, burnished to a deep amber after it comes out of the oven. But it's about more than the visuals: Cooking chicken on the bone pays great dividends, adding flavor and preventing the meat from drying out. While guests wait for the chicken to cook, we serve them a salad made from the legs, which we cook slowly in duck fat. You can do the same at home. Because of multiple steps that don't allow the cook much time at the table, we recommend this as a dish for couples or friends enjoying a leisurely evening in or near the kitchen, perhaps cooking together. Pour some good red wine and hang out while one or both of you make the salad, serving it as a starter, then finish and carve the chicken. If you like, serve the roasted chicken with a seasonal side dish; we especially recommend the Root Vegetable Gratin (page 283), which you can bake in the oven starting at the same time the chicken goes in.

To Prep

1 (3½- to 4-pound) chicken,
    preferably organic
Kosher salt
About 2 quarts duck fat (see
    Sources, page 321)

Use a chef's knife to cut the wings off the chicken. Remove the legs by cutting with a kitchen knife where the leg meets the body, then turning the leg until it pops out of the socket, cutting it away with the knife. Set the legs aside and either discard the wings or save them for another use, such as stock. Turn the chicken over so the breasts face downward. Use kitchen shears to cut around and through the perimeter of the ribs in an oval pattern, cutting away and removing

the ribs and backbone (save them for stock as well, if desired) to expose the cavity. The chicken's body can be refrigerated for up to 2 days; unlike most meats, it is best refrigerated uncovered on a plate, which keeps spoilage-inducing moisture from collecting and lets the skin air-dry—this will produce a crackling result when cooked.

To make the chicken confit, season the chicken legs generously with salt, set on a plate, cover loosely with plastic wrap, and refrigerate for 24 hours.

When ready to proceed, preheat the oven to 275°F. Brush the salt off the legs, rinse under cold running water, and pat dry with paper towels. Put the legs in a pan that holds them snugly.

Melt the duck fat in a separate pot over medium heat until liquefied but not boiling, then pour it over the legs. Cover with aluminum foil or a lid, transfer to the oven, and cook until the chicken meat is tender and easily pulls away from the bone, about 3 hours.

Remove the pan from the oven, uncover, and let rest for 1 hour. Use tongs or a slotted spoon to transfer the legs to a cutting board and, when cool enough to handle, remove the bones, discarding them, and shred the meat by hand. Use right away or refrigerate for up to 24 hours for this dish (the rest of the chicken must be cooked by then), or for up to 2 weeks if using the meat for another use; cover the meat with the duck fat to preserve it for more than 24 hours.

To Serve

Kosher salt and freshly ground black pepper

2 tablespoons extra-virgin olive oil, plus more for the salad

2 tablespoons unsalted butter

1 head of garlic, top cut off to expose the cloves

3 fresh thyme sprigs

1 Granny Smith apple

1 celery root

2 teaspoons chopped cornichons

2 teaspoons chopped brine-packed capers

2 teaspoons minced peeled celery

2 teaspoons sliced scallion whites

4 teaspoons fines herbes (see page 44) or thinly sliced fresh flat-leaf parsley leaves

¼ cup mayonnaise (for homemade, make Aioli, page 193, omitting the garlic)

1 teaspoon a black truffle paste (see Sources, page 321)

1 teaspoon sherry vinegar, plus more for serving

1 white button mushroom, shaved on a mandoline

1 fresh black truffle (see Sources, page 321)

Fleur de sel

Preheat the oven to 350°F.

Season the chicken's cavity and exterior generously with salt and pepper. Heat the olive oil in a wide, deep sauté pan over high heat until shimmering. Add the chicken and sear until nicely golden brown on all sides, turning it as it browns, about 8 minutes.

Add the butter to the pan, along with the garlic and thyme. Reduce the heat slightly and continue to cook, basting the chicken with the butter, for 2 minutes. Transfer to the oven and roast until cooked through and medium-hot inside, 20 to 25 minutes, basting occasionally; check for doneness with a cake tester (see page 4), inserting it into the thickest part of the chicken; it should be medium-hot.

While the chicken is roasting, make and serve the salad: Peel the apple and celery root, cut them into thin slices, preferably on a mandoline, and punch out ¾-inch pieces with a biscuit cutter or cut into similar shapes with a knife. Set aside.

Put the chicken leg meat in a large bowl. Add the cornichons, capers, celery, scallions, herbs, mayonnaise, and truffle paste. Season to taste with salt and pepper and fold together well with a rubber spatula. Add the vinegar and just enough olive oil to lightly moisten and fold them into the salad.

Divide the salad between two small bowls and top with the apple, celery root, and mushroom slices. Shave black truffle over each serving with a truffle slicer, or shave on a mandoline and scatter over the salads. Finish with a drizzle of olive oil. Enjoy the salad while you wait for the chicken to finish roasting.

Finish and serve the roasted chicken: Remove the chicken from the oven and let rest in a warm place for about 10 minutes, with the cavity facing downward over a heatproof bowl to catch the juices.

To serve, cut off the breasts. Season the flesh side of the breasts with fleur de sel and pepper, lifting the tenderloin to season underneath it. Whisk a little olive oil into the juices in the bowl, and season with pepper and a splash of vinegar. Arrange one breast on each of two plates, spoon the juices over the chicken, and serve.

Chicken Albufera

Serves 4

The uncomplicated beauty of Chicken Albufera, another classic from the Ducasse canon, doesn't even begin to hint of the many steps that go into making it indelibly delicious. The recipe pulls out all the stops to create a rich and complex sauce that features chicken bones, Madeira, cognac, and even Foie Gras Confit trimmings in its makeup. (If you do not have any foie gras confit on hand, which we realize is a distinct possibility, you can use a cooked foie gras preparation, such as a terrine.) If you are proficient in breaking down a chicken, debone the breast and legs to provide the necessary bones for the sauce.

To Prep

Albufera Sauce

2 pounds chicken bones (wings, thighs, or neck)

¼ cup extra-virgin olive oil

1 small celery stalk, cut into large dice

1 small onion, cut into large dice

1 small carrot, cut into large dice

2 garlic cloves, smashed with the side of a chef's knife and peeled

1 fresh thyme sprig

1 bay leaf, preferably fresh

¼ cup white port

¼ cup Madeira

Splash of cognac

About 3 cups chicken stock, preferably homemade (page 317)

1 tablespoon cornstarch

2 tablespoons unsalted butter

2 tablespoons trimmings from Foie Gras Confit (page 92)

Preheat the oven to 325°F

Use a cleaver or heavy chef's knife to chop the chicken bones into small chunks.

Heat the olive oil in a small cast-iron or ceramic Dutch oven over medium heat. When the oil shimmers, add the celery, onion, and carrot and cook, stirring, until softened but not browned, about 5 minutes. Stir in the garlic, thyme, and bay leaf and cook, stirring, until aromatic, about 1 minute. Pour in the port and Madeira and cook, stirring to loosen any flavorful bits cooked onto the bottom of the pot, until the port simmers and reduces and the pan is almost dry, about 4 minutes. Stir in the cognac, bring to a simmer, and cook until the pan is almost dry, about 1 minute. Pour in enough chicken stock to cover the bones, bring to a simmer, cover with a tight-fitting lid, and transfer to the oven. Cook until the flavors have intensified, about 1 hour 30 minutes. During this time, periodically check to be sure the liquid is just barely simmering; if it's bubbling aggressively, reduce the oven temperature by 25°F; if not bubbling at all, raise it by 25°F.

Remove from the oven and strain the sauce through a chinois or fine-mesh strainer set over a large pot. Set the pot over high

heat, bring to a boil, and cook to further enhance the flavor, about 5 minutes. Put the cornstarch in a small bowl, add about 1 tablespoon cold water, and stir together to make a slurry, dissolving the cornstarch. Stir the slurry into the sauce, then transfer the sauce to a blender and blend. Add the butter and foie gras and blend just until emulsified. Strain the sauce through a chinois or fine-mesh strainer into a heatproof vessel. Use right away, set aside for up to 2 hours at room temperature, or refrigerate in an airtight container for up to 2 days.

Vegetables

1 tablespoon extra-virgin olive oil

2 tablespoons unsalted butter

1 garlic clove, smashed with the side of a chef's knife and peeled

1 fresh thyme sprig

4 baby carrots, halved

2 celery stalks, peeled and cut into spears

4 cipollini onions, peeled

4 scallions, outer layers removed, cut on an angle into 2 or 3 pieces

8 baby turnips, trimmed and shaped with a paring knife

Kosher salt and freshly ground black pepper

½ cup chicken stock, preferably homemade (page 317)

Heat the olive oil with 1 tablespoon of the butter over medium heat in a small pot or sauté pan with a tight-fitting lid. When the butter foams, add the garlic and thyme and cook, stirring, for 1 minute to flavor the fats. Add the carrots, celery, onions, scallions, and turnips, season with salt and pepper, and cook, stirring occasionally, until slightly softened but not browned, about 5 minutes. Pour in the chicken stock, bring to a simmer, cover, and cook until the vegetables are done, testing with a cake tester or knife tip and removing each one when cooked through; the cooking times will range from about 5 minutes for the celery to 10 to 12 minutes for the carrots. Gather the cooked vegetables in a small heatproof bowl. Use a spoon to fish out and discard the garlic and thyme.

If the cooking liquid has not reduced during the vegetables' cooking time, bring it to a boil over high heat and cook until nicely thickened and flavorful. Use right away or set aside for up to 2 hours at room temperature.

To Serve

4 boneless, skin-on chicken breasts (about 6 ounces each)

Kosher salt and freshly ground black pepper

1 tablespoon unsalted butter

Sherry vinegar

Cognac

¼ cup whipped cream (from about 2 tablespoons heavy cream)

Preheat the oven to 350°F.

Pour the Albufera sauce into a wide, deep sauté pan with a tight-fitting lid and heat over medium heat to 170 to 180°F. Season the chicken breasts generously with salt. Add them to the Albufera sauce, cover, and gently poach, adjusting the heat to maintain the temperature of the sauce at 170 to 180°F, lifting the lid to check the temperature and baste periodically. Check the chicken throughout with a cake tester (see page 4) until the cake tester is medium-hot, about 12 minutes. When the chicken reaches the desired temperature, use a slotted spoon to transfer the breasts to a rimmed baking sheet.

(continued)

Meanwhile, reheat the vegetables in their glaze over medium heat. Reheat the sauce, adjust the seasoning with salt and/or pepper, add the butter, swirling to melt it, then add a dash of sherry vinegar and a few drops of cognac.

Transfer the chicken breasts to the oven and warm them through for 1 minute, then remove the chicken from the oven, peel off the skin, discarding it, and set one breast on each of four plates. Spoon some vegetables alongside the chicken on each plate, either together, or artfully arranged as shown in the photo.

Fold the cream into the sauce, but do not completely integrate, instead leaving it somewhat marbled. Spoon the sauce over the chicken breasts and serve.

Stuffed Quail with Peas and Cipollini Onions

Serves 4

Like the rabbit dish on page 232, these stuffed quail require a bit of careful advance work, but can be a secret weapon when entertaining because they can be prepared up to two days ahead of time and quickly finished when the time comes to serve them. The cipollini and peas are a homey, familiar accompaniment that lend this dish the casual air of rustic home cooking.

To Prep

Stuffed Quail

1 tablespoon plus 1 teaspoon
  extra-virgin olive oil

¼ cup diced bacon

¼ cup minced shiitake mushroom caps

¼ cup minced white button mushroom caps

1 tablespoon unsalted butter

½ Spanish onion, minced

2 garlic cloves, thinly sliced

2 tablespoons chopped fresh sage leaves

4 cups diced crust-on country bread

About 1 cup chicken stock, preferably homemade (page 317)

2 tablespoons fines herbes (see page 44)
  or thinly sliced fresh flat-leaf
  parsley leaves

2 tablespoons finely grated
  Parmigiano-Reggiano cheese

2 tablespoons finely grated
  Pecorino Romano cheese

1 large egg

4 semi-boneless quail

Heat 1 teaspoon of the olive oil in a wide, deep pot. Add the bacon and cook, stirring occasionally, until it is nicely browned and has rendered most of its fat, about 6 minutes. Add the shiitake and button mushrooms and the butter and cook, stirring occasionally, to lightly brown the mushrooms, about 5 minutes. Add the onion and garlic and cook, stirring occasionally, until softened but not browned, about 3 minutes. Add the sage, bread, and stock and cook, stirring occasionally, until the bread absorbs the stock, about 5 minutes. Transfer the mixture to a medium heatproof bowl and let cool. Once cool, add the herbs, the remaining 1 tablespoon olive oil, the cheeses, and the egg, stirring just until the ingredients are incorporated.

Clip the quail's wings at the second joint (the "elbow") with kitchen shears, and set them aside. Fill each cavity with a small ball of the herb-and-cheese mixture. Use a paring knife to cut a slit in one leg on each quail and push the end of the other leg through to close the cavity. Cook right away or put the quail on a plate, cover tightly with plastic wrap, and refrigerate for up to 2 days.

(continued)

Glazed Cipollini Onions

2 tablespoons unsalted butter

12 cipollini onions, peeled

Kosher salt

2 tablespoons sugar

Melt the butter in a medium pan over medium-high heat, letting it brown slightly, then add the onions, season with salt, and cover with a lid. Cook until the onions are slightly softened (test with a cake tester or knife tip), then stir in the sugar, coating the onions with the sugary butter. Cover and cook, lifting the lid to stir occasionally, until the onions are very soft (test with a cake tester or knife tip) and nicely glazed. The onions can be served right away or kept in the pot, covered, at room temperature for up to 2 hours.

To Serve

¼ cup extra-virgin olive oil

Kosher salt and freshly ground black pepper

5 tablespoons unsalted butter

1 garlic clove, smashed with the side of a chef's knife and peeled

8 fresh sage leaves

1½ cups shelled English peas, blanched and shocked (page 313)

1 cup chicken stock, preferably homemade (page 317)

If the stuffed quail have been refrigerated, let them come to room temperature.

Preheat the oven to 350°F.

Heat the oil in a large, deep sauté pan over medium-high heat. Season the quail with salt and pepper, add them to the pan, and cook until lightly browned all over, turning with tongs as they cook, about 10 minutes. Add 2 tablespoons of the butter, the garlic, sage, and wings to the pan. Baste the quail continuously with the melted butter for 5 minutes, then transfer the pan to the oven and cook until the quail is done and the filling within is cooked through; test for doneness with a cake tester (see page 4; it should be medium-hot).

While the quail is cooking, combine the peas, ½ cup of the chicken stock, and remaining 3 tablespoons butter in a small pot. Bring to a simmer over medium-high heat and cook gently, swirling occasionally, until the stock and butter reduce and emulsify into a glaze, about 6 minutes.

Reheat the onions in their pot over medium heat.

Transfer the quail to a plate or platter and let rest. Discard the wings. Fish out and reserve the sage leaves.

Drain all but 2 tablespoons of fat from the pan, stir in the remaining ½ cup chicken stock, and cook over high heat, stirring, until the stock reduces slightly and the fat emulsifies, about 3 minutes.

Spoon some peas onto each of four plates. Top with a stuffed quail and garnish with 3 onions per plate. Spoon some sauce over the quail on each plate and garnish each serving with 2 sage leaves. Serve.

Duck Breast with Quince and Radishes

Serves 4

Duck is traditionally served with sweet, tart, and/or spicy accompaniments that cut the fattiness of the meat. Here, quince are poached in a sweet verjus mixture and peppery radishes are glazed with a sweet-and-sour mix of vinegar and sugar, and the resulting flavors and textures stand up beautifully to the duck. The combination is so complete that no sauce is required.

To Prep

Poached Quince

1 quince

2 cups white verjus (dry white wine with 3 tablespoons sugar stirred in can be substituted)

2 tablespoons sugar

Pinch of kosher salt

Cut off the top and bottom of the quince, reserving them. Peel and quarter the quince, then cut out and discard the cores (see page 61).

Put the quince trimmings and quarters in a small pot. Add the verjus, sugar, and salt. Bring to a simmer over low heat and cook until tender to a cake tester or knife tip, 30 to 40 minutes. Use right away or let cool and refrigerate the quince in its liquid in an airtight container for up to 24 hours.

Radishes

5 red radishes

1 tablespoon extra-virgin olive oil

1 garlic clove, smashed with the side of a chef's knife and peeled

Pinch of sugar

1 tablespoon unsalted butter

Kosher salt

1 tablespoon sherry vinegar

Shave 1 radish and hold it in ice water. Cut the remaining radishes into 8 wedges each.

Heat the olive oil in a small pot over medium heat. Add the garlic and cook for 1 minute, without browning, to flavor the oil. Add the radish wedges, sugar, and butter and season with salt. Cook, stirring occasionally, until the radishes are tender to a cake tester or knife tip, about 10 minutes. Pour in the vinegar and stir to loosen any flavorful bits cooked onto the bottom of the pot. Cook for a minute or two, stirring to coat the radishes, then remove the pot from the heat. The radish wedges can be refrigerated in their cooking liquid in an airtight container for up to 24 hours. The shaved radish can be covered and refrigerated for up to 24 hours.

To Serve

4 duck breasts (about 8 ounces each)

Kosher salt and freshly ground black pepper

1 teaspoon extra-virgin olive oil

1 tablespoon unsalted butter

Score the duck breasts on the fat side with a sharp paring knife, taking care to not cut through to the flesh. Season them on the flesh side with salt and pepper.

Heat the olive oil in a wide, deep sauté pan over medium heat. Add the duck breasts, skin-side down, and cook gently, occasionally carefully pouring off the fat as it renders. Cook until the skin is brown and crispy and the fat has fully rendered, 8 to 10 minutes. Turn the duck over, add the butter to the pan, and cook, basting, for 3 minutes. Transfer the duck to a clean, dry surface to rest for 5 minutes.

Meanwhile, drain all but 2 tablespoons of fat from the pan, add the quince to the pan, and brown slightly over medium heat, about 4 minutes. At the same time, gently reheat the radish wedges in a small pot over medium heat.

Thinly slice each duck breast and fan the slices of one duck breast on each of four plates. Spoon the quince and radishes alongside. Drain the shaved radishes and scatter the slices over each serving. Serve.

Grilled Rabbit Legs with Grilled Vegetables and Bagna Cauda

Serves 4

This recipe offers a powerful reminder that grilling can produce results just as complex as what we do on our stovetops or in the oven: Pounded-out rabbit legs are preseasoned with a slightly spicy rub, and a bagna cauda sauce, fashioned after the famous garlicky dip, is spooned over grilled summer vegetables at the table. It's a perfect dish for entertaining because it doesn't take much more work than making, say, marinated chicken and vegetables, but makes a much bigger impression at the table. Incidentally, if you buy your rabbits whole, this is a good way to use the parts not used in the recipe on page 232.

To Prep

Marinated Rabbit Legs

4 rabbit legs

1 teaspoon fennel seed

½ teaspoon whole black peppercorns

½ teaspoon coriander seed

½ teaspoon coarse Korean chili powder (see Sources, page 321)

6 garlic cloves, smashed with the side of a chef's knife and peeled

5 fresh thyme sprigs

3 fresh rosemary sprigs

Extra-virgin olive oil

Remove the bottom bone of each rabbit leg. Working with one leg at a time, set the leg between two pieces of plastic wrap and gently pound with a meat mallet or the bottom of a heavy pan to a uniform thickness of ¼ inch, being careful to not break through the flesh. The leg should resemble a paillard or Milanese preparation, with the bone protruding.

Toast the fennel seed, peppercorns, and coriander seed together (see page 314). Once they have cooled, gently crush them together using a mortar and pestle or the bottom of a heavy pan. Transfer them to a small bowl. Add the chili powder to the bowl and stir together to make a rub.

Put the pounded-out rabbit legs in a baking dish just large enough to hold them in a single layer. Sprinkle the spice rub over both sides of the legs. Scatter the garlic, thyme, and rosemary over the legs and drizzle generously with olive oil. Cover the legs with plastic wrap, gently pressing the plastic down on the legs to keep them from oxidizing.

Set aside to marinate in the refrigerator for at least 2 hours or up to 2 days.

Bagna Cauda Sauce

1 garlic clove, halved

4 cloves garlic confit (see page 315)

2 teaspoons brine-packed capers, drained

6 anchovy fillets

2 tablespoons balsamic vinegar

1 teaspoon sherry vinegar

¼ cup extra-virgin olive oil

1 tablespoon whole-grain mustard

Freshly cracked black pepper

Put the fresh garlic, garlic confit, capers, and anchovies in the bowl of a food processor fitted with the steel blade and pulse to a paste. Add the balsamic vinegar and sherry vinegar. With the motor running, slowly drizzle in the oil to make an emulsified sauce. Transfer the mixture to a bowl or container and fold in the mustard. Stir in a few grinds of cracked pepper.

Use right away or refrigerate in an airtight container for up to 24 hours.

To Serve

1 zucchini, cut crosswise into
   ½-inch-thick slices

1 summer squash, cut crosswise
   into ½-inch-thick slices

1 Japanese eggplant, cut crosswise
   into ½-inch-thick slices

4 scallions, white and light green
   parts, outer layer peeled

12 whole shishito peppers (available
   from specialty and Asian markets,
   or see Sources, page 321)

1 red onion, cut into 6 rings

Extra-virgin olive oil

Kosher salt and freshly ground black pepper

4 slices country bread

Heat a charcoal grill, letting the coals burn until covered with white ash, or heat a gas grill to high.

Meanwhile, put the zucchini, squash, eggplant, scallions, peppers, and onion in a medium bowl. Drizzle them with olive oil, season with salt and pepper, and toss to coat.

Remove the rabbit legs from their marinade. Brush off any solids and let the legs drain of any excess oil to avoid flare-ups on the grill. Season the legs with salt.

Grill the rabbit and vegetables until nice grill marks form and they are cooked through, about 4 minutes per side. Meanwhile, put the bagna cauda sauce in a small, serving-appropriate casserole and reheat it on the grill. Drizzle the bread lightly with olive oil and grill until lightly charred, about 1 minute per side.

As each type of vegetable is done, 5 to 12 minutes based on the thickness of the vegetable and the heat of the grill, transfer it to a large serving platter. When the rabbit legs are done, transfer them to a cutting board. Cut the legs into strips and arrange on the platter as well. Serve family-style, passing the sauce and bread alongside.

Stuffed Rabbit with Spring Greens

Serves 4

This stuffed rabbit is a bit of a workout, but we think it's well worth the trouble to produce a visually stunning and memorable main course. It's also, ironically, very convenient, because the rabbit can be readied up to three days ahead of time, leaving you to simply heat it and prepare a pan sauce when the time comes to serve. It's ideal to grind the stuffing ingredients in a meat grinder, but you can also pulse them in a food processor. You will need to start with a whole rabbit; ask your butcher to break it down for you; the shoulders can be used in the pasta dish on page 154.

To Prep

1 fryer rabbit (about 3 pounds),
    legs and shoulders removed by
    your butcher, liver reserved

2 tablespoons plus 1 teaspoon extra-virgin
    olive oil

½ garlic clove, thinly sliced

4 cups loosely packed greens, such as Swiss
    chard, spinach, arugula, and/or dandelions,
    ideally a combination of 2 or more

Kosher salt

½ bunch Swiss chard

¼ cup finely diced pancetta or bacon

1 tablespoon minced shallot

1½ tablespoons fines herbes (see page 44), or
    thinly sliced fresh flat-leaf parsley leaves

½ tablespoon chopped fresh marjoram

1½ piquillo peppers (see Sources,
    page 321), minced

1½ tablespoons toasted bread
    crumbs (page 315)

1 large egg

Freshly ground black pepper

2 pieces caul fat (see Sources, page 321),
    cut into 10 x 14-inch rectangles

Remove the bones from the rabbit (see photos). Debone 1 rabbit leg, coarsely chop the bones, and set them aside. Coarsely chop the meat and set it aside separately.

Heat 2 tablespoons of the oil in a wide, deep sauté pan over medium-high heat. Add half the garlic and cook, stirring occasionally, until softened but not browned, about 2 minutes. Add the greens, season with salt, and cook, stirring, until wilted and bright green, 2 to 3 minutes. Line a plate with a clean kitchen towel or paper towels and spread the greens out on the plate. Transfer to the refrigerator briefly to cool.

Cut off the Swiss chard stems and set aside. Soak the leaves in a bowl of cold water, agitating them by hand, to remove any grit, then spin them dry in a salad spinner. Peel and finely dice the stems.

Heat the remaining teaspoon of olive oil in a sauté pan over medium-high heat. Add the pancetta and sauté until it is lightly golden brown and has rendered enough fat to coat the bottom of the pan, about 4 minutes. Add the remaining garlic, the shallot, and the diced chard stems and season with salt. Cook, stirring, until the stems are softened, about 6 minutes. Add the Swiss chard leaves and cook, stirring continuously, until very soft, about 6 minutes. Transfer the contents of the pan to a plate and set aside.

Put the rabbit liver and the leg meat in the bowl of a food processor fitted with the steel blade, season with salt, and pulse to

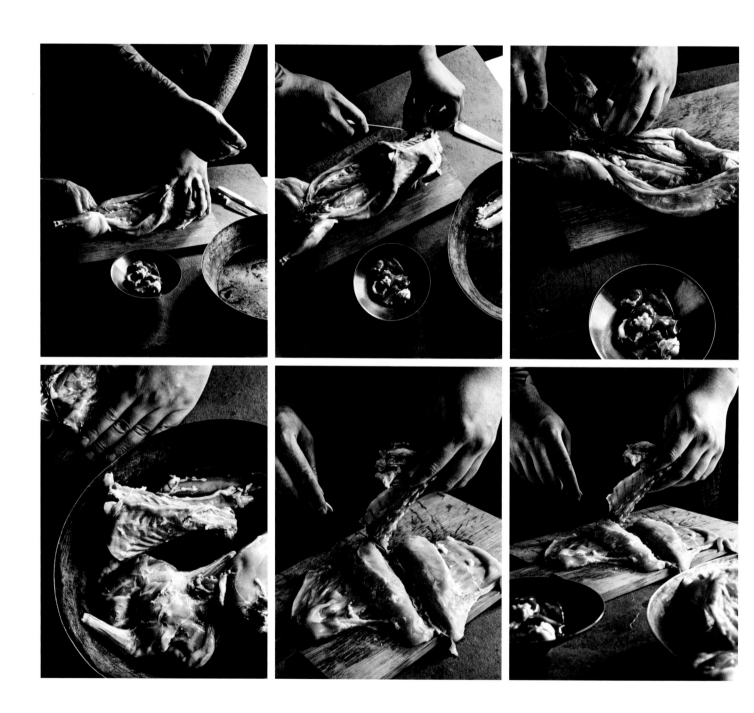

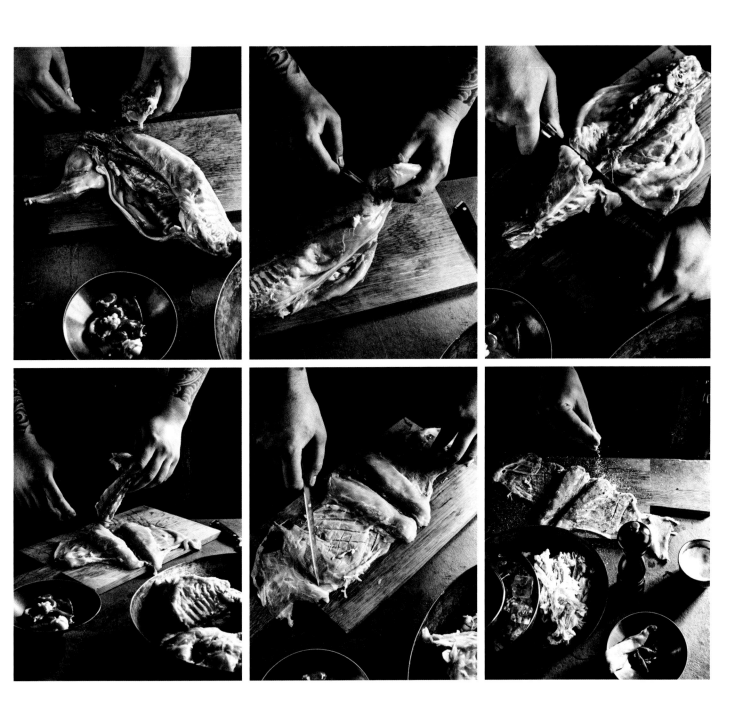

a coarse consistency. Squeeze any excess liquid from the cooked, cooled greens and add them to the bowl. (If using a grinder, just feed individual components through the grinder, collecting them in the same bowl.) Add the herb mix, marjoram, piquillo peppers, and bread crumbs. Crack the egg into a small bowl, beat it gently with a fork, and add half the egg to the bowl, discarding the rest. Season with salt and pepper and pulse just to combine. You cannot eat raw rabbit, but if you'd like to test the seasoning, wrap a small piece in plastic wrap and poach in gently simmering water until cooked through; taste the cooked piece and adjust the seasoning as needed.

Season the rabbit with salt and pepper, and lay the stuffing over it. Arrange the caul fat pieces on your work surface, slightly overlapping them, then roll the rabbit around the stuffing and set the rabbit on the caul fat. Roll the caul fat around the rabbit twice to encase it. Tie the ends with kitchen string, then tie at the middle, tying firmly but not too tightly. Tie with one additional piece of string between the middle and ends on both sides. Roll the prepared rabbit snugly in plastic wrap to shape it. Use right away, or refrigerate the rabbit in the plastic wrap for up to 2 days.

To Serve

Kosher salt and freshly ground black pepper

3 tablespoons extra-virgin olive oil, plus more for serving

2 tablespoons unsalted butter

3 garlic cloves, smashed with the side of a chef's knife and peeled

2 fresh thyme sprigs

2 tablespoons minced shallot

2 anchovy fillets (optional)

1 tablespoon sherry vinegar

½ cup chicken stock, preferably homemade (page 317)

Preheat the oven to 350°F.

Carefully remove the rabbit from the plastic wrap by cutting one end and sliding it out. Season the outside with salt and pepper.

Heat the olive oil in a roasting pan or cast-iron pan over medium-high heat. Add the rabbit. Add the reserved chopped leg bones to the pan to brown them for the sauce. Brown the rabbit, turning it as it browns, until browned on all sides, about 10 minutes. Add the butter, 2 garlic cloves, and the thyme to the pan. Baste the rabbit with the melted butter, then transfer the pan to the oven and roast for about 5 minutes; check for doneness with a cake tester (see page 4; it should be medium-hot). Transfer the rabbit to a clean, dry surface and let it rest while you make the sauce.

Pour off all but about 2 tablespoons of the fat from the pan. Add the remaining garlic clove, the shallot, and the anchovies (if using) and cook, stirring occasionally, until the garlic and shallot are softened but not browned, about 2 minutes. Add the vinegar and cook, stirring to loosen any flavorful bits cooked onto the bottom of the pan, about 1 minute. Add the stock, bring to a boil, and cook until reduced by a little more than half, about 5 minutes. Strain the sauce through a chinois or fine-mesh strainer into a medium, heatproof vessel and set aside.

Cut the strings from the rabbit and cut the rabbit into 1-inch slices. Divide the slices among four plates and top with the sauce and a drizzle of olive oil. Serve.

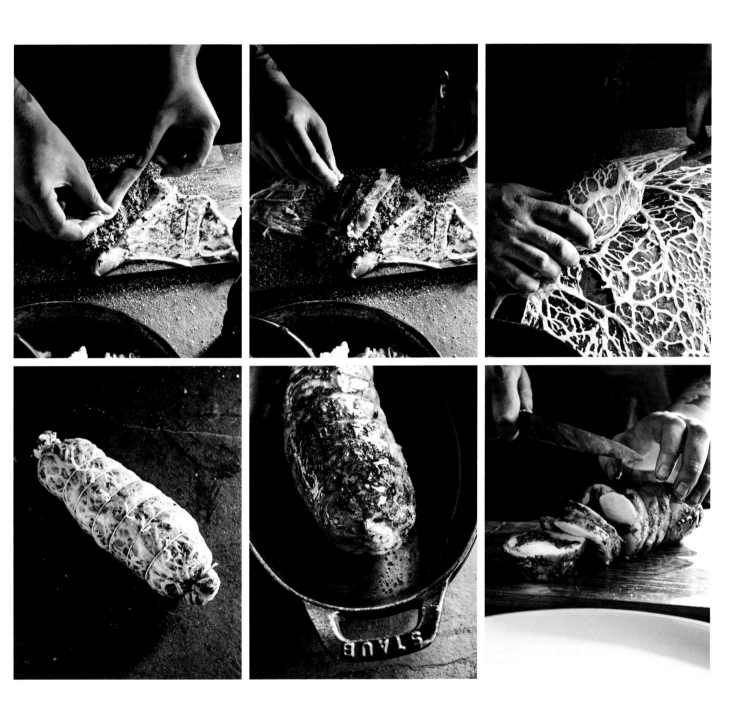

Grilled Pork Chop with Kimchi

Serves 4

This summertime dish epitomizes the casual cooking we often seek when grilling. Brining the pork chop ahead of time makes it super tender, and the kimchi is made by dolling up a store-bought condiment with fresh ingredients, elevating it to something that tastes homemade.

To Prep

¼ cup salt

2 tablespoons sugar

1 bay leaf, preferably fresh

½ teaspoon fresh thyme

3 garlic cloves, peeled and smashed

½ teaspoon red pepper flakes

½ teaspoon mustard seed

½ teaspoon juniper seed

½ teaspoon ground allspice

½ teaspoon whole cloves

½ teaspoon ground cinnamon

1 (1-inch) piece fresh ginger, peeled and thinly sliced

4 boneless pork chops (about 7 ounces each), preferably from the rack

Put 4 cups water, the salt, sugar, bay leaf, thyme, garlic, red pepper flakes, mustard seed, juniper seed, allspice, cloves, cinnamon, and ginger in a medium pot. Bring to a boil over high heat, then remove the pot from the heat and let the mixture cool completely. Put the pork chops in a baking dish or other vessel. Pour the brine over the chops, cover, and refrigerate for 6 hours.

Remove the pork chops from the liquid, pat dry with paper towels, and use right away, or wrap individually in plastic wrap and refrigerate for up to 2 days.

To Serve

About ¼ cup Korean chili powder
  (see Sources, page 321) or
  other dried chili powder

Extra-virgin olive oil

1 tablespoon thinly sliced scallion whites,
  plus 12 scallions, white and green parts

4 cups store-bought kimchi

Juice of ½ lime

1 tablespoon white sesame seeds,
  toasted (see page 314)

1 teaspoon sesame oil

1 teaspoon fish sauce

1 tablespoon chopped fresh cilantro

Kosher salt and freshly ground black pepper

Prepare a charcoal grill for grilling, letting the coals burn until covered with white ash, or heat a gas grill to high.

Dust the pork chops with chili powder and drizzle sparingly with olive oil. Place on the grill and cook until nice grill marks form and the pork is cooked through (check with a cake tester— see page 4; it should be medium-hot), about 6 minutes per side. Transfer to a plate and let rest while you grill the whole scallions, turning them to char them all over, about 6 minutes.

While grilling the pork chops and scallions, put the kimchi in a bowl. Add the chopped scallion, lime juice, sesame seeds, sesame oil, fish sauce, and cilantro. Season with salt and black pepper.

Cut the pork into ½-inch-thick slices. Spoon the kimchi onto the center of a platter and arrange the pork slices over the kimchi. Arrange the scallions around the perimeter of the plate and serve family-style.

Pork Belly Parmesan

Serves 4

Our restaurants are located in south Brooklyn, which has a deep-seated Italian-American history; to this day, family-owned specialty butcher and pastry shops offering quintessential Italian-American specialties continue to thrive. This dish is a bit of a tribute to our environment, a fancified take on a traditional Parmesan sandwich. You can serve it with the gnudi and artichokes on page 122 (as pictured here); the broccoli on page 268; or even in a sandwich. The best pork for this is Berkshire, for its flavor and marbling.

Note that there are multiple places in this recipe where you can stop the cooking and then pick it up again a day or more later.

To Prep

Pork Belly

Kosher salt

1 tablespoon minced garlic

¼ cup sugar

1 tablespoon coarsely cracked
   black peppercorns

1 tablespoon fennel seed

1 tablespoon coarsely chopped
   fresh thyme leaves

1 (1½-pound) fresh pork belly

1½ to 2 quarts duck fat (see
   Sources, page 321)

¾ cup all-purpose flour

3 large eggs

½ cup plain bread crumbs, preferably
   panko, pulsed in a food processor

Put ½ cup of salt in a small bowl. Add the garlic, sugar, peppercorns, fennel seed, and thyme and stir together.

Set the pork belly on a piece of plastic wrap. Coat the pork all over with the spice mixture and wrap loosely with the plastic. Refrigerate for 24 hours.

The next day, preheat the oven to 250°F. Put the duck fat in a pot and melt it over medium heat until liquefied but not boiling.

Remove the plastic wrap from the pork, brush off the solids, and rinse the pork briefly under cold running water. Pat it dry and set it in a baking dish or casserole just large enough to comfortably hold it. Add enough duck fat to cover it, cover with a lid or aluminum foil, and cook in the oven until the pork is very soft, about 7 hours.

Remove the baking dish from the oven and let the pork cool in the fat. Once cooled, remove it from the fat, wrap it in plastic wrap, and set it on a baking sheet. Top with another baking sheet and set heavy weights, such as canned tomatoes, on top to

press the pork down to an even thickness. Refrigerate that way overnight, or up to 3 days.

The next day, cut the pork belly into 4 strips, about 1½ inches thick. (You may have more pork belly than you need for this dish; use the extra to make sandwiches or in ragùs, or finely chop as a filling for tortellini, see page 156.)

Set up three wide, shallow bowls for breading: Put the flour in one, the eggs in another, whisking them with 1 tablespoon water, and the bread crumbs in a third. One by one, dredge the pork strips in the flour, then the egg, letting any excess drip back into the bowl, then turn the strips in the bread crumbs. Then dip in the egg again, letting any excess drip back into the bowl, and finally in the bread crumbs again.

Use right away or wrap loosely in plastic wrap and refrigerate for up to 24 hours.

Tomato Sauce

2 tablespoons extra-virgin olive oil

3 garlic cloves, thinly sliced

½ Spanish onion, minced

1 (15-ounce) can whole peeled tomatoes, preferably San Marzano or organic, crushed by hand, juices drained

Pinch of sugar

Kosher salt

Heat the olive oil in a wide, deep sauté pan over medium heat. When the oil is shimmering, add the garlic and onion and cook, stirring occasionally, until softened but not browned, about 3 minutes. Add the tomatoes, a pinch of sugar, and season with salt. Bring to a simmer and cook, stirring occasionally, until the mixture is thickened and almost dry, about 20 minutes; it should resemble a condiment more than a sauce. Use right away or refrigerate in an airtight container for up to 3 days.

To Serve

2 tablespoons diced fresh basil leaves

2 teaspoons sherry vinegar

Freshly cracked black pepper

Canola oil

1 ball mozzarella (about 1 pound), sliced as thin as possible, at room temperature

If necessary, let the tomato sauce come to room temperature, about 1 hour. Stir in the basil and vinegar and season with a few grinds of cracked pepper.

Preheat the oven to 400°F or preheat the broiler to low.

Pour canola oil into a sauté pan to a depth of about ¼ inch. Heat it over medium heat until shimmering. Add the pork and brown it on both sides, about 3 minutes per side. Transfer the pork to a rimmed baking sheet and bake until warmed through (check for doneness with a cake tester—see page 4; it should be medium-hot), about 5 minutes. Remove from the oven and top each piece of pork with the tomato condiment, then drape slices of mozzarella over each piece.

Return the baking sheet to the oven and bake until the cheese is lightly browned and melted, about 4 minutes.

Serve the pork with the desired accompaniments (see headnote).

Short Rib Pastrami with Braised Cabbage and Red Bliss Potatoes

Serves 4

The centerpiece of this hearty wintertime meal isn't thinly sliced pastrami, but rather a generous portion of short rib that's been brined, then rubbed with black pepper and coriander seed, and steamed. The accompanying elements are a potent braised cabbage made with green apple, sherry vinegar, and Dijon mustard, and Red Bliss potatoes that offer starchy relief to all of the big flavors that surround it. You can also add a crunchy element by scattering thin slices of Granny Smith apple dressed with olive oil and lemon juice around the plate. Although it involves a multiday process, this is a very easy recipe and produces a showstopping result.

To Prep

Braised Short Ribs
¼ cup plus 2 tablespoons kosher salt

¼ cup sugar

2 garlic cloves, smashed with the side of a chef's knife and peeled

1 tablespoon pickling spices

2 pounds boneless beef short rib (plate cut, weighed without the bone), in 4 pieces

1 tablespoon coriander seed, toasted (see page 314) and ground

1 tablespoon whole black peppercorns, toasted (see page 314) and ground

Put 2 quarts water, the salt, sugar, garlic, and pickling spices in a pot and bring to a boil over high heat. Remove the pot from the heat and let the liquid cool, then transfer it to an airtight container and refrigerate until it has been chilled to 40°F.

Put the short ribs in a bowl or plastic container and pour the brine over the ribs. Cover and brine in the refrigerator for 3 days.

Remove the ribs from the brine and pat them dry with a clean kitchen towel or a paper towel. Rub the coriander seed and peppercorns over the short ribs, set them on a plate, and refrigerate, unwrapped, for at least 8 hours or overnight.

To cook the pastrami, bring an inch of water to a simmer in a pot sized to hold a steamer. Add the short rib pieces to the steamer in a single layer, cover the pot, and steam for 2 hours 30 minutes; the pastrami will jiggle when done. Remove the pastrami from the steamer and immediately wrap each piece individually in plastic wrap. Use right away or refrigerate for up to 24 hours.

Braised Cabbage

1 medium head green or savoy cabbage (about 1¼ pounds), quartered through the root end, core removed, thinly sliced crosswise

½ cup dry white wine

1 teaspoon sugar

Kosher salt

1 teaspoon extra-virgin olive oil

1 teaspoon unsalted butter

1 smoked bacon slice (about 1 ounce)

½ Spanish onion, halved through the root end and thinly sliced (to approximate the shape of the cabbage)

Freshly ground black pepper

1 garlic clove, thinly sliced

1 bay leaf, preferably fresh

1 teaspoon caraway seed

1 small Yukon Gold or Idaho potato, peeled and coarsely grated

1 medium Granny Smith apple, peeled, cored, and coarsely grated

1 cup chicken stock, preferably homemade (page 317)

Put the cabbage in a shallow pan or bowl and pour the wine over it. Sprinkle the sugar and 1 teaspoon of salt over it and toss well. Cover the cabbage with plastic wrap and marinate in the refrigerator for 1 hour, or up to 24 hours (the longer the better).

Position a rack in the center of the oven and preheat the oven to 350°F.

Heat a heavy ovenproof pot over medium-high heat. Add the oil and butter and melt the butter. Add the bacon and cook until it renders some fat but do not let it brown, 1 to 2 minutes. Add the onion and sweat it for 2 to 3 minutes, then season with a generous pinch of salt and a few grinds of pepper. Add the garlic, bay leaf, and caraway seed, stir, and cook for 2 to 3 minutes. Stir in the cabbage; it will seem like a lot for the pot, but will wilt down over 8 minutes of cooking time. (To wilt it faster, cover the pot with a lid.) Stir in the potato and apple, being careful to not let them scorch. Season with more salt. Stir in the chicken stock, bring to a simmer, and cover the pot with a lid.

Transfer the covered pot to the oven and braise until the cabbage is tender and the potato and apple are cooked into the mix, 1 hour 15 minutes to 1 hour 30 minutes. Use tongs or a slotted spoon to fish out and discard the bacon and bay leaf. Use right away or refrigerate in an airtight container for up to 24 hours.

Red Bliss Potatoes

12 ounces Red Bliss potatoes, ideally 12 small potatoes

Kosher salt

1 garlic clove, smashed with the side of a chef's knife and peeled

1 fresh thyme sprig

1 teaspoon whole black peppercorns

1 bay leaf, preferably fresh

Put the potatoes in a large pot, cover by a few inches with cold water, and generously salt the water. Add the garlic, thyme, peppercorns, and bay leaf. Bring to a boil and cook until the potatoes are tender to a cake tester or knife tip, 15 to 20 minutes, depending on the size of the potatoes. Drain the potatoes and, when cool enough to handle but still warm, use a paring knife to peel them. (Discard the garlic, thyme, peppercorns, and bay leaf.)

Use right away or refrigerate in an airtight container for up to 4 hours.

To Serve

½ cup chicken stock, preferably homemade (page 317)

2 tablespoons unsalted butter

Kosher salt

1 tablespoon Dijon mustard

¼ cup minced fresh herbs, ideally a mix
   of flat-leaf parsley, dill, and tarragon

½ small shallot, minced

A few drops of apple cider vinegar,
   sherry vinegar, or lemon juice

Freshly ground black pepper

Position a rack in the center of the oven and preheat the oven to 350°F.

Unwrap the short rib pastrami and set them in a medium pan. Pour water into the pan to come ½ inch up the sides of the pan. Bring to a simmer over medium-high heat, cover with a tight-fitting lid or aluminum foil, and transfer to the oven. Cook until the short rib pastrami are heated through, about 8 minutes.

Meanwhile, put the potatoes in a small pot, add the stock and 1 tablespoon of the butter, and heat over medium-high heat until the potatoes are warmed through. Put the cabbage in a separate small pot and reheat it over medium-high heat. Season with salt and stir in the Dijon mustard, herbs, shallot, vinegar, and a few grinds of pepper, then stir in the remaining 1 tablespoon butter. The cabbage might seem very assertive and mustardy if tasted on its own, but bear in mind that it is an accompaniment to the pastrami.

To serve, spoon some cabbage onto the center of four plates. Top with the pastrami and arrange potatoes around the meat and cabbage on each plate. Serve.

Beef Sirloin with Pont Neuf Potatoes and Shallot Marmalade

Serves 4

A high-class take on "meat and potatoes" with the potatoes elegantly shaped (the name comes from a bridge in Paris) and cooked in clarified butter and a shallot marmalade that brings essential acid and sweetness to the plate. If you like, fold diced raw bone marrow into the marmalade at the end to enrich it.

To Prep

Shallot Marmalade

1½ cups thinly sliced shallots

½ cup red wine

¼ cup balsamic vinegar

¼ cup red wine vinegar

1 teaspoon sugar

Pont Neuf Potatoes

3 large Idaho potatoes

Kosher salt

2 cups clarified butter (see page 315)

2 fresh thyme sprigs

5 garlic cloves, smashed with the side of a chef's knife and peeled

Put the shallots in a small pot. Add the wine, balsamic vinegar, red wine vinegar, and sugar and bring to a simmer over medium heat, stirring to dissolve the sugar. Reduce the heat to low and simmer until the shallots are very soft, about 30 minutes. Use right away or let cool and refrigerate in an airtight container for up to 3 days.

Preheat the oven to 300°F.

Fill a large bowl halfway with cold water. Peel and cut each potato into 4 pont neuf crescents (see photographs, page 250), or rectangles if easier. As you cut them, put the crescents in the water to keep them from oxidizing and turning brown. Once all the potatoes have been shaped and gathered in the water, gently agitate the bowl to rinse off any starch.

Remove the potatoes from the bowl, pat dry with paper towels, and season with salt. Let rest for 10 minutes to absorb the salt.

After 10 minutes, heat the clarified butter in a large ovenproof pot over medium heat. Add the thyme and garlic and cook for 1 minute to flavor the butter. Add the potatoes. Transfer the pot to the oven and cook for 15 minutes. Use tongs or a spoon to turn the potatoes over and cook for 15 minutes more, or until lightly golden all over and a cake tester or paring knife slides in and out of a potato easily.

Remove the pot from the heat and let the potatoes cool in the fat. Use right away or hold the potatoes in the fat for up to 4 hours at room temperature.

To Serve

2 tablespoons extra-virgin olive oil

Kosher salt and freshly ground black pepper

2 sirloin steaks (about 1 pound each)

5 garlic cloves, smashed with the side
   of a chef's knife and peeled

2 fresh thyme sprigs

6 tablespoons (¾ stick) unsalted butter

Coarsely ground black pepper

1 tablespoon fines herbes (see page 44) or
   thinly sliced fresh flat-leaf parsley leaves

Fleur de sel

Preheat the oven to 450°F.

Use a slotted spoon to lift the potatoes out of the fat. Discard any thyme or garlic that adheres to them. Arrange them on a small baking sheet and heat in the oven for 10 minutes.

Heat the olive oil in a sauté pan over medium-high heat. Season the steaks with salt and pepper. When the oil is shimmering, add the steaks to the pan and cook until nicely seared on both sides, about 5 minutes per side. Add the garlic, thyme, and 4 tablespoons of the butter and cook, basting the steaks with the butter as it melts, until the steaks reach your desired doneness.

Transfer the steaks to a clean, dry work surface or a plate and let them rest for 5 minutes.

Meanwhile, reheat the marmalade in a small pot, folding in the remaining 2 tablespoons butter to melt it. Stir in a few coarse grinds of pepper.

When the potatoes are cooked through, transfer them to a large heatproof bowl, add the herbs, toss to coat, and season with salt and pepper.

Spoon some marmalade on each of four plates. Cut each steak into thick slices and plate the steak and potatoes alongside the marmalade. Sprinkle a few grains of fleur de sel on each piece of meat and serve.

Lamb Loin with Spring Vegetables and Snail Butter

Serves 4

The conventional wisdom when including several vegetables in the same dish is to blanch or sauté many of them separately to preserve their individual characteristics. This recipe diverts from that rule by cooking most of the spring vegetables together, adding them to the pan based on how long each will take to cook, allowing their flavors to mingle slightly while still keeping each one al dente.

To Prep

2 tablespoons extra-virgin olive oil

Kosher salt

1 garlic clove, thinly sliced

4 baby carrots, thinly sliced on an angle

2 small artichokes, trimmed (see page 124), bottoms halved

1 baby turnip, thinly sliced

1 tablespoon unsalted butter

4 scallions, white and light green parts, cut on an angle

4 asparagus stalks, tip quartered, stalk thinly cut on an angle

1 zucchini, thinly sliced on an angle

1 cup chicken stock, preferably homemade (page 317)

Heat the olive oil in a wide, deep sauté pan over medium heat.

Season with salt after adding each of the following vegetables: Add the garlic and cook, stirring occasionally, until softened but not browned, about 2 minutes. Add the carrots and cook, stirring occasionally, until slightly softened, about 2 minutes. Add the artichoke pieces and cook, tossing, for 30 seconds. Add the turnips and cook, tossing, for 2 minutes. Add the butter, scallions, asparagus stalks and tips, and zucchini and cook, tossing, for 1 minute.

Pour in the stock, bring to a simmer, and cook until it has evaporated and the vegetables are soft, about 4 minutes.

Use right away or spread the vegetables out on a baking sheet, cool, cover loosely with plastic wrap, and refrigerate for up to 6 hours.

To Serve

4 (6-ounce) pieces lamb loin

Kosher salt

Piment d'Espelette or freshly
ground black pepper

¼ cup extra-virgin olive oil, plus more for
serving

4 tablespoons (½ stick) unsalted butter

4 garlic cloves, smashed with the side
of a chef's knife and peeled

1 fresh thyme sprig

1 fresh rosemary sprig

¼ cup dry white wine

¼ cup plus 2 tablespoons chicken stock,
preferably homemade (page 317)

½ lemon

12 small lettuce leaves, preferably baby romaine

¼ cup shelled English peas, blanched
and shocked (see page 313)

¼ cup peeled shelled favas (see page 313)

8 ramps (optional)

4 tablespoons Snail Butter (page 129)

Fleur de sel

If necessary, allow the reserved vegetables to come to room
temperature.

Season the lamb with salt and piment d'Espelette.

Heat ¼ cup of the olive oil in a wide, deep sauté pan over
medium-high heat. Add the lamb and cook until nicely seared on
the bottom, then turn over and cook on the other side until seared,
about 6 minutes. Add 2 tablespoons of the unsalted butter, the
garlic, thyme, and rosemary and baste the lamb with the butter as it
melts for 2 to 3 minutes.

Transfer the lamb to a plate or platter and tent with aluminum
foil. Drain the fat from the pan. Add the wine to the pan and stir to
loosen any flavorful bits cooked onto the bottom of the pan. Bring
to a simmer and cook until almost completely reduced, about 4
minutes. Add ¼ cup of the stock and the remaining 2 tablespoons
unsalted butter and swirl to emulsify the fats, about 3 minutes.
Strain the sauce through a chinois or fine-mesh strainer into a
heatproof bowl. Add a squeeze of lemon juice, catching the seeds in
your hand and discarding them. Keep the sauce covered and warm.

Heat the vegetables in a wide, deep sauté pan over medium
heat. Add the lettuce, peas, favas, and ramps (if using). Pour in the
remaining 2 tablespoons stock and simmer until the vegetables are
cooked and the stock has reduced, about 2 minutes. Swirl in the
snail butter, melting it and emulsifying the liquids into a sauce.
Taste and adjust the seasoning with salt and/or pepper, if necessary.
Add a squeeze of lemon juice.

To serve, divide the vegetables among four plates, spreading
them out to show off their colors. Slice the lamb crosswise and
arrange the slices over the vegetables. Spoon the sauce over and
around the lamb. Finish with a sprinkling of fleur de sel and a
drizzle of olive oil. Serve.

Grilled Lamb Ribs with Japanese Eggplant

Serves 4

When you hit on a winning combination in the kitchen, it's useful to keep it in mind and find ways to adapt it. We introduced this main course when we opened our sister restaurant, Dover, borrowing a few bits from our kale salad (page 49), namely the Thai dressing and the inclusion of crushed peanuts, a textural touch expanded on here with fried garlic and shallots. The dressing, like many Thai condiments, has a terrific affinity for grilled meats, and the steamed Japanese eggplant drinks it up as well.

To Prep

Confit Lamb Ribs
2 Denver ribs (about 1½ pounds each)

Kosher salt

About 2 quarts duck fat (see
  Sources, page 321)

Season the ribs generously with salt, cover loosely with plastic wrap, and refrigerate for 24 hours.

When ready to proceed, preheat the oven to 275°F. Brush the salt off the ribs, rinse them under cold running water, and pat dry with paper towels. Put the ribs in a pan that holds them snugly; you can cut the ribs if necessary, or allow them to overlap slightly.

Put the duck fat in a separate pot and melt it over medium heat until liquefied but not boiling, then pour it over the ribs. Cover with aluminum foil or a lid, transfer to the oven, and cook until the lamb meat is tender and pulls easily away from the bone, about 4 hours.

Remove the pan from the oven, remove the cover, and let rest for 1 hour. Use tongs or a slotted spoon to transfer the lamb to a cutting board and, when cool enough to handle, remove the fat from the ribs, discarding it. Cut the ribs into eight 2-rib sections. The ribs can be refrigerated for up to 2 days.

(continued)

Steamed Japanese Eggplant

2 Japanese eggplants (about
   1 pound total), peeled
Kosher salt and freshly ground black pepper

Season the eggplants generously with salt and pepper. Let rest for 10 minutes to absorb the seasoning.

Meanwhile, bring a few inches of water to a simmer in a pot fit to hold a steaming basket. Add the eggplant to the basket, halving them if necessary to fit, cover, and steam until slightly softened, about 8 minutes. Let cool, then wrap in plastic and chill in the refrigerator for at least 1 hour, or up to 24 hours. Cut crosswise into 2-inch pieces.

To Serve

1 tablespoon extra-virgin olive oil
Kosher salt and freshly ground black pepper
¾ cup Thai Dressing (page 51)
2 shallots, thinly sliced and
   fried (see page 314)
6 garlic cloves, thinly sliced and
   fried (see page 314; you can use
   the same oil as the shallots)
¾ cup crushed roasted salted peanuts
2 cups loosely packed roughly equal parts
   fresh Thai basil, cilantro, and mint leaves

Prepare a charcoal grill for grilling, letting the coals burn until covered with white ash, or heat a gas grill to high. Alternatively, heat a grill pan over high heat on the stovetop.

Heat a cast-iron pan over high heat; if cooking on a grill, simply heat the pan over the grill. Add the olive oil to the pan. Season the eggplant pieces with salt and pepper. Add the eggplant pieces to the pan and brown all over, turning as they brown, about 6 minutes.

Meanwhile, grill the ribs just to heat them through and create grill marks, 2 to 3 minutes per side. (Alternatively, you can reheat them on a baking sheet in a preheated 375°F oven for about 5 minutes.)

Put 2 pieces of eggplant and 2 rib segments on each of four plates. Spoon some dressing over the eggplant and ribs on each plate, then scatter the shallots, garlic, and peanuts over them. Finish with a scattering of herbs and serve.

Roasted Rack of Lamb with Boulangère Potatoes and Braised Lettuce

Serves 4

The most unusual element of this rack of lamb composition is the way the lettuces are tossed with the potatoes and briefly cooked just before serving. That quick step enriches the lettuces in a surprising way, and helps unify the different components on the plate. (See photo on page 211.)

To Prep

2 large Yukon Gold potatoes

Kosher salt

Extra-virgin olive oil

¼ cup diced smoked bacon

3 garlic cloves, smashed with the side
  of a chef's knife and peeled

½ Spanish onion, cut into small dice

Freshly ground black pepper

About 2 cups chicken stock,
  preferably homemade (page 317)

Cut each potato into 1½-inch slices and punch out circles with a 2-inch round cutter. Rinse the discs under cold running water to wash off any excess starch. Pat dry with paper towels, season generously with salt, and let rest for 10 minutes to absorb the salt.

Preheat the oven to 300°F.

Heat the olive oil in a wide, deep sauté pan over medium-high heat. Add the potatoes and cook until lightly browned on both sides, about 5 minutes per side, turning them over with a spoon. Gently stir in the bacon and cook, stirring occasionally, until the bacon is crispy and most of its fat has rendered, about 6 minutes. Carefully pour off any excess fat from the pan, then add the garlic and onion. Season with salt and pepper and cook, stirring, until they are lightly caramelized, about 4 minutes. Pour in enough stock to come halfway up the sides of the potatoes, bring to a simmer, cover with a lid, and cook in the oven just until the potatoes are tender to a cake tester or knife tip, about 15 minutes.

Remove the potatoes from the oven. Use right away or let cool and refrigerate in an airtight container overnight.

To Serve

2 tablespoons extra-virgin olive oil

1 (8-bone) rack of lamb,
   Frenched by your butcher

Kosher salt

Korean chili powder (see Sources,
   page 321) or piment d'Espelette

Juice of ½ lemon

½ cup chicken stock, preferably homemade (page 317)

1 tablespoon unsalted butter

4 small heads of lettuce, such as
   baby romaine or little gem

4 pieces of tomato confit (see page 313)

Preheat the oven to 350°F.

Heat 1 tablespoon of the oil in a large, cast-iron pan over medium-high heat. Season the lamb with salt and chili powder. Add the rack of lamb to the pan, fat-side down, and sear for about 5 minutes. Turn the rack on its side so it's resting on the bone, transfer to the oven, and cook until nicely browned and cooked through, testing for doneness with a cake tester (see page 4; it should be medium-hot), about 12 minutes.

Transfer the lamb to a cutting board and let it rest for 10 minutes. Do not turn off the oven.

Meanwhile, pour the fat from the cast-iron pan, and return the pan to the stovetop over medium heat. Add the lemon juice and stir to loosen any flavorful bits cooked onto the bottom of the pan. Stir in the chicken stock, then the remaining 1 tablespoon olive oil and the butter, and stir to emulsify the liquids with the fats in the pan, letting the mixture reduce for about 5 minutes.

Transfer the potato mixture to an ovenproof sauté pan or casserole and reheat in the oven. Add the lettuces and tomato confit to the pan and let wilt in the oven for a minute or two.

Slice the rack of lamb into 4 chops. Spoon some of the potato, lettuce, and tomato confit onto each of four dinner plates. Set a portion of lamb alongside, and spoon some sauce over the lamb. Serve.

Veal Loin with Swiss Chard, Tomato, and Green Garlic

Serves 4

As delicious as veal can be, the star of this dish is the accompaniment, with Swiss chard leaves and stems, spring garlic, and oven-roasted tomatoes each bringing their own high-impact flavors to bear. A last-second hit of lemon juice, and the capers added to the sauce just before serving, add acid and salinity that effortlessly elevate the entire dish.

To Prep

2 beefsteak tomatoes, peeled
  (see page 313)
Kosher salt and freshly ground black pepper
Pinch of sugar
1 garlic clove, thinly sliced
½ teaspoon minced fresh thyme leaves
1 tablespoon balsamic vinegar
1 tablespoon extra-virgin olive oil

Preheat the oven to 200°F.

Halve the tomatoes crosswise, then cut the halves into quarters, yielding 8 pieces from each tomato. Squeeze out some of the seeds and put the pieces in a medium bowl. Season with salt, pepper, and the sugar. Add the garlic, thyme, vinegar, and olive oil and toss well to coat the tomatoes.

Line a baking sheet with parchment paper or aluminum foil and spread the tomato pieces out so they are not touching each other. Bake in the oven until shriveled but still moist, about 1 hour, turning them over with a spatula or fork after 30 minutes.

Remove the sheet from the oven and let the tomatoes cool. Use right away or refrigerate in an airtight container for up to 3 days.

To Serve

1 bunch Swiss chard with nice thick stems

½ lemon

6 tablespoons (¾ stick) unsalted butter

1 piece small tender green garlic, cut
   on an angle into 1½-inch pieces, 2
   outer layers removed, or 2 scallions,
   white and light green parts

Kosher salt

½ cup dry white wine

1¼ cups chicken stock, preferably homemade (page 317)

¼ cup plus 3 tablespoons extra-virgin olive oil

4 pieces veal loin (about 6 ounces each)

Freshly ground black pepper

4 garlic cloves, smashed with the side
   of a chef's knife and peeled

1 fresh thyme sprig

1 fresh rosemary sprig

1 teaspoon brine-packed capers, drained

Preheat the oven to 350°F.

To make the Swiss chard, cut the Swiss chard stems from the leaves and set aside. Wash the leaves in a colander and set aside in the sink to drain. Peel the stems with a paring knife or vegetable peeler, pulling away the fibrous outer layer. Cut the stems on an angle at 2-inch intervals, put in a small bowl, cover with cold water, and add a squeeze of lemon juice, catching the seeds in your hand and discarding them. Set aside.

Melt 1 tablespoon of the butter in a wide, deep sauté pan over medium-high heat. When the butter foams, add the green garlic, season with salt, and cook until just softened, 2 to 3 minutes. Drain the chard stems, pat them dry with a paper towel, and add them to the pan. Cook, stirring, until slightly softened, 2 to 3 minutes. Pour in ¼ cup of the wine, bring to a simmer, and cook until reduced by half, about 3 minutes. Pour in 1 cup of the stock, bring to a boil, and cook until reduced by about two-thirds, then swirl in 3 tablespoons of the olive oil and 1 tablespoon of the butter, emulsifying them. Remove the pan from the heat and keep the chard covered and warm.

To cook the veal, season the meat with salt and pepper. Heat the remaining ¼ cup of olive oil in a wide, deep sauté pan over medium-high heat. Add the veal and cook until nicely seared on the bottom, then turn over and cook on the other side until seared, about 6 minutes total cooking time. Add 2 tablespoons of the butter, the garlic, thyme, and rosemary and baste the veal with the butter as it melts for 2 to 3 minutes. Transfer the pan to the oven and cook until the veal is heated through (check for doneness with a cake tester—see page 4; it should be medium-hot), about 4 minutes.

Transfer the veal pieces to a plate or platter and tent with aluminum foil. Drain the fat from the pan. Add the remaining ¼ cup wine to the pan and stir to loosen any flavorful bits cooked onto the bottom of the pan. Bring to a simmer and cook until almost completely reduced, about 4 minutes. Add the remaining ¼ cup stock and remaining 2 tablespoons butter and swirl to emulsify the fats, about 3 minutes. Strain the sauce through a chinois or fine-mesh strainer into a heatproof bowl. Add a squeeze of lemon juice. Keep the sauce covered and warm.

Reheat the Swiss chard in its pan over medium heat for a minute or two. Swirl the tomatoes and Swiss chard leaves in just to warm them. Remove the pan from the heat and stir in a squeeze of lemon juice.

To serve, cut the veal into 1-inch slices, dividing them among four wide, shallow bowls. Spoon some Swiss chard and tomatoes alongside. Swirl the capers into the sauce and spoon some sauce over the veal on each plate. Serve.

Side Dishes

Romaine Lettuce with Crème Fraîche Dressing

Serves 4

This salad might not seem like much but the combination of clean, crunchy lettuce and tart crème fraîche makes a wonderful sidecar to grilled and roasted meats; at our restaurants we serve it alongside the sirloin with pont neuf potatoes dish on page 249.

To Prep

½ cup crème fraîche
1 tablespoon fresh lemon juice
1 tablespoon extra-virgin olive oil
Kosher salt and freshly ground black
  pepper

Make the dressing by putting the crème fraîche, lemon juice, and olive oil in a medium bowl. Season with salt and pepper and whisk together. Use the dressing right away or refrigerate it in an airtight container for up to 24 hours.

To Serve

Leaves from 2 romaine hearts,
  halved, washed, and spun dry

If the dressing has been refrigerated, let it come to room temperature for a few minutes.

Put the leaves on a small platter and drizzle with the dressing. Serve family-style.

Creamed Corn with Bacon

Serves 4 to 6

With a combination of whole corn kernels and a corn puree, this side dish, enriched with bacon and lightened up with tarragon, is summery and complex. Serve it with white fish such as cod or bass, or with lobster, shrimp, or chicken.

To Prep

1 tablespoon unsalted butter

1 tablespoon minced shallot

1 garlic clove, smashed with the side of a chef's knife and peeled

1 cup corn kernels (from about 2 cobs)

Kosher salt

½ cup chicken stock, preferably homemade (page 317)

Melt the butter in a sauté pan over medium heat. When the butter foams, add the shallot and garlic and cook, stirring occasionally, until softened but not browned, about 2 minutes. Add the corn, season with salt, and cook, stirring occasionally but without allowing it to brown, for 5 minutes. Pour in the stock, bring to a simmer, and cook until the kernels are very soft, 8 to 10 minutes.

Transfer the mixture to a blender and puree. Strain the puree through a fine-mesh strainer into a bowl, pressing down with a rubber spatula to extract as much puree as possible. Use right away or refrigerate in an airtight container for up to 2 days.

To Serve

¼ cup finely diced smoked bacon

1 tablespoon minced shallot

1 garlic clove, thinly sliced

3 cups corn kernels (from about 6 cobs)

½ cup chicken stock, preferably homemade (page 317)

Kosher salt and freshly ground black pepper

2 tablespoons coarsely chopped fresh tarragon

⅓ cup lightly whipped cream (from 3 tablespoons heavy cream)

Cook the bacon in a large sauté pan over medium heat, stirring occasionally, until it is crispy and enough fat has rendered to coat the bottom of the pan, about 6 minutes. Add the shallot and garlic and cook, stirring occasionally, until softened but not browned, about 2 minutes. Add the corn kernels and stock, bring to a simmer, and cook until the corn is softened but still al dente and the stock has reduced by half, about 5 minutes. Stir in the corn puree, bring to a boil, and stir to emulsify with the stock, about 2 minutes. Season with salt and pepper and stir in the tarragon. Off the heat, fold in the whipped cream.

Divide among individual plates or serve family-style from a bowl.

Roasted Broccoli with Watercress, Lemon, and Pecorino

Serves 4

Broccoli seems an unlikely candidate for charring, but the intense contrast creates a compelling effect that gets along as a side dish to any number of fish or meats. The acidic lemon and peppery watercress round out and pull the flavors together. Don't cut the broccoli florets to uniform size; the smallest ones will darken, adding variety and punctuation to the plate. This is one case where zesting your lemon as you work makes a big difference, because you get the oil along with the zest, perfuming the finished dish. Serve this with just about anything, from white-fleshed fish to roasted chicken or duck to beef.

To Prep

3 heads of broccoli (about 8 ounces each), cut into florets
Kosher salt

Cut the stems off the florets, and discard the stems or save them for another use. You should have about 6 cups of florets. Cut especially large ones in half.

Bring a large pot of salted water to a boil. Fill a large bowl halfway with ice and water and set aside. Add the broccoli to the boiling water and cook until al dente, 1 to 2 minutes. Drain in a colander and transfer to the ice water to stop the cooking and preserve the color. Drain again, dry on paper towels, and use right away or refrigerate in an airtight container for up to 8 hours.

To Serve

About ¾ cup plus 2 tablespoons
extra-virgin olive oil

¼ cup fresh lemon juice, reserve 1 lemon
half for grating ¼ teaspoon of zest

2 teaspoons minced shallot

1 tablespoon fines herbes (see page 44) or
thinly sliced fresh flat-leaf parsley leaves

Kosher salt and freshly ground black pepper

4 cups loosely packed watercress leaves

½ cup finely grated aged pecorino
cheese, such as Ginepro, Toscano,
or d'Oro (see Sources, page 321)

Select a sauté pan wide and deep enough to accommodate all
the broccoli in an even layer (or cook it in two batches or in two
pans). Heat ½ cup of the oil in the pan over high heat until almost
smoking. Turn off the heat to avoid splattering or flare-ups and add
the broccoli carefully. (The broccoli has a tendency to soak up oil,
so add more if necessary.) Cook, turning with a spoon or fork, to
brown the broccoli all over, then transfer to a heatproof bowl. Add
the remaining ¼ cup plus 2 tablespoons olive oil, the lemon juice,
shallot, and herbs. Season with salt and pepper and toss.

Transfer the broccoli to a serving platter. Top with the
watercress and a scattering of cheese. Finely grate about ¼ teaspoon
of lemon zest over the dish. Serve family-style from the center of
the table.

Roasted and Raw Cauliflower with Currants, Capers, and Hazelnuts

Serves 4

An amalgam of mostly Italian ingredients that eats like an Asian dish thanks to the combination of fish sauce, acid, herbs, and nuts. You can change up the ingredients here, varying the type of onion, adding minced dried fruits, or incorporating minced anchovy fillets along with the other ingredients at the end of the recipe as an alternative to the *colatura*. Serve this with fish and chicken, or as part of an antipasti-type spread at the outset of a party or meal.

To Prep

1 head cauliflower (about 1½ pounds)

Cut off and discard the stem of the cauliflower, then cut out the core and discard it as well. Trim one-quarter of the head into very small pieces, tiny enough that they would be pleasant to eat raw; you should have about ⅔ cup. Trim the remaining cauliflower into medium pieces; you should have about 2 cups. (These approximate amounts needn't be exact.)

Use right away or refrigerate in an airtight container for up to 24 hours.

To Serve

¾ cup extra-virgin olive oil

3 tablespoons fresh lemon juice

2 tablespoons *colatura* (see page 51 and
Sources, page 321) or fish sauce

½ cup currants, soaked in warm water
for 5 minutes and drained

½ cup coarsely chopped fried or
toasted hazelnuts (see page 314)

¼ cup thinly sliced red onion

½ cup thinly sliced peeled celery

1 tablespoon brine-packed capers, drained

1 cup loosely packed fresh
flat-leaf parsley leaves

1 tablespoon fines herbes (see page 44)
or fresh flat-leaf parsley leaves

Kosher salt and freshly ground black pepper

Heat ½ cup of the olive oil in a medium, heavy pan until shimmering. Add the medium pieces of cauliflower and cook until golden brown, 5 to 6 minutes, turning the pieces as they brown. Use a slotted spoon to transfer the cauliflower to a large heatproof bowl, leaving the oil behind. Once the oil cools, discard it.

Add the small cauliflower pieces to the bowl, then add the remaining ¼ cup olive oil, the lemon juice, *colatura*, currants, hazelnuts, onion, celery, capers, parsley, and herbs. Season with salt and pepper, toss well, and transfer to a serving plate. Serve family-style.

Sunchokes with Orange, Pistachio, and Aged Pecorino

Serves 4

Like baby artichokes, sunchokes can be eaten raw when they're thinly sliced. Here, slivers of raw sunchokes are tossed with citrus and crunchy components for a quick and simple side dish that's a terrific balance to the char of grilled meats. As with a few of the recipes in this chapter, there's no prep step here, but this can be quickly prepared from start to finish.

6 medium sunchokes, scrubbed and
    thinly shaved on a mandoline
2 oranges, peeled and cut into
    supremes (see page 313)
¼ cup fried or toasted pistachio
    nuts (see page 314)
3 tablespoons extra-virgin olive oil
2 tablespoons fresh lemon juice
Kosher salt and freshly ground black pepper
¼ cup loosely packed fresh
    flat-leaf parsley leaves
Small piece of aged pecorino, such
    as Ginepro, Toscano, or d'Oro
    (see Sources, page 321)

Put the sunchokes, orange supremes, pistachios, olive oil, and lemon juice in a large bowl, season with salt and pepper, and toss well.

Divide among individual plates or serve family-style from a large bowl. Top with the parsley and a grating of cheese.

Roasted Carrots with Yogurt, Quinoa, and Dill

Serves 4

This super-convenient side dish is easy to make, and hits all the flavor and texture marks with caramel-glazed carrots, cool, creamy yogurt, fragrant dill, and crunchy fried quinoa. It actually tastes best at room temperature, making it a valuable recipe to have in your repertoire for entertaining. In addition to serving it as a freestanding side dish, these carrots can be plated alongside braised lamb shank or roasted leg of lamb for a composed dish.

For a more dramatic presentation, use a variety of different-colored carrots.

To Prep

12 carrots, ends trimmed, well washed and scrubbed

12 fresh dill sprigs, picked

¼ cup extra-virgin olive oil

Kosher salt

1 teaspoon caraway seed, lightly crushed, ideally with a mortar and pestle

½ cup sugar

Preheat the oven to 350°F.

Fill a medium bowl halfway with ice and water. Halve one of the carrots lengthwise, and shave it, ideally on a mandoline. Put the shavings in the ice water, add the dill, and set aside.

Cut the remaining carrots on an angle into 2 or 3 pieces each.

Heat a heavy, ovenproof sauté pan over high heat, letting it get very hot. Add the olive oil and briefly heat it until it is almost smoking. Add the carrots and a generous pinch of salt and the caraway seed and toss to coat the carrots for about 1 minute. Scatter the sugar over the carrots and stir. Cook, tossing the carrots, until they are nicely caramelized and the sugar has browned and starts to bubble, about 6 minutes. Pour in ½ cup water, bring it to a simmer, and cook until slightly reduced and the sugar and water begin to come together in a caramel, about 2 minutes.

Transfer the pan to the oven and roast until the carrots are tender to a knife tip, 10 to 12 minutes, adding more water as necessary to keep the caramel from drying out.

Transfer the carrots to a large bowl and let cool to room temperature. Use right away or keep covered with plastic wrap, at room temperature, for up to 2 hours.

To Serve

½ cup Greek yogurt

2 teaspoons fresh lemon juice

1 tablespoon plus 1 teaspoon extra-virgin olive oil, plus more for serving

Freshly ground black pepper

Few dashes sherry vinegar

Fleur de sel

Crispy Fried Quinoa (page 25)

Put the yogurt in a bowl. Stir in the lemon juice and 1 tablespoon of the olive oil, and season with a few grinds of black pepper.

Drain the reserved, shaved raw carrots and dill and pat dry with paper towels.

Shake a few dashes of sherry vinegar and drizzle the remaining 1 teaspoon olive oil over the roasted carrots. Spoon the yogurt into the bottom of a serving bowl, top with the roasted carrots, season with a pinch of fleur de sel, and finish with the raw carrots, dill, and quinoa.

Bomba Rice with Soffrito and Saffron

Serves 4

We sometimes serve this alongside the chicken for two (page 217) at our sister restaurant, Dover. Bomba is a short-grain Spanish rice with an irresistible name that is sometimes used to make paella because it absorbs the perfect amount of stock, similar to how Italian Arborio rice behaves in risotto. We stir a *soffrito*, the base of pan-fried vegetables and garlic that is the starting point for many Mediterranean recipes (this one includes tomatoes and smoked paprika) into the rice for a piquant flavor. It's good with any roasted meat or fish or on its own as a vegetarian option, or topped with a poached egg. It's also the prefect accompaniment to a grilled sausage and a cold beer. The *soffrito* recipe produces only about half a cup, but that's more than you need for this recipe. Spread the extra on toast for a snack or starter to another meal.

To Prep

1 teaspoon extra-virgin olive oil

1 Spanish onion, minced

Kosher salt

3 garlic cloves, minced

¼ teaspoon smoked paprika
(see Sources, page 321)

1 red bell pepper, peeled and minced

3 beefsteak tomatoes, peeled (see
page 313), deseeded, and minced

Freshly ground black pepper

Heat the olive oil in a medium pot over medium heat. When the oil shimmers, add the onion, season with salt, and cook, stirring, until softened but not browned, about 3 minutes. Add the garlic and paprika, season with salt, and cook, stirring, until softened but not browned, about 2 minutes. Add the bell pepper, season with salt, and cook, stirring, until it begins to give off its liquid and the liquid dries, about 3 minutes, then stir in the tomatoes, season with salt, bring to a simmer, and cook until very dry, about 20 minutes. Season with black pepper and remove the pot from the heat.

Use right away or let cool and refrigerate in an airtight container for up to 2 days.

To Serve

1¼ cups chicken stock, preferably homemade (page 317)

1 teaspoon extra-virgin olive oil

½ garlic clove, thinly sliced

½ cup Bomba rice

Pinch of saffron

1 teaspoon sherry vinegar

Kosher salt and freshly ground black pepper

1 teaspoon unsalted butter

Preheat the oven to 350°F.

Bring the stock to a simmer in a small pot over medium-high heat.

Meanwhile, heat the oil over medium heat in a medium pot with a tight-fitting lid. Add the garlic and cook, stirring occasionally, until golden, about 3 minutes. Add the rice and saffron and cook, stirring, to lightly toast the rice, about 1 minute. Stir in 2 tablespoons of the *soffrito*, then pour in the hot stock all at once. Stir in the vinegar and season with salt and pepper. Cover and cook in the oven for 15 minutes. Remove the pot from the oven and let rest, covered, for 5 minutes. Stir in the butter, fluff with a fork, and transfer to a serving dish.

Crushed Yukon Gold Potatoes with Olive Oil, Brown Butter, and Parsley

Serves 4

An elegant, lighter alternative to mashed potatoes, this side dish is simply prepared by lightly mashing steamed potatoes with a combination of fresh and browned butter. Amazingly, it can be made a couple of hours ahead of time and reheated in the microwave. It's terrific with chicken, fish, veal, and lamb.

To Prep

4 large Yukon Gold potatoes
Kosher salt
3 tablespoons extra-virgin olive oil
1 tablespoon unsalted butter
2 tablespoons browned butter (page 315)
Freshly ground black pepper

Peel the potatoes and cut them into 1-inch pieces. Put the pieces in a steamer basket, season with salt, and let rest for 5 minutes to allow the potatoes to absorb the salt.

Bring an inch of water to a simmer in a pot fitted to hold the steamer basket. Set the basket over the water, cover, and steam the potatoes until they are tender but still hold their shape, 12 to 15 minutes.

Transfer the potatoes to a bowl. Add 1½ tablespoons of the olive oil, ½ tablespoon of the unsalted butter, and 1 tablespoon of the browned butter and mash with a fork to incorporate the fats. Fold in the remaining 1½ tablespoons olive oil, ½ tablespoon unsalted butter, and 1 tablespoon browned butter and season with salt and pepper.

Use right away, or cover with plastic wrap and hold at room temperature or, ideally, in a warm place, for up to 2 hours.

To Serve

¼ cup coarsely chopped fresh
  flat-leaf parsley leaves

If they have been prepared in advance, reheat the potatoes in the microwave (be sure the bowl they are in is microwave-safe) according to your model's settings.

Fold in the parsley, transfer to a serving dish, and serve family-style.

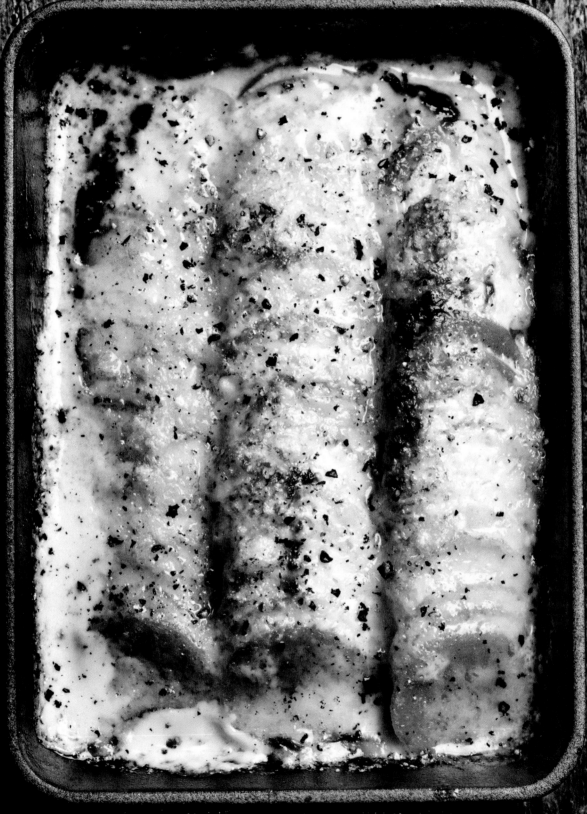

Root Vegetable Gratin

Makes 2 single-serving gratins

This gratin complements earthy autumn vegetables with a black truffle cream and Comté cheese. It's a bit labor intensive, but not particularly complicated. Note that you will need two 4 x 6 x 1-inch (deep) casseroles, ideally made of cast iron or enamel for the nicest presentation, although Pyrex dishes will work as well.

To Prep

1 small celery root

1 small sweet potato

1 small rutabaga

1 small turnip

1 small butternut squash

Kosher salt and freshly ground black
    pepper

Pinch of sugar

2 teaspoons unsalted butter

½ tablespoon chicken stock or water

2 fresh thyme sprigs

2 garlic slices

¼ cup heavy cream

1 teaspoon black truffle paste

About 3 ounces Comté cheese or other
    Alpine cheese, such as Gruyère
    or Emmenthal, thinly sliced

Preheat the oven to 350°F.

Peel the celery root, sweet potato, rutabaga, turnip, and squash and slice them on a mandoline 1/16 inch thick. You will need 32 slices of each. Use a 1-inch round cutter to punch out circles from each slice. Save the trimmings of the vegetables for other uses. (If you like, you can use all but the sweet potato in the soup; see page 287.)

Arrange two individual casseroles, ideally 4 x 6 x 1-inch (deep), on your work surface. Stack the vegetable slices in stacks of 20, alternating types and keeping the white and orange vegetables separate. Lift each stack, holding it between your thumb and forefinger, and tilt it into the casseroles, fanning the slices out. It should take two stacks of vegetables to fill each dish. (You may need to adjust the quantities slightly if using different-size casseroles.)

Season the vegetables with salt, pepper, and the sugar. Top the vegetables in each dish with 1 teaspoon of the butter and sprinkle each gratin with chicken stock. Top each gratin with a thyme sprig and a slice of garlic.

(continued)

Wrap the gratins individually in aluminum foil, sealing them tightly.

Set the dishes on a rimmed baking sheet and bake until the vegetables are soft to a cake tester or knife tip, 45 to 50 minutes.

Toward the end of the cooking time, bring the cream to a boil in a medium pot over medium-high heat. Cook until reduced by half, about 5 minutes. Reduce the heat and stir in the truffle paste. Season with pepper. Remove the vegetables from the oven and pour the cream over the vegetables in both dishes.

Preheat the broiler.

Cover the vegetables with overlapping slices of cheese. Return the baking sheet to the oven and broil until the cheese is melted and the cream is bubbling around the edges, about 3 minutes. Remove the sheet from the oven and let rest for 5 minutes. Finish and serve immediately, or let the gratins rest for up to 2 hours at room temperature.

To Serve

1 fresh black truffle (see Sources, page 321)

If the gratins have rested and cooled for much more than 5 minutes, preheat the oven to 350°F, set them on a rimmed baking sheet, and reheat for a few minutes to warm them through and re-melt the cheese. If they have only been resting for 5 minutes and are still hot, skip this step.

Top each gratin with truffle slices, either slicing right over them with a truffle slicer or by slicing the truffle on a mandoline, then scattering the slices over the gratins. Serve.

→   **PUREED VEGETABLE SOUP**   *Serves 4*

If you're looking for a good way to use the vegetable trimmings produced by making these gratins, here's a quick soup you can make with just a few additional ingredients.

2 tablespoons extra-virgin olive
    oil, plus more for serving
4 tablespoons (½ stick) unsalted butter
½ Spanish onion, thinly sliced
3 garlic cloves, smashed with the side
    of a chef's knife and peeled
About 4 cups vegetable trimmings from
    the gratin (except the sweet potato)
½ Granny Smith apple, peeled and cored
Kosher salt
1 tablespoon sugar
4 cups vegetable stock or chicken
    stock, preferably homemade
    (pages 316, 317), or water
3 tablespoons browned butter (see page 315)

Heat the oil with 2 tablespoons of the unsalted butter in a large pot over medium-high heat. When the butter foams, add the onion and garlic and cook, stirring occasionally, until softened but not browned, about 4 minutes. Stir in the vegetable trimmings and apple and season with salt and the sugar. Cook, stirring occasionally, until the vegetables are softened but not browned, about 8 minutes. Pour in the stock, bring to a simmer, and cook for 8 to 10 minutes.

Add the remaining 2 tablespoons unsalted butter and the browned butter and puree the soup directly in the pot with an immersion blender, or, working in batches, transfer it to a standing blender and puree.

Serve the soup right away or let cool and refrigerate in an airtight container for up to 2 days, reheating gently before serving. After ladling into bowls, drizzle with olive oil just before serving.

Spaetzle with Bacon, Egg, and Mushrooms

Serves 4

Spaetzle, the little dumplings common in German and Austrian cooking, are a terrific alternative to pasta or potato as a side dish, or even as a starter. We toss spaetzle with bacon, mushrooms, and an invigorating mix of sherry vinegar and herbs, then top each serving with a baked egg. When the egg is broken and the yolk is incorporated into the dish, it eats like a fancified carbonara. Serve this with roasted poultry and meats; it's especially good with chicken and pork.

To Prep

1 large egg

1 large egg yolk

6.25 ounces (1 cup) all-purpose flour

¼ cup milk

3 ounces (5 tablespoons) crème fraîche

Kosher salt

In the bowl of a stand mixer fitted with the paddle attachment, combine the egg, egg yolk, flour, milk, crème fraîche, and ¼ teaspoon salt. Beat for 4 to 5 minutes to develop the gluten; the batter will smooth out slightly but not change appreciably in appearance. Transfer to a bowl, cover with plastic wrap, and let rest for 1 hour at room temperature, or up to 24 hours in the refrigerator.

Bring a large pot of salted water to a boil. Fill a large bowl halfway with ice and water.

Press the batter through the holes of a spaetzle maker or colander into the boiling water, it will naturally break off in approximately ½-inch pieces. Cook until the spaetzle rise to the surface and toughen, 1 to 2 minutes. Use a slotted spoon to transfer them to the ice water to stop the cooking and set their shape.

Drain, pat dry with paper towels, and use right away, or refrigerate in an airtight container overnight.

To Serve

2 tablespoons unsalted butter, plus more for greasing

4 large eggs

1 tablespoon extra-virgin olive oil

2 slab bacon slices, diced

12 shiitake mushrooms, ends trimmed, larger ones halved or quartered

2 teaspoons minced shallot

1 teaspoon fines herbes (see page 44) or thinly sliced fresh flat-leaf parsley leaves

1 teaspoon sherry vinegar

¼ cup finely grated Parmigiano-Reggiano cheese

Preheat the oven to 325°F.

Grease a large, ovenproof, nonstick rimmed baking sheet with butter. Working with one egg at a time, crack the eggs onto the baking sheet. Transfer the baking sheet to the oven and cook until the whites are cooked and the yolks are set, about 5 minutes.

Meanwhile, heat the oil with 1 tablespoon of the butter in a wide, deep sauté pan. Add the bacon and mushrooms and cook, stirring occasionally, until the bacon renders much of its fat and the mushrooms begin to give off their liquid, about 6 minutes. Add the spaetzle and toss well until lightly golden brown, about 3 minutes. Add the remaining 1 tablespoon butter and toss to melt it and further coat and enrich the spaetzle.

Add the shallot, herbs, vinegar, and cheese and toss well.

Divide the spaetzle among four plates. Remove the baking sheet from the oven and use a spatula to top each serving with an egg. Serve.

Crispy Brussels Sprouts with Sriracha, Honey, and Lime

Serves 4 to 6

We've come a long way since the days when Brussels sprouts were only cooked with bacon. What was once a staple of home cooking has become an improbably popular item in restaurants, with each chef doing his or her own thing with them; this sweet-and-spicy treatment is one of our favorites.

To Prep

½ cup fresh lime juice

½ cup honey

2 tablespoons Sriracha

1 tablespoon sesame oil

2 tablespoons soy sauce

2 tablespoons rice wine vinegar

To make the dressing, put the lime juice, honey, Sriracha, sesame oil, soy sauce, and vinegar in a small container and stir together. Use right away or cover with plastic wrap and refrigerate for up to 2 days.

To Serve

Canola oil or other neutral oil, such as grapeseed, for frying

1 pound Brussels sprouts, trimmed and quartered

Kosher salt and freshly ground black pepper

¼ cup coarsely chopped shallots

3 tablespoons white or black sesame seeds, toasted (see page 314)

¼ cup loosely packed fresh cilantro leaves

If necessary, let the dressing come to room temperature.

Set up a deep-fryer, heating the oil to 350°F, or pour oil one-third of the way up the sides of a heavy pot and heat the oil over medium-high heat to 350°F.

Carefully add the Brussels sprouts to the oil and fry, turning them with a slotted spoon, until crispy and dark brown, about 2 minutes, adjusting the heat level as necessary to maintain the temperature. Lift them out of the oil with the slotted spoon and drain on paper towels. Season immediately with salt and pepper.

Transfer the Brussels sprouts to a serving bowl. Drizzle with the dressing and add the shallots, sesame seeds, and cilantro. Toss well and serve hot.

Desserts

Fennel Seed Panna Cotta with Lemon Confit

Serves 8

Our take on the classic Italian dessert infuses the cream with the anise flavor of fennel seed and tops it with tart candied lemon peel. The two components create a back and forth, the sweet citrus cleansing the palate, preparing it to receive the next hit of fennel. If you have some fresh fennel on hand, garnish the finished desserts with a frond, as shown in the photo.

To Prep

Lemon Confit Topping

2 lemons, zest removed in strips
    with a vegetable peeler, no
    pith attached, and juiced
2 tablespoons sugar
½ tablespoon fennel seed,
    toasted (page 314)

Panna Cotta

4 cups heavy cream
½ cup sugar
¼ teaspoon kosher salt
¼ cup fennel seed, toasted (see page
    314) and coarsely ground (ideally
    with a mortar and pestle)
1 envelope powdered gelatin
    (2¼ teaspoons)

Put the lemon zest in a small pot and cover with cold water. Bring the water to a boil, then immediately drain. Repeat two times. Add the lemon juice, sugar, and fennel seed to the pot and bring to a simmer over very low heat. Continue to simmer very gently until the zest is tender, about 1 hour 30 minutes. Remove the pot from the heat and let the zest cool in its syrup. Use right away or store the confit in its syrup in an airtight container in the refrigerator for up to 3 days.

Put the cream, sugar, and salt in a medium pot and bring to a simmer, stirring to dissolve the sugar. Turn off the heat, stir in the fennel seed, cover, and let steep for 15 minutes to infuse the cream with fennel flavor.

Meanwhile, put ¼ cup plus 2 tablespoons cold water in a wide, spouted, heatproof measuring cup, such as a Pyrex cup, with a capacity of at least 4 cups. Sprinkle the gelatin over the water and let it bloom for at least 5 minutes.

After the cream has steeped, pour it through a fine-mesh strainer into the measuring cup with the gelatin. Discard the crushed fennel seed and whisk the mixture to dissolve the gelatin. Pour the mixture into eight ½-cup serving vessels, let cool, then cover with plastic wrap and refrigerate until set, at least 3 hours, or up to 2 days.

To Serve

Remove the panna cottas from the refrigerator and let them come to room temperature for 10 minutes. Garnish with the lemon confit and serve.

Date and Almond Cigars with Honey and Whipped Cream

Serves 4

One last nod to Ducasse: These "cigars," filled with a date and almond paste, are, no exaggeration, one of the best things we have ever tasted. The combination of sweet filling, crunchy filo, and honeyed whipped cream are utter perfection. Because they can be frozen, you might want to make these in batches and keep them on hand.

To Prep

Date and Almond Cigars

17.5 ounces (about 2¼ cups) marzipan

½ cup chopped pitted dates

½ cup almonds, toasted (see page 314) and chopped

Finely grated zest and juice of 1 orange

Kosher salt

24 filo dough sheets

3 tablespoons butter, melted

Put the marzipan, dates, almonds, orange zest and juice, and ½ teaspoon of salt in a medium bowl and mix well with a spatula; the mixture will be pasty and firm.

To assemble the cigars, stack 2 sheets of filo on a clean, dry work surface. Brush them with melted butter. Spoon a cigarette-size roll of filling about 1 inch from the end closest to you and roll the filo up tightly around the filling. Repeat with the remaining filo and filling to make 12 cigars.

Use right away or wrap the prepared cigars in plastic and refrigerate for up to 24 hours, or freeze for up to 1 month. They are easiest to cook from the frozen state and do not need to be defrosted.

Honey Whipped Cream

¾ cup heavy cream

1 tablespoon honey

½ vanilla bean, halved lengthwise and seeds scraped

In the bowl of a stand mixer fitted with the whisk attachment, combine the cream, honey, and vanilla bean seeds and whip on medium speed until soft peaks form. Use right away or refrigerate in an airtight container for up to 1 hour.

To Serve

Canola oil or other neutral oil, such as grapeseed, for frying

Honey, for drizzling

Pour the oil into a medium pot so it comes one-third of the way up the sides and heat until shimmering. Working in batches, add the cigars, without crowding, to the oil, and fry until crispy and golden brown, 3 to 4 minutes.

As they are done, drain the cigars briefly on paper towels. Transfer 3 cigars to each of four plates, drizzle with honey, and serve with the whipped cream alongside for dipping.

Pan-Roasted Fruits with Vanilla Mascarpone

Serves 4

Vary the fruits in this dessert according to what's in season or looks good at the market; tossing them in butter and sugar will pull all the flavors together, allowing for almost any combination to work.

To Prep

8 ounces mascarpone cheese

2 tablespoons sugar

1 vanilla bean, halved lengthwise and seeds scraped

In the bowl of a stand mixer fitted with the whisk attachment, combine the mascarpone, sugar, and vanilla bean seeds and whip on the highest speed until smooth, about 1 minute. Use right away or refrigerate in an airtight container for up to 24 hours.

To Serve

2 tablespoons unsalted butter

1 pear, peeled, quartered, cored (see page 61), and cut into wedges

1 peach, peeled, pitted, and cut into wedges

1 banana, thinly sliced

1 cup strawberries, hulled, larger ones halved

½ cup blueberries

About 2 teaspoons sugar

1 tablespoon fresh lemon juice

8 fresh mint leaves

Spread the vanilla mascarpone onto four plates and set them aside.

Heat a wide, deep sauté pan over medium-high heat. Add the butter and when it foams, add the pear, peach, banana, strawberries, and blueberries. Season with sugar (the sweeter the fruits, the less sugar you will need) and cook, tossing, until lightly caramelized, about 5 minutes. Toss in the lemon juice and spoon the fruits over the mascarpone on each plate. Garnish with mint and serve.

Buttermilk Biscuits with Macerated Strawberries and Sweet Cream

Serves 4

This rather straightforward version of strawberry shortcake gets a strong hit of flavor from macerating the berries in Armagnac.

To Prep

2 cups all-purpose flour, plus
    more for dusting
8 tablespoons (1 stick) unsalted butter
1 teaspoon kosher salt
1 teaspoon sugar
1 tablespoon baking powder
¾ cup heavy cream

Preheat the oven to 350°F.

Put the flour, butter, salt, sugar, and baking powder in a large bowl and knead by hand until they come together in a coarse crumb. Add the cream all at once, kneading it in to form a dough just until it comes together, without overworking.

Dust a clean, dry work surface with flour. Press the dough down and roll it out to a ½-inch-thick rectangle. Gently fold it over once as though closing a book and use a 2½-inch cutter to punch out 4 circles.

Line a baking sheet with parchment paper and arrange the circles on the parchment about 1 inch apart. Transfer the baking sheet to the refrigerator and chill for at least 10 minutes. Bake until lightly golden, 18 to 20 minutes. (Alternatively, the circles can be held in the refrigerator for up to 24 hours—bake in a preheated 350°F oven as directed.)

Remove the baking sheet from the oven and let the biscuits cool to room temperature. Use right away or store in an airtight container at room temperature for up to 8 hours.

To Serve

1 quart hulled, quartered strawberries
1 tablespoon sugar
2 tablespoons Armagnac,
    cognac, or Grand Marnier
Whipped cream (see page 315)

Put the strawberries in a bowl. Dust with the sugar and sprinkle with the Armagnac. Toss gently and let macerate for 10 minutes.

To serve, set one biscuit in each of four bowls. Spoon some strawberries over each biscuit and finish with a heaping tablespoon of whipped cream. Serve.

Blueberry Clafoutis

Serves 4

Our clafoutis are different from most, more custardy than cakelike, thanks to some unusual ingredients, especially heavy cream. You can adapt this recipe to make it with any fruit you like without altering any of the other quantities; cherries, berries, and peaches are terrific.

To Prep

Unsalted butter or nonstick
   cooking spray, for greasing

1 cup sugar, plus more for sprinkling

4 large eggs

1 cup cornstarch

1 cup almond flour

1½ cups heavy cream

1 tablespoon honey

1 teaspoon pure vanilla extract

Kosher salt

1 cup blueberries

Preheat the oven to 400°F. Butter four 6-ounce soufflé molds, then sprinkle sugar into each one, turning the molds to coat with the sugar, and pour out any excess sugar.

In the bowl of a stand mixer fitted with the whisk attachment, combine the eggs, sugar, cornstarch, almond flour, cream, honey, and vanilla. Season with a pinch of salt. Whip on medium speed until well incorporated, 2 to 3 minutes. Remove the bowl from the mixer. Set aside 20 blueberries for garnish and fold the remaining blueberries into the batter by hand.

Pour the batter into the molds, but do not fill them all the way—the clafoutis will rise when baked. Set the molds on a rimmed baking sheet and bake for 8 minutes, then rotate and bake until a cake tester or toothpick inserted into the center of a clafoutis comes out clean, the batter is set, and the clafoutis are puffy and browned, 8 to 10 minutes more. Use right away, while still hot, or hold at room temperature for up to 2 hours.

To Serve

Confectioners' sugar

1 pint ice cream of your choice (optional)

If the clafoutis have cooled, reheat them on the baking sheet in a preheated 400°F oven for a few minutes.

Carefully invert the clafoutis onto individual plates, unmold them, and garnish with the reserved blueberries and confectioners' sugar. Serve with ice cream alongside, if desired.

Olive Oil Cake with Mascarpone and Candied Orange Peel

Serves 8

Olive oil cakes are almost foolproof because they are so moist, made with lots of egg and, of course, olive oil, that they don't require a deft baker's touch and almost never dry out in the oven. Ours gets extra flavor from an application of amaretto syrup that soaks into the cake just before serving, and a topping of flavored mascarpone and candied orange zest. If you plan to make this, save the skins of mandarin oranges for the zest; they have no pith, making them ideal for candying. If making with mandarin zest, simply break it up into pieces rather than peeling it into strips for a rustic effect; multiply the amounts of sugar and honey as necessary to cover it when candying.

To Prep

Candied Orange Peel

Zest of 1 orange, removed in strips with a vegetable peeler, no pith attached

½ cup fresh orange juice (use the orange above after zesting; you may need a second orange depending on size and yield)

1 cup sugar

2 tablespoons honey

1 vanilla bean, halved lengthwise and seeds scraped

Put the orange zest in a small pot and cover with cold water. Bring the water to a boil, then immediately drain. Repeat two times. Add ½ cup cold water, the orange juice, sugar, honey, and vanilla pod and seeds to the pot and bring to a simmer over very low heat. Continue to gently simmer until the zest is tender, about 1 hour 30 minutes. Remove the pot from the heat and let the zest cool in its syrup (remove the vanilla pod and use in the Amaretto Syrup or reserve for another use). Use right away or store the candied peel in its syrup in an airtight container in the refrigerator for up to 3 days.

Amaretto Syrup

1 cup sugar

1 vanilla bean (you can use the same bean pod used in the orange zest confit)

About 2 tablespoons amaretto

Put the sugar, vanilla bean, and 1 cup cold water in a small pot and heat over medium-high heat, whisking continuously, until the sugar has dissolved, about 5 minutes. Remove the pot from the heat and let the syrup cool, then whisk in the amaretto, adding more to taste, if you like. The syrup can be used right away or refrigerated in an airtight container for up to 24 hours.

Mascarpone Cream

4 ounces mascarpone cheese

1 cup heavy cream

1 tablespoon sugar

½ teaspoon pure vanilla extract

½ vanilla bean, halved length-wise and seeds scraped

In the bowl of a stand mixer fitted with the whisk attachment, combine the mascarpone, cream, sugar, vanilla extract, and vanilla bean seeds and whisk on low speed until fluffy, about 3 minutes. Use right away or refrigerate in an airtight container for up to 4 hours.

Olive Oil Cake

Nonstick cooking spray

1½ cups all-purpose flour, plus more for dusting

3 large eggs

¼ cup milk

¾ cup extra-virgin olive oil

1 cup sugar

Finely grated zest of 2 lemons

Finely grated zest of 1 orange

⅔ cup almond flour

½ teaspoon kosher salt

2 teaspoons baking powder

Preheat the oven to 350°F. Spray a 9-inch round cake pan with nonstick cooking spray, dust with flour, turning the pan to coat it with the flour, and pour out any excess flour.

Put the eggs, milk, olive oil, sugar, lemon and orange zest, almond flour, all-purpose flour, salt, and baking powder in a medium bowl. Whisk together by hand until well incorporated.

Pour the batter into the prepared pan and set the pan on a rimmed baking sheet. Bake until the cake rises and is golden brown, and a cake tester or toothpick inserted into the center comes out clean, 45 to 50 minutes.

Remove the cake from the oven, unmold onto a cooling rack, and let cool. Use right away or let rest at room temperature on a covered cake stand for up to 8 hours.

To Serve

Slice the cake into individual portions. Set each portion on a plate and spoon the amaretto syrup over the cake, letting the cake soak it up and using all the syrup. Top each serving with mascarpone cream and confit orange peel. Serve.

Banana Lime Tart with Dulce de Leche

Serves 4

The sweet caramel dulce de leche might seem an unlikely pairing with bananas and lime zest, but the three get along great in this easy-to-assemble dessert. If you've never made dulce de leche from sweetened condensed milk, you're in for a treat—the transformation, arrived at by simply boiling the milk in the can, is amazing, and the dulce has many applications, from spreading on toast to topping desserts.

To Prep

1 (14-ounce) can sweetened condensed milk

Set the can in a large pot and cover with cold water by a few inches, leaving a few inches between the water and the top of the pot. Bring the water to a boil over high heat, then reduce the heat to low, cover the pot, and simmer for 3 hours, periodically checking the water level and adding more if necessary to keep the can covered. Remove the lid and use tongs to remove the can from the pot; it will be very hot. Set the can aside to cool for at least 2 hours. Do not attempt to open it during this time because the heat creates pressure inside that can cause the hot dulce de leche to "explode."

Once completely cooled, open the can and use a rubber spatula to transfer the dulce de leche to an airtight container. Use right away or refrigerate for up to 3 days.

To Serve

2 bananas, cut crosswise into ⅛-inch slices

Zest and juice of 1 lime

1 tablespoon sugar

8 (2-inch) round tart shells (recipe follows)

Whipped cream (see page 315)

Put the banana slices in a medium bowl, add the lime zest and juice and the sugar, and toss very gently to coat the bananas. Set aside.

Spoon 1 tablespoon of dulce de leche into each tart shell and gently spread it with a spatula to cover the bottom. Layer the banana slices in overlapping circles over the caramel. Top with whipped cream and serve.

Tart Shell Dough

Makes 8 (2½-inch) round, 4 (4-inch) round, or 4 (5 x 2-inch) rectangular tart shells

Our recipe for a basic tart shell. The trick to baking it successfully is to have it at just the right temperature for rolling; it should be neither too warm nor too cold, but just in between, pliable but not too soft. If you find yourself with extra dough, you can make cookies with it by rolling it out, cutting it into desired shapes, arranging them on a parchment paper–lined baking sheet, topping them with Sugar in the Raw, and baking them at 350°F until light golden brown; the baking time will vary based on size.

8 tablespoons (1 stick) plus 3 tablespoons unsalted butter

½ cup sugar

½ vanilla bean, halved lengthwise and seeds scraped

½ teaspoon pure vanilla extract

1 large egg

1¾ cups all-purpose flour, plus more for dusting

In the bowl of a stand mixer fitted with the paddle attachment, combine the butter, sugar, vanilla bean seeds, vanilla extract, and egg and beat on medium-low speed until just incorporated, about 3 minutes, then beat in the flour until incorporated.

Turn out the dough onto your work surface, press it down into a flat shape to make it easier to roll, wrap in plastic, and refrigerate until firm; timing will depend on a number of factors, but you want it pliable but not too soft. If it becomes too cold or firm in the refrigerator, leave it out at room temperature briefly before rolling.

When ready to proceed, preheat the oven to 375°F.

Unwrap the dough, dust a work surface with flour, and roll the dough out with a floured rolling pin to a thickness of ⅛ inch. You will need to constantly reflour the rolling pin and occasionally turn the dough over to keep them from sticking to each other.

Cut the dough into shapes slightly larger than your mold(s). For example, for 2½-inch molds, punch out 3 ¼-inch circles with a cutter. Press the dough into the mold(s) and press it to the sides. Trim any overhang with a paring knife and discard it or use it to make cookies (see headnote). (For the rectangular tarts on page 310, simply cut rectangles from the rolled-out dough.)

Prick the dough all over with a fork, line with parchment paper, fill with dried beans or pie weights, and bake until light golden, about 16 minutes. Remove the shell(s) from the oven. When cool enough to handle, remove the pie weights, and let the shell(s) cool completely. The tart shell(s) can be held for up to 1 day, covered, at room temperature.

Apricots with Honey and Sweet Ricotta

Serves 4

This exceedingly simple dessert hails from the days before we had a pastry chef at Battersby and needed our desserts to be quick to plate and serve. We change the fruits in this tart seasonally. This is one of our favorite versions. It is also wonderful made with cherries or figs in the summer. (See photo on page 293.)

To Prep

1 cup ricotta cheese

2 tablespoons honey

Finely grated zest of 1 lemon

1 tablespoon fruity extra-virgin olive oil (optional)

In the bowl of a food processor fitted with the steel blade, combine the ricotta, honey, lemon zest, and olive oil (if using), and process just until incorporated and smooth, about 1 minute.

Use right away or refrigerate in an airtight container for up to 24 hours.

To Serve

2 large or 4 small apricots, cut into thin wedges (eighths or sixteenths, depending on the size of the apricots)

Juice of ½ lemon

4 (5 x 2-inch) rectangular tart shells (see page 308)

Honey

½ cup crushed nuts of your choice, such as almonds or walnuts

Put the apricots and lemon juice in a medium bowl and toss together. Top the tart shells with the apricots, drizzle with honey, and top with the nuts. Serve.

Chocolate Bread Pudding

Serves 6

This conventional chocolate bread pudding balances the decadence of chocolate with the airiness of brioche. The ice cream is optional but a high-quality, vanilla-based flavor makes a perfect foil for the rich pudding.

To Prep

2 to 3 tablespoons unsalted butter, for greasing

¾ cup sugar, plus more for sprinkling

1 cup milk

1½ cups heavy cream

½ vanilla bean, halved lengthwise and seeds scraped

½ teaspoon pure vanilla extract

1 large egg yolk

2 large eggs

3 ounces dark chocolate, coarsely chopped

1 ounce milk chocolate, coarsely chopped

½ pound brioche loaf, crusts removed, cut into ½-inch cubes

Preheat the oven to 350°F. Butter six ½-cup ramekins, then sprinkle sugar into each one, turning the ramekin to coat it with the sugar, and pour out any excess sugar.

Put the milk, cream, sugar, vanilla bean seeds, and vanilla extract in a large pot and bring to a boil over medium-high heat. Remove the pot from the heat and whisk in the egg yolk and whole eggs gradually, so as not to scramble the eggs. Whisk in 2 ounces of the dark chocolate and the milk chocolate until melted, then fold in the brioche cubes.

Pour the brioche mixture into the ramekins, layering in the remaining pieces of chopped dark chocolate (they will melt and create pockets of chocolate as the dessert bakes).

Set the ramekins in a roasting pan and pour warm water about ¼ inch up their sides. Bake until set but not overly dry, about 16 minutes. Use tongs or oven mitts to remove the ramekins from the roasting pan.

Use right away or cover loosely with plastic wrap and hold at room temperature for up to 8 hours.

To Serve

1 pint ice cream of your choice (optional)

If the bread puddings have cooled, reheat them briefly on a rimmed baking sheet in a preheated 350°F oven.

Serve the pudding with ice cream on top or alongside, if desired.

Basic Techniques and Recipes

CUTTING CITRUS SUPREMES   To make citrus supremes, cut off both ends of the citrus, then stand the fruit on one of its flat ends on the cutting board. Remove the peel—pith and membrane—by cutting from top to bottom and following the contours of the fruit; continue to cut off strips of the peel until it's all removed and the pulp is exposed. Hold the peeled fruit in one hand and slice between the membrane and pulp of each segment, removing each membrane-free segment as you work your way around the fruit. Take care to keep the segments intact.

BLANCHING AND SHOCKING VEGETABLES   To blanch vegetables, fill a large pot two-thirds full with salted water and bring to a boil over high heat. Fill a large bowl halfway with ice and water. When the salted water is boiling, add the vegetables and blanch until al dente, 1 to 3 minutes depending on size, density, and thickness. Drain the vegetables in a colander or strainer, then transfer the vegetables to the ice water to "shock" them, stopping the cooking and preserving their natural color. Drain again.

    FOR FAVA BEANS: Fava beans require two steps to be fully peeled. Working with one fava bean pod at a time, pull the "string" that runs along the seam and open up the pod. Blanch the fava beans and shock them. Drain. Squeeze each fava bean between your thumb and forefinger to force the fava out of its skin. The favas can be used right away or refrigerated in an airtight container for up to 24 hours.

PEELING TOMATOES   To peel tomatoes, bring a medium pot of water to a boil over high heat. Fill a large bowl halfway with ice and water. Use a paring knife to cut out the core from the top of the tomato, where the stem meets the flesh, then cut a shallow "X" in the bottom of the tomato. Lower the tomatoes into the boiling water and cook until the peel begins to pull away, about 15 seconds. Use tongs or a slotted spoon to transfer the tomatoes to the ice water to stop the cooking. Once cooled, use the paring knife to help you pull off the skin.

TOMATO CONFIT   To make these oven-dried tomato petals, preheat the oven to 275°F. Peel 3 plum tomatoes (see above) and cut the pulp from them. (If making the tomato confit for the gazpacho on page 100, save the pulp.) Set a piece of aluminum foil on a rimmed baking sheet and brush it with extra-virgin olive oil. Set the tomatoes on the foil with the cut sides up. Season with salt and sugar; the paler the tomatoes, the more sugar you should add. Drizzle with olive oil and bake until slightly shriveled and dry, about 90 minutes, turning the tomatoes over after about 45 minutes. The tomatoes can be used right away or refrigerated in an airtight container for up to 3 days. To make more tomato confit, simply use more tomatoes.

TOASTING NUTS AND SPICES Put nuts or spices in a wide sauté pan, set over medium-high heat, and cook, shaking the pan slightly to prevent scorching and ensure even cooking, until lightly toasted and fragrant, usually 2 to 3 minutes.

FRYING GARLIC OR SHALLOTS To fry garlic or shallots, simply heat an inch or two of canola oil, or another neutral oil such as grapeseed, in a small pot over medium-high heat. Thinly slice the desired quantity of garlic or shallots, dredge in all-purpose flour, shaking off any excess, and add to the oil (if the oil doesn't bubble around the first piece, it's not hot enough yet). Fry just until crispy and golden, a few seconds, then use a slotted spoon to transfer the garlic or shallots to paper towels to drain and season immediately with salt. The fried shallots or garlic are best fresh from frying, but can be held in an airtight container at room temperature for up to 24 hours.

BRIOCHE CROUTONS To make brioche croutons, remove and discard the crust from a section of brioche and cut enough bread into ½-inch cubes to yield ½ cup. (You should use about one 3-inch section of brioche.) Put the bread in a large bowl, drizzle with 1 tablespoon extra-virgin olive oil, and season with salt and pepper. Toss well, then spread out the bread cubes on a rimmed baking sheet and bake until lightly golden, shaking the baking sheet occasionally to ensure even cooking, about 8 minutes. Remove the baking sheet from the oven and let the croutons cool. The croutons can be used right away or stored in an airtight container at room temperature for up to 24 hours. Makes ½ cup; to make more, simply multiply the ingredients according to desired yield.

For more flavorful croutons, use the same amount of diced brioche as above. Melt 2 tablespoons unsalted butter in a small pan over medium-high heat. When the butter foams, add the brioche. Cook, tossing or stirring every 30 seconds, until lightly golden brown on all sides, 2 to 3 minutes. Add 1 smashed garlic clove, 1 fresh thyme sprig, and a pinch of salt and toss for a few seconds. Drain on paper towels, discarding the garlic and

thyme. The croutons can be held at room temperature for up to 2 hours. Makes ½ cup; to make more, simply multiply the ingredients according to desired yield.

FRYING NUTS To fry nuts, first make a simple syrup by cooking equal quantities water and sugar over high heat, whisking until the sugar dissolves. You want about the same volume of syrup as nuts, so let that be your guide for how much to make. Add a pinch of sugar and reduce the heat so the syrup is simmering. Add the desired type of nut and simmer very gently, covered, until very tender; the time will vary greatly depending on the type of nut, with pine nuts being the fastest, 25 to 35 minutes, and walnuts and pecans taking a bit longer; very hard nuts can take up to 1 hour. To test for doneness, remove a nut with a slotted spoon, let it cool, and eat it. Drain the nuts in a fine-mesh strainer, saving the syrup for another use or discarding it. Set the nuts aside while you heat a few inches of canola oil or other neutral oil in a deep, heavy pot to a temperature of 325°F, then carefully add the nuts and cook for 5 to 8 minutes or until the bubbles stop, indicating that the nuts have given up all their moisture.

Transfer the nuts to a baking sheet and let cool, then drain on paper towels. (Do not go directly from the pot to paper towels, or the coating on the nuts will stick to the paper.) Fried nuts can be used right away or stored in an airtight container at room temperature for up to 1 week.

PICKLING VEGETABLES To pickle vegetables, clean and trim the vegetables to be pickled and transfer them to an 8-ounce mason jar, filling the jar. Add 1 tablespoon pickling spices and 1 crushed garlic clove. Make a brine by putting ¼ cup plus 3 tablespoons water, 3 tablespoons rice wine vinegar, 3 tablespoons sugar, and 1 tablespoon kosher salt in a small pot and bringing the mixture to a boil over high heat. When the salt and sugar have dissolved, pour the brine over the vegetables in the mason jar and let cool. The pickled vegetables can be used right away but are best after being covered and refrigerated for at least 24 hours; they will keep in the refrigerator for up to 1 year. To make 16-ounce batches, use a 16-ounce mason jar and double the ingredients.

GARLIC CONFIT   To make these soft, spreadable cloves of garlic, preheat the oven to 275°F. Separate the cloves of a head of garlic, leaving the skin on, and gather them in a small baking dish. Pour in just enough extra-virgin olive oil to cover them and cook in the oven until a cake tester or knife tip slides into the cloves with no resistance, 45 minutes to 1 hour. Remove the dish from the oven and let the garlic cool in the oil. Once cool enough to handle, squeeze the soft garlic from the skins. Use right away or refrigerate in an airtight container for up to 3 days.

TOASTED BREAD CRUMBS   To make toasted bread crumbs, preheat the oven to 275°F. Dice day-old bread and put it in a bowl. (If you do not have any day-old bread, you can lightly toast bread in a low oven until just hardened.) Grate 1 or 2 garlic cloves, depending on the intensity of flavor desired, into the bowl using a Microplane. Pick the thyme leaves from 2 or 3 sprigs and add them to the bowl, then drizzle with extra-virgin olive oil and season with salt and pepper. Spread the bread out on a rimmed baking sheet and bake, shaking occasionally to ensure even cooking, until lightly golden, completely dry, and hardened, 30 to 35 minutes. Transfer to the bowl of a food processor fitted with the steel blade and pulse to crumbs, but do not overprocess or they will become sandy. Bread crumbs can be held in an airtight container at room temperature for several weeks.

BROWNED BUTTER   We suggest making browned butter in large quantities because it keeps well in the refrigerator for several weeks and it's almost impossible to make smaller amounts without leaving the fat in; by making a large quantity, you have the luxury of straining out the fat for a "clarified" effect. To make browned butter, put a stick or more of unsalted butter in a sauté pan and slowly melt it over low heat, then continue to cook until the butter browns and the fats separate. Strain the butter through a fine-mesh strainer,

ideally but not necessarily lined with cheesecloth, discarding the fat, and use right away, or let cool and refrigerate in an airtight container for up to 2 weeks. You can stir it into recipes without tempering it, letting it melt into preparations as they cook.

CLARIFIED BUTTER   To clarify butter, put it in a small, heavy pot and melt it over low heat, not allowing it to brown. When the butter melts and the milk solids separate, remove the pot from the heat. Use a tablespoon to skim off the solids that have risen to the top and carefully pour out the butterfat, leaving any remaining solids at the bottom of the pot behind. Two sticks of butter will yield about ¾ cup clarified butter.

WHIPPED CREAM   To make whipped cream, put ½ cup heavy cream and 1 teaspoon sugar in the bowl of a stand mixer fitted with the whisk attachment and beat until soft peaks form, about 5 minutes. (You can also whip the cream in a bowl with a hand mixer or by hand with a whisk, although it will take longer.) Use the whipped cream right away or refrigerate in an airtight container for up to 24 hours. You may need to briefly whisk by hand to reincorporate any liquid before serving.

Vegetable Stock

2 tablespoons canola oil or other
  neutral oil, such as grapeseed
½ fennel bulb, thickly sliced
1 large carrot, cut into 3 large pieces
1 leek, white and light green parts
  only, quartered through the
  root and well washed
1 celery stalk, cut into 3 large pieces
½ Spanish onion, cut into 3 large pieces
3 garlic cloves, smashed with the side
  of a chef's knife and peeled
4 fresh flat-leaf parsley sprigs
3 bay leaves, preferably fresh
Kosher salt

Makes about 2 quarts

Note: *You do not have to use all of the vegetables listed, although it's best to do so.*

Heat the oil in a deep pot over medium heat. Add the fennel, carrot, leek, celery, onion, garlic, parsley, and bay leaves. Season with a generous pinch of salt and cook, stirring, until the vegetables are softened but not browned, about 6 minutes.

Pour in enough cold water to cover the vegetables by 2 inches, bring to a simmer, reduce the heat to low, and continue to simmer for 1 hour.

Strain the stock through a chinois or fine-mesh strainer into a heatproof container. Use right away, or let cool and refrigerate in an airtight container for up to 3 days or freeze in batches for up to 1 month.

Shrimp Stock

1 pound medium head-on shrimp
  (about 16 shrimp)
2 tablespoons extra-virgin olive oil
1 large shallot, thinly sliced
1 large celery stalk, thinly sliced
1 large carrot, thinly sliced
½ sliced fennel bulb, thinly sliced
4 garlic cloves, smashed with the side
  of a chef's knife and peeled
½ tablespoon tomato paste
3 tablespoons cognac
¼ cup dry white wine
6 cups chicken stock, preferably homemade (page 317)
1 teaspoon fresh lemon juice
Kosher salt and freshly ground black
  pepper

Makes about 1½ quarts

Coarsely chop the shrimp in their shells using a cleaver or heavy kitchen knife, to make a coarse paste. (They can also be pulsed in the bowl of a food processor fitted with the steel blade.)

Heat the oil in a medium pot over medium-high heat. Add the shrimp and cook, stirring occasionally, until bright red, about 2 minutes. Add the shallot, celery, carrot, fennel, and garlic and cook, stirring occasionally, until softened but not browned, about 6 minutes. Add the tomato paste, stirring to coat the vegetables, and cook for 2 minutes. Stir in the cognac, bring to a simmer, and simmer until almost completely evaporated, about 2 minutes. Pour in the wine, bring to a simmer, and simmer until almost completely evaporated, about 4 minutes. Pour in the stock, bring to a simmer, and simmer until intensely flavored, 20 to 30 minutes.

Strain the stock through a chinois or fine-mesh strainer into a heatproof container. Stir in the lemon juice and season with salt and pepper. Use right away, refrigerate in an airtight container for up to 3 days, or freeze in batches for up to 1 month.

Chicken Stock

Makes about 2½ quarts

6 pounds chicken bones, hacked into large
   pieces with a cleaver or heavy knife

1 Spanish onion, coarsely chopped

1 large carrot, coarsely chopped

1 celery stalk, coarsely chopped

1 head of garlic, halved

2 fresh thyme sprigs

3 fresh flat-leaf parsley sprigs

1 teaspoon whole black peppercorns

1 bay leaf, preferably fresh

Put the chicken bones in a large pot and add enough cold water to cover them by 2 inches. Bring to a gentle simmer over medium-high heat, then add the onion, carrot, celery, garlic, thyme, parsley, peppercorns, and bay leaf. Skim any fat and impurities that rise to the surface. Reduce the heat to low and continue to simmer, uncovered, for 6 hours, or up to overnight, to further focus the flavor.

Strain the stock through a chinois or fine-mesh strainer into a heatproof container. Use right away, or let cool and refrigerate in an airtight container for up to 3 days, or freeze in batches for up to 1 month.

Sources

00 flour
buonitalia.com

Ascorbic acid powder (vitamin C)
amazon.com

Black truffle
dartagnan.com

Black truffle paste
deananddeluca.com

Calabrian chilies (sold by Tutto
Calabria brand as "hot long chili
peppers")
buonitalia.com

Castelvetrano olives
amazon.com

Caul fat
heritagefoodsusa.com

Cheeses
murrayscheese.com

Colatura
zingermans.com

Cookware
staubusa.com

Dried shrimp
amazon.com

Duck and duck fat
dartagnan.com

Foie gras and foie gras terrine
dartagnan.com

Kaffir lime leaves
kalustyans.com

Korean chili powder
kalustyans.com

Meredith Dairy sheep and goat
cheese blend
igourmet.com

Palm sugar
kalustyans.com

Pickled ramps
blackberryfarm.com

Pimentón de la Vera
spicehouse.com

Pink curing salt (sodium nitrite)
amazon.com

Piquillo peppers
kalustyans.com

Ponzu
kalustyans.com

Porcini powder
kalustyans.com

Sea urchin
catalinaop.com

Shishito peppers
melissas.com

Smoked paprika
spicehouse.com

Squid ink
almagourmet.com

Sweetbreads
dartagnan.com

Verjus
wolffer.com

Vin jaune
chateauchalon.com

Acknowledgments

Our great thanks to…

Our agent, David Black, for helping to conceive the book and seeing it through from proposal to publication.

Photographer Tuukka Koski, for his great eye and one-of-a-kind dramatic visuals; and to Tuukka's team: prop stylist Pamela Silver, photographic assistant Martin Scott Powell, and prop assistant Dylan Wilde.

Designer Lotta Nieminen, for bringing a distinct and elegant look to this book.

Our editor, Karen Murgolo, for her early belief and enthusiasm, and for letting us keep the rabbit.

Editorial assistant Morgan Hedden, for her help along the way.

The food media of New York City and the United States, for their support and attention.

Our teams at Battersby and Dover, for helping us get it done every day.

And to our customers—it's our sincere honor to cook for you.

Index

scallions (*cont.*)
    Grilled Rabbit Legs with
        Grilled Vegetables and
        Bagna Cauda, 230–31
scallops
    how to cook, 175
    Marinated Scallops with
        Cherries, Almonds,
        and Tarragon
        Tempura, 66, *67*, 68
    Seared Scallops with
        Spinach and Aromatic
        Vegetable Broth, 174–75
seafood cocktail
    Cóctel de Mariscos, 32–33
sea urchin
    Spaghetti alla Chitarra
        with Sea Urchin and
        Chili, 130, *131*, 132
shallots
    frying, 314
    Shallot Marmalade, 249
shishito peppers
    Garganelli with Chicken
        Sugo and Peppers,
        133, *134*, 135
    Grilled Rabbit Legs with
        Grilled Vegetables and
        Bagna Cauda, 230–31
    Watermelon Salad with
        Shishito Peppers and
        Feta, 46, *47*, 48
Short Rib Pastrami with
    Braised Cabbage and
    Red Bliss Potatoes,
    246–48
shrimp
    cleaning tip, 33
    Cóctel de Mariscos,
        32–33
    Corn Soup with Shrimp,
        106
    Shrimp Sauce, 69
    Shrimp Stock, 316
    Shrimp with Pimentón
        Pepper, Potato, and
        Chorizo, *176*, 177–78

Vegetables à la Grecque
    with Shrimp, 69, *70*,
    71
Snail Butter, 129
    Lamb Loin with Spring
        Vegetables and Snail
        Butter, 253–54, *255*
    Risotto-Style
        Strozzapreti with
        Spring Vegetables and
        Snail Butter, 126–27,
        128, 129
snow peas
    Crudités with Aioli, 22,
        23
    Spring Peas with Lemon
        and Manchego, *41*,
        45
Sofrito, 279
soups. *See* broths;
    consommé; gazpacho;
    stocks; velouté; *specific
    soups*
sour cream
    Caviar Pie, 29, *30*, 31
Sourdough Croutons, 52
Spaetzle with Bacon, Egg,
    and Mushrooms,
    288–89
Spaghetti alla Chitarra
    with Sea Urchin and
    Chili, 130, *131*, 132
spinach
    Seared Scallops with
        Spinach and Aromatic
        Vegetable Broth,
        174–75
Squid Ink Tagliatelle, *144*,
    145–46, 166
Sriracha, 33
    Crispy Brussels Sprouts
        with Sriracha, Honey,
        and Lime, *290*, 291
    Steak Tartare with Crispy
        Artichokes and an
        Herb Salad, 82, *83*,
        84

stocks
    Chicken Stock, 317
    Corn Stock, 106
    Shrimp Stock, 316
    Vegetable Stock, 316
strawberries
    Buttermilk Biscuits
        with Macerated
        Strawberries and
        Sweet Cream, 300, *301*
    Pan-Roasted Fruits with
        Vanilla Mascarpone,
        299
    Tomato and Strawberry
        Soup with Basil and
        Balsamic Vinegar, *20*, 21
    Striped Bass with Braised
        Fennel and Tomato
        Confit, 197, *198*, 199
    Strozzapreti, Risotto-Style,
        with Spring Vegetables
        and Snail Butter,
        126–27, *128*, 129
    Summer Fruit Panzanella,
        212, 213–14
sunchokes
    Greek Yogurt with Root
        Vegetable Muesli, 24
    Sunchokes with Orange,
        Pistachio, and Aged
        Pecorino, 274, *275*
sweet potatoes
    Greek Yogurt with Root
        Vegetable Muesli, 24
    Root Vegetable Gratin,
        282, 283, *284–85*, 286
Swiss chard
    Stuffed Rabbit with
        Spring Greens, 232,
        233–35, 236, *237–39*
    Veal Loin with Swiss
        Chard, Tomato, and
        Green Garlic, 262–63

syrups
    Amaretto Syrup, 305
    simple syrup, 314

Tagliatelle, Squid Ink, *144*,
    145–46, 166
tarragon
    fines herbes, 44
    Herbs and Lettuces with
        Crispy Quinoa and
        White Mushroom, 42,
        43, 44
    Marinated Scallops with
        Cherries, Almonds,
        and Tarragon
        Tempura, 66, *67*, 68
    Steak Tartare with
        Crispy Artichokes and
        an Herb Salad, 82,
        83, 84
tarts
    Apricots with Honey and
        Sweet Ricotta, 310
    Banana Lime Tart with
        Dulce de Leche, *306*,
        307
    Tart Shell Dough, 308,
        309
tempura batter, 66
Thai Coconut Broth with
    Mussels and Bok
    Choy, 107, *108*, 109
Thai Dressing, 51
tomatoes
    Bomba Rice with Soffrito
        and Saffron, 279–80
    Eggplant Caponata with
        Mozzarella, 55, *56*, 57
    Heirloom Tomatoes
        with Burrata and
        Sourdough Croutons,
        52, *53*, 54
    Marinated Tomatoes, 52
    peeling tomatoes, 313
    Pici with Braised Rabbit,
        Tomato, and Fennel,
        154–55

About the Authors

Joseph Ogrodnek and **Walker Stern**, chef-owners of Brooklyn's popular Battersby and Dover restaurants, first met as classmates at the Culinary Institute of America, then became friends when they worked together in the kitchen of Alain Ducasse at the Essex House in New York City. Both trained at acclaimed restaurants early in their careers: Ogrodnek, a Philadelphia native, at Washington Square Café and Tabla in New York City; Stern, who grew up in California and Atlanta, at La Folie and the Dining Room at the Ritz-Carlton in San Francisco, and at Alain Ducasse's Mix restaurant in Las Vegas. After the two classmates reconnected at Alain Ducasse in New York City, Ogrodnek worked at Gramercy Tavern, then became chef at Anella in Brooklyn, while Stern cooked at Blue Hill, and was the opening sous chef at 81 on Manhattan's Upper West Side, before taking over the kitchen at the Vanderbilt in Brooklyn.

In 2011, eager to have greater control over their futures and explore their own culinary style, Ogrodnek and Stern decided to collaborate on a restaurant, pooling their resources, talent, and creativity to open Battersby on Cobble Hill's thriving Smith Street. When the restaurant debuted in fall 2011, accolades followed almost immediately, including a place on *Bon Appétit*'s list of the top ten best new restaurants in the country. In 2013, the duo opened their second restaurant, Dover, also in Brooklyn, and in 2014, *Food & Wine* named Ogrodnek and Stern to its prestigious Best New Chefs list.

Stern and Ogrodnek both live in Brooklyn, New York.

Andrew Friedman has collaborated on more than twenty-five cookbooks and other projects with some of America's finest and most well-known chefs, including Michael White, Paul Liebrandt, Alfred Portale, and former White House chef Walter Scheib. He coedited the popular anthology *Don't Try This at Home* and is a two-time winner of the IACP award for Best Chef or Restaurant Cookbook. Friedman is an editor at large for *Tennis* magazine and the coauthor of American tennis star James Blake's *New York Times*–bestselling memoir *Breaking Back*. In 2009, he published his first nonfiction book, *Knives at Dawn*. He is also the creator of and chief contributor to the chef-focused website Toqueland.com.